HOW MASS ATROCITIES END

Given the brutality of mass atrocities, it is no wonder that one question dominates research and policy: what can we, who are not at risk, do to prevent such violence and hasten endings? But this question skips a more fundamental question for understanding the trajectory of violence: how do mass atrocities *actually* end?

This volume presents an analysis of the processes, decisions, and factors that help bring about the end of mass atrocities. It includes qualitatively rich case studies from Burundi, Guatemala, Indonesia, Sudan, Bosnia, and Iraq, drawing patterns from wide-ranging data. As such, it offers a much needed correction to the popular "salvation narrative" framing mass atrocity in terms of good and evil. The nuanced, multidisciplinary approach followed here represents not only an essential tool for scholars, but an important step forward in improving civilian protection.

BRIDGET CONLEY-ZILKIC is Research Director of World Peace Foundation, where she currently leads research on the How Mass Atrocities End project. She is also an assistant research professor at The Fletcher School, Tufts University. Professor Conley-Zilkic has published multiple essays on mass atrocity prevention and response, and on the potential for museums to engage human rights issues. She received a PhD in Comparative Literature from Binghamton University in 2001.

How Mass Atrocities End

STUDIES FROM GUATEMALA, BURUNDI, INDONESIA, SUDAN, BOSNIA-HERZEGOVINA, AND IRAQ

Edited by

BRIDGET CONLEY-ZILKIC

CAMBRIDGE
UNIVERSITY PRESS

CAMBRIDGE
UNIVERSITY PRESS

32 Avenue of the Americas, New York, NY 10013-2473, USA

Cambridge University Press is part of the University of Cambridge.

It furthers the University's mission by disseminating knowledge in the pursuit of education, learning, and research at the highest international levels of excellence.

www.cambridge.org
Information on this title: www.cambridge.org/9781107124370

First published 2016

A catalog record for this publication is available from the British Library.

Library of Congress Cataloging in Publication Data
How mass atrocities end : studies from Guatemala, Burundi, Indonesia, the Sudans, Bosnia-Herzegovina, and Iraq / edited by Bridget Conley-Zilkic.
pages cm
Includes bibliographical references and index.
ISBN 978-1-107-12437-0 (Hardback)
1. Atrocities–Prevention–Case studies. 2. Genocide–Prevention–Case studies. 3. Atrocities–Case studies. 4. Genocide–Case studies. I. Conley-Zilkic, Bridget.
HV6322.7.H69 2015
363.34–dc23 2015018947

ISBN 978-1-107-12437-0 Hardback

Contents

Figures

Tables

Boxes

Contributors

Roddy Brett is a lecturer in the School of International Relations and co-directs the Masters Programme in Peace and Conflict Studies at the University of St. Andrews. At present, he is Visiting Research Associate at the Latin America Centre, at the University of Oxford. His fields of research include conflict, peace processes/peace building, political violence and genocide, and post-conflict reconstruction. He has published a total of eight books and various articles, including most recently *The Post-Conflict Legacy of Genocide: Political Violence in Guatemala* (Palgrave Macmillan 2015). At present, he is preparing a new monograph on the history of Colombia's FARC guerrillas. Dr. Brett has acted as Advisor to the UNDP and the UNHCHR in Guatemala and Colombia and as Advisor on Indigenous Affairs to the Norwegian Embassy in Guatemala. He worked with the Centre for Human Rights Legal Action in Guatemala, as a member of the original team that prepared the evidence against former dictator General Ríos Montt, leading to his conviction in May 2013 for eighty years for genocide and crimes against humanity. He is a member of the Academic Advisory Board for the International Center on Non-Violent Conflict, in Washington, D.C., and of the Advisory Council of the Institute of Humanitarian Studies (OCHA) in Bogota.

Bridget Conley-Zilkic is Research Director of the World Peace Foundation (WPF) and Assistant Research Professor at The Fletcher School. At WPF, she is the lead researcher on the How Mass Atrocities End project. She previously worked as Research Director for the U.S. Holocaust Memorial Museum's Committee on Conscience. She led the Museum's research and projects on contemporary threats of genocide, including curating an exhibition, *From Memory to Action: Meeting the Challenge of Genocide Today*, providing analysis of at-risk countries, and producing educational resources. She has published multiple essays on mass atrocity prevention and response, and on the potential for museums to engage human rights issues. She received a PhD in Comparative Literature from Binghamton University in 2001.

Alex de Waal is Executive Director of the World Peace Foundation and a research professor at The Fletcher School of Law and Diplomacy, Tufts University. During 2009–2011, he served as Senior Advisor to the African Union High Level Implementation Panel for Sudan. He was also Program Director at the Social Science Research Council, with responsibilities for research programs on humanitarian issues and HIV/AIDS and social transformation. His academic research has focused on issues of famine, conflict, and human rights in Africa. He was awarded an OBE in the UK New Year's Honors List of 2009, was on the *Prospect/Foreign Policy* list of hundred public intellectuals in 2008, and the *Atlantic Monthly* list of twenty-seven "brave thinkers" in 2009.

Fanar Haddad (B.Sc [LSE], M.Phil. [Cantab], PhD [Exon]) is a Senior Research Fellow at the Middle East Institute, National University of Singapore. Previously lectured in modern Middle Eastern history at the University of Exeter and, most recently, at Queen Mary, University of London. Prior to obtaining his PhD, Haddad was a research analyst at the Foreign and Commonwealth Office where he worked on North Africa. He has since published widely on issues relating to historic and contemporary Iraq. His main research topics are identity, historical memory, nationalism, communal conflict, and minority politics. He is the author of *Sectarianism in Iraq: Antagonistic Visions of Unity* (London/New York: Hurst/ Columbia University Press 2011).

Claire Q. Smith (B.A. Hons [Oxford], MIA [Columbia], PhD [LSE]) is an assistant professor in the Department of Politics at the University of York. She researches and teaches in the fields of conflict, peace, democratization, and development. Prior to York, she held Teaching Fellowships at the London School of Economics and Political Science (LSE) and the School of Oriental and African Studies (SOAS). Claire's postdoctoral research (co-funded by the World Peace Foundation) concentrates on the comparative political history of post war and post genocide state and peace building in Indonesia and Timor-Leste, on which she is currently writing her first book. Claire has research and policy experience in Indonesia, Timor-Leste, Cambodia and Lao PDR, where she has worked with the World Bank, UNICEF, UNDP and UNHCHR, and The Asia Foundation.

Noel Twagiramungu is a research fellow and lead researcher on the Liberation Movements in Power project at World Peace Foundation at The Fletcher School. A former Scholar-at-Risk Fellow at Harvard University, Noel has taught at the University of Dar es Salaam and Smith College. Previously, he served as the executive director of the Ligue des droits de la person dans la région des Grands Lacs (LDGL), a leading human rights umbrella organization in the Great Lakes region, where he oversaw for five years plans to improve human rights documentation and monitoring in conjunction with twenty-seven human rights NGOs in

Rwanda, Burundi, and the DRC. He was also the founder and coordinator of the Documentation Centre on Genocide Trials in Rwanda. He has served over the past decade as a consultant and country expert on Rwanda for numerous organizations, including the United Nations, the Clingendael Institute (Netherlands), and the Nordic Africa Institute (Sweden). Noel holds an LL.M. in International and European Human Rights Law from Utrecht University and a PhD from The Fletcher School at Tufts University. Author of a doctoral thesis devoted to "Explaining Variation in the Transition from Genocidal Violence to Rebel Governance in Contemporary Rwanda and Burundi" and winner of the African Studies Association's 2011 Best Graduate Paper Prize, Noel's teaching, research, publications, and fieldwork focus on human rights, sustainable development, identity-based violence, ethnopolitics, peace processes and post-conflict governance, with a regional focus on east and central Africa.

Acknowledgments

This book has been a long time in the making. The idea of studying actual endings first occurred to Alex de Waal more than ten years ago as he reflected on his experience working with Sudan's Nuba population during the height of attacks against them in 1992. The assault subsided in ways that did not conform to assumptions about endings that framed the burgeoning anti-atrocity movement. Intrigued by the discrepancy, de Waal suggested that we launch a cross-case comparative study. Over the subsequent years, the project has taken many forms and benefitted from discussions with a wide range of case experts, theorists, and policymakers, too numerous to name. We thank all who participated in these discussions and who generously shared their insights. The possibility to focus the project and sponsor new research to develop the core ideas coalesced when de Waal and I were able to work together at the WPF. This volume would not be possible without Alex de Waal's intellectual and organization leadership, or the contributions by our chapter authors. To all of them, I express my deepest gratitude.

Introduction

Bridget Conley-Zilkic

How do mass atrocities end? *Badly*, the research, policy, and popular consensus asserts. Illustrating this point are the cruel remains of genocides past: a trail of Armenian death across Anatolia, the ashes that to this day cover the ground at Auschwitz, the bones still visible in Cambodia's killing fields, the image of a frozen embrace as a mother grasps her child against the chemical weapon onslaught in Kurdish Iraq, the annual re-burials of identified remains from Srebrenica, and the churches and schools transformed into massacre memorials across Rwanda. Atrocities end, these scenes inform us, with the annihilation of the victim population.

Given the depths of human brutality on display in the perpetration of mass atrocities, it is no wonder that one question dominates the entire body of work on genocide and mass atrocities: *what can we, who are not at risk, do to prevent such violence and hasten endings?* Drawing on selective memory, the imagination of how *we* might help end mass atrocities overemphasizes military defeats – timely or tardy. They represent the last hope and most powerful tool in the toolbox to staunch what otherwise appears as unstoppable escalation of violence directed against entire civilian groups. While such interventions are not always possible, they are imagined as the most robust and efficacious response in the anti-atrocities toolbox. Thus, the question that sparked development of tools for responding to atrocities was: *how and when can the international community justify armed intervention to save populations?* Even when armed intervention does not occur, as it most often does not, this question orients the imagination of atrocities prevention and response (Conley-Zilkic 2015), and is the logical outcome of the obsession with the question of what "we" can do.

Thus are endings conceived as part of a salvation narrative: the international community rescues the innocent, halts violence, and punishes the guilty. The story and all its characters are fixed within an ideal ending. In this version, not only does the killing stop, but the innocent are vindicated, the guilty punished and a new political dispensation is installed that protects the future. There is nothing wrong with this story as an expression of hope, but it does not describe actual endings.

Understanding actual endings requires a different story. Mass atrocities end in ways that are always compromised and incomplete. There is no redemption in the wake of such extensive and brutal violence. Our definition of endings focuses on a limited factor: *significant declines* in violence organized to target civilians on a widespread and systematic scale. We recognize that this is not the same as ending the suffering and vulnerability of victims, achieving justice, or, in many cases, a conclusion of all violence. Further, as will be addressed more below, several of our cases do not sustain even this very limited definition of an ending; in those cases, we explore the dynamics of why violence rises and falls. But part of the story we can tell about the endings defined as declines in mass civilian targeted violence is that they are, in fact, often not synonymous or coterminous with broader human rights or state-building agenda. Actual atrocity endings require separate analysis.

Our question is simple: how and why do mass atrocities *actually* end? This is the central question that must precede the one of what 'we' can do. The answer reveals a tale of the processes, decisions, and factors that influence how and when atrocities decline. Actual endings demand our attention, because regardless of whether perpetrators "succeed," atrocities do always end, and understanding the processes by which they do so offers insights into the initiation and escalation of violence against civilians.These processes cannot be taken for granted, idealized into a better future ending or simply mourned; they must be queried in all their complexity. While there is no cause to celebrate the atrocity endings addressed in this volume, there is much to be learned.

In this book, we define mass atrocities as widespread and systematic violence against civilians, largely characterized by killing, but we address a wider range of harms. Endings are marked by significant reductions in killing and are studied in detailed analysis of six country cases: Guatemala, Burundi, Sudan (including southern/South Sudan[1]), Indonesia (including Papua and East Timor/Timor-Leste[2]), Yugoslavia (focusing on Bosnia-Herzegovina[3]), and Iraq. The cases suggest many cross-cutting themes, some of which are discussed in this Introduction. The order of their presentation draws out some of these themes: the volume begins with Guatemala and Burundi, both of which have experienced endings that are thus far firm and aligned with the articulation of a liberal state. However, Burundi appears

[1] South Sudan became independent from Sudan in 2011; previously, it was the southern region, states, or provinces of Sudan.

[2] East Timor claimed its independence from Indonesia under the name Timor-Leste in 2002. In this Introduction, we refer to the area as East Timor while addressing the period during which it was part of Indonesia.

[3] Bosnia-Herzegovina became an independent state in April 1992.

to have moved beyond the ethnic logic that animated atrocities, while in Guatemala, it is largely confirmed by the severe inequality the victim group continues to experience. Nonetheless, in neither country is violence a thing of the past: political violence continues in Burundi in 2015 and Guatemala has an exceptionally high homicide rate. In both countries, continuing violence provides testimony to the underlying political dysfunction that serves as the backdrop for historic episodes of mass killing. The Sudans and Indonesia both offer a multitude of atrocity events with several distinct victim groups within states that have recently transitioned out of military dictatorship. Endings demonstrate important differences in the capacities of a more institutionalized and internationally integrated state like Indonesia in comparison with either Sudan or South Sudan.

Our third pairing, Bosnia and Iraq, offer two extremes within the anti-atrocity agenda: Bosnia occupies a misplaced seat of honor as an example of what the international community can accomplish when it decides to halt atrocities. Iraq, despite exceptionally high levels of civilian killing, was completely absent from the anti-atrocity agenda through its worst violence, finding resonance only after the reduction in U.S. forces in Summer 2014, when the call to action was to increase U.S. military engagement. Each chapter provides a broad historical and political context of mass atrocities, focuses on a limited number of episodes, and asks: how and why did mass atrocities end?

To the question of *why study endings*, we emphatically reply that this woefully underexamined aspect of mass atrocities offers valuable insight into the patterns, politics, decision making, and potential for influencing endings of mass violence against civilians. Four key stories emerge. The first is the political rationality of perpetrators. Second, is a tale of the place of violence in historical political economy. Third, is the intersection of mass atrocity and armed conflict, a story that adds nuance the current consensus that conflict is frequently the context for atrocities. Finally, is the story of "us" – those who are not immediately at risk and whose actions might help those who are. Commitment to the principle that mass atrocities are not an inevitable part of human existence has borne fruit; but precisely *why* and *how* it has, in addition to what further might be done to hasten endings, requires revision.

THE WRONG STORY: THE LIMITS OF "GENOCIDE"

Most of our authors are not genocide scholars, but area experts whose vocabulary and analytical tools draw on a wide range of theoretical, disciplinary, and subdisciplinary frameworks. They have selected the vocabulary that they felt best fit the dynamics of violence in their cases, with the term "mass atrocities" providing a broad general framework across chapters.

We intentionally depart from the conceptual framework introduced by the legal definition of genocide which is poorly designed to inform a study of endings. At its core, "genocide" attempts to qualitatively differentiate one form of violence from all other forms (Bogossian 2010); as such, the conceptual, legal, and practical implications of the term obscure the variations in the degree of violence that we feel are of utmost concern to studying endings. Further limitations arise from the definition of the group and the requirement of a criminal "intent to destroy."

The legal definition of genocide limits the victims to ethnic, national, racial or religious groups. While such "groupness" often describes victim selection, it rarely can account for endings. Thus, several authors use vocabulary related to groupness: Bridget Conley-Zilkic refers to "ethnic cleansing" in her chapter on Bosnia, Noel Twgiramungu addresses "ethnic violence" in Burundi, Alex de Waal engages with the literature on Sudan's "identity politics," and Fanar Haddad discusses "sectarian violence" in Iraq. In each case these terms describe the major social schism across which violence occurs, but are less relevant when it comes time for analyzing why violence declines. These terms, regardless if viewed within essentialist or constructivist framework, are not equipped to analyze the evolution of political dynamics and calculations that inform endings.

Genocidal intent requires a goal of destroying a group, regardless of motive or context for violence. This implies evil in the very mindset of the perpetrator. Given the brutality of violence involved in the cases of genocide, there is little reason to object to such a classification. But it is a short and misguided step from the assumption of evil to the assumption that perpetrators by nature will not alter their actions absent outside force. The idea of 'evil' obscures study of endings. Neither the evil of the violence perpetrated nor the parallel assumption that outside actors are comparatively "good" is of much value when it comes to analyzing how and why violence ends.

At the height of violence in each of our cases, there can be little doubt that they fit even more limited definitions of mass killing or genocide. But our cases move beyond these dismal peaks, and explore the relationship between spikes and valleys of violence, as well as the potential for recurrence. Some of our insights may be the product of analyzing a wider range of violent episodes than generally are considered genocide. This decision echoes contemporary application, whether consciously or not, of the anti-atrocity agenda to lower levels and a wider range of violence than historical cases of genocide. In short, we follow a more agnostic approach to differentiating specific types of violence against civilians in favor of examining the politics of escalation and decline. Thus, we learn from other theorists of political violence who question how far we can currently disaggregate different forms of violence and the political mechanisms that set them into motion, or, as we note, cause them to end. For example, Cunningham and Lemke have recently argued that many of the factors considered by quantitative analysts to be relevant to civil war studies are also relevant to understanding a much broader range of forms of violence (2014).

While we eschew the language of "genocide" as an organizing principle, we frame our analysis in conversation with what Scott Straus (2012a) describes as the new consensus in genocide studies. Scholarly research increasingly recognizes that this form of violence against civilians most often occurs during armed conflict, and follows a strategic logic whereby civilians are targeted because of their relationship to what perpetrators view as a real and present threat. Ideology remains an important theme within genocide studies, but scholars have shifted from viewing group hatred as *causing* mass violence, to understanding it as a filter through which political elites' ideals and strategies are articulated and targets for violence selected. Further, research shows that genocidal violence tends to radicalize over time, rather than beginning as a fully planned program to physically eliminate the targeted group.

ACTUAL MASS ATROCITIES ENDINGS: SIX CLUSTERS OF INCIDENTS

Given our broad definitional parameters, there are many cases we could have selected for inclusion in this volume. The cases presented offer important geographical, temporal, and regime type diversity. Additionally, they include widely recognized examples (Bosnia, Darfur, Sudan) and understudied mass atrocities (eg., East Timor and Papua in Indonesia, Sudan's Nuba Mountains, Burundi, Guatemala, and Iraq).

Within each country case are multiple episodes. The chapter on Burundi describes five episodes of mass violence: in 1965, 1972, 1998, 1993, and 1994–2005. The Guatemala chapter focuses on one, in the context of the long civil war, when violence increased from 1982 to 1983, but it also analyzes the conditions for indigenous populations thereafter. The instances of mass atrocities discussed in Sudan include only the highest spikes of violence, with discussion of four instances chosen from more than seven candidates. As noted in our Indonesia chapter, the country witnessed at least five periods of heightened civilian killing, but the chapter focuses on a comparison of two in East Timor and Papua. The former Yugoslavia witnessed three periods of mass atrocities in the twentieth century: during the Balkan Wars through the end of World War I, World War II through 1948, and the 1990s. The chapter discusses each and offers an in-depth study of Bosnia-Herzegovina during 1992–1995. Finally, the chapter on Iraq itemizes the periods of violence under Saddam Hussein, but concentrates on the post-2003 violence, which continues into drafting this volume. The dynamics captured in these cases are not merely descriptions of the decline of a particular episode of mass violence, but also the relationship between spikes, declines, the purpose and control of violence, and the potential for renewed or continued mass atrocities.

Our approach to examining endings requires reliable data, and we recognize that the quality of the available data varies enormously. In some instances, we have high confidence that the best-researched numbers do a good job capturing the scale and pattern of violence, but in other cases, even the best estimates are subject to considerable question. For instance, Guatemala, Bosnia-Herzegovina between 1992 and 1995, East Timor 1999, and Iraq from 2003– present are, among instances of mass atrocities, well documented by either a range of governmental or non-governmental organizations or, in the cases of East Timor and Guatemala, truth commissions which carried out credible studies that produced death tolls. On the other hand, periods of violence in Sudan before the 2000s, Papua and Burundi throughout the periods of violence are quite poorly documented. Counting civilian deaths is a somewhat recent endeavor, and while it is improving, considerable challenges remain. As Keith Kraus cautions, "critical occlusions and limitations associated with *what is counted* and *how it is counted* pose serious challenges to the goal of developing adequate conflict resolution and violence reduction policies and program" (Kraus 2013, pp. 265–266). Each author addresses this concern in greater depth.

Dynamics of endings

In Burundi, the central question is: how did this country, beset by violence throughout its post-colonial history arrive at what appears to be, as Noel Twagiramungu argues, a "transformative ending," such that the core dynamics feeding ethnic mass killing seem to have concluded? The first three documented periods of violence ended with a similar pattern: Hutu efforts to mount a coup or attack Tutsi civilians were halted when the Tutsi-dominated military responded with overwhelming force. This violence subsided as the government and military consolidated control and "restored order." Endings post-1993 varied, in that Hutu armed opposition increased its capacity and held territory. The combination of key leaders' commitment to moderation, the "mutually hurting stalemate" (Zartman 1989) in the armed conflict, the influence of events in neighboring Rwanda, and international pressure created a context whereby the gains of political moderation outpaced those of ethnic extremism. These dynamics fueled a transformational ending – whereby disputes between groups shifted to the political plane, and importantly, no longer occurred solely along the ethnic divide. However, this does not translate into an end to political violence, but a change in its scale, dynamics and logic.

Armed conflict in Guatemala began in 1965 and did not end until 1995, but as Roddy Brett illustrates, the phase of mass atrocities, characterized by an articulated plan to kill significant portions of the indigenous Maya population and reorganize the survivors in securitized population centers, is concentrated between 1981 and 1983. This phase ended when the army achieved its goals: not to physically eliminate the Maya, but to create a modern, institutionalized state with a consolidated, Ladino identity. The army further managed, as Brett argues, to secure a seat for itself at the nation's economic table, previously dominated by a social and business elite. An internationally mediated peace process provided the final touch on the emergence of the modern Guatemalan state: the peace agreement, despite its credentials and rights-oriented mechanisms, protected the army's gains and did nothing to alter the structural marginalization of the Maya. The result, as Brett argues, is ongoing genocidal effects for this targeted population, where overt, large-scale violence is no longer necessary.

Across the many instances of mass atrocities in Sudan's contemporary history, Alex de Waal chronicles two kinds of endings: one, the government achieves its immediate goals; and two, perpetrator groups can no longer sustain high levels of violence because of internal dissent, resistance by the targeted groups, and organizational and resource constraints. All kinds of endings are incomplete, with unresolved conflicts risking recurrent mass violence. De Waal argues that the greatest risk for mass atrocities arises when the central government and provincial military elites both have interests in mass violence, creating an escalatory spiral. Sudan's "endings" are better understood as shifts from high-level mass atrocities to lower-level violence when there is a breakdown in coordination between these two sets of actors.

Indonesian atrocities, as Claire Smith demonstrates, ended in dramatically different fashion during the Suharto period of military dictatorship during the Cold War and under the semi-democratic state that followed. However, this historical line cannot explain additional differences between her two key cases, Papua and East Timor, both of which suffered violence before and after political transition. Her chapter asks why the post-Suharto governments pursued different policies, each involving violence against civilians, to very different ends. A number of arguably unique factors aligned to enable East Timor to exit a cycle of systematic violence through independence: an extremely capable Timorese leadership inspired a transnational activist network, thereby internationalizing their political agenda. The first Indonesian leader after Suharto's military dictatorship, B. J. Habibie, saw himself as a reformer and tried to liberalize the state. While he was unable to consolidate his agenda within either the military or the government, the internal dissent created an opening seized by the Timorese and backed by threat of international force. This opening swiftly closed, as Papua demonstrates. There, the government and military decided that there would be no further independence for Indonesian territories. Instead, they experimented with a range of policies to quiet separatist hopes: increased cultural and political expression, militarized crackdowns and attempts to co-opt the elite into the status quo.

The analysis of endings in Bosnia, Bridget Conley-Zilkic argues, raises two questions: first, why has NATO airpower been overemphasized in what was a complex, compromised ending? And second, why has the simplified version been adopted as a model for anti-atrocities response? The initial phase of conflict in 1992 witnessed an enormous spike of killing and displacement, as the Bosnian Serbs made quick use of their military superiority to claim and then consolidate control of over seventy percent of Bosnian territory. This initial phase of mass atrocities halted due to the "success" of the campaign, the government's armed resistance, and the Bosnian Serbs' internal limitations. Violence continued throughout the conflict but not at the same intensity of killing except following the fall of Srebrenica in 1995. The conflict was halted as regional alliances shifted, consensus emerged on the political framework for the Yugoslav successor states, an offensive by the Bosnian government and Croat army reduced the area held by the Bosnian Serbs, and bold U.S. diplomacy seized the moment. NATO airpower played a role in this mix, particularly in relation to breaking the siege of Sarajevo, but cannot be accurately assessed without the broader context.

Iraq since 2003 is the major blind spot of the anti-atrocities movement. Despite some human rights-based arguments backing the initial intervention, the U.S.-led intervention followed a political–military, not humanitarian or anti-atrocities logic; a framing that anti-atrocity activists never challenged. Nonetheless, modern Iraq has suffered almost every "remedy" for mass atrocities that the anti-atrocity toolbox has to offer: condemnation, sanctions, no-fly zones, trials, regime change, the full policy attention of the United States, and a seemingly endless flow of development funds – and it has experienced more than a decade's worth of fluctuating violence consistently characterized by targeting of civilians with no end in sight. Fanar Haddad examines the ongoing cycle of violence to answer the question: why have atrocities not ended?

Before 2003, large-scale violence against civilians in Iraq ended when the Iraqi state deployed overwhelming force to accomplish its goals. After 2003, despite (or because of) the U.S. occupation, there is no force capable of asserting sufficient state control to subdue violence. Haddad demonstrates the core incompatibility of Shi'ite and Sunni views of both history and the State. Violence escalates when various incentives converge: anti-state, anti-Shi'ite, and anti-occupation violence on the one hand, concentrated against pro-State, anti-Sunni, and anti-terrorist violence on the other hand. An "ending" of sorts was possible in 2007–2008, as Sunni leaders realized they were losing the armed conflict and reached out to the United States to bolster their position within the new Iraq. Simultaneously, the U.S. counterinsurgency policy shifted to a more population-centric approach that not only increased numbers of American boots on the ground, but helped drive a wedge between mainstream Sunni leaders and al-Qaeda elements. And, the Iraqi state began behaving like a state rather than a coalition of Shi'ite interests. But the moment of contingency when these factors aligned was short-lived: sectarian interests reasserted dominance over state politics, and re-confirmed violence as the preferred means through which politicians would pursue their incompatible goals.

FOUR STORIES OF HOW MASS ATROCITIES END

By shifting the perspective from *what we can do*, to *what happened*, these studies of mass atrocity endings introduce a new set of stories. First is a story of perpetrator logic: the studies demonstrate that endings follow a strategic logic. Second, is a geo-historical narrative whereby perpetrator regimes often met their goals during Cold War-era mass atrocity episodes by applying overwhelming armed force against the victim group and any organized resistance associated with it. The scale of violence is lower in post–Cold War instances (with the exception of Iraq) and endings are influenced by a wider array of factors. Salient among these factors is the increased international attention to and willingness to impose penalties for regimes that commit atrocities. However, as we will discuss below, this influence does not function as a one-to-one application of tools with subsequent outcomes, nor does it achieve more ideal endings. Rather, what we see is a complex set of factors that contribute to greater variation and contingency in endings.

Third, while the cases largely confirm the widely noted correlation between mass atrocities and conflict, we find widely disparate patterns across cases in the timing and dynamics of these two phenomena. Finally, endings force us to revise the story we tell about ourselves, as those who might hasten endings and help protect vulnerable populations.The point is not to dismiss this question of international policies that might decrease violence, but to arrive at it from an understanding of how mass atrocities actually end, rather than the imagination of how they ought to end.

Perpetrator logic governing atrocity endings

The first story captured by our study of endings is that of perpetrator logic. The crucial actor in endings is the perpetrator, whose actions must change for violence to halt or decline. The logic that animates violence in all of our cases aligns with one of the key insights of recent work on genocide: campaigns of mass killing are launched in relation to a strategic goal.[4] A parallel insight is that endings occur when actors realize that their interests are better served by decreasing violence than by continuing it.

In our cases, those implementing policies that assault civilians are mostly states and the armed forces associated with them. Nonetheless, non-state actors played significant roles in atrocity campaigns in Sudan, South Sudan, Iraq, Bosnia-

[4] This point resonates with cross-case studies of mass atrocities and genocide. See Benjamin Valentino (2004) especially on this point.

Herzegovina, and Burundi. Further, dissent within a coalition of perpetrators can quicken endings, but dissent is not synonymous with reform. A significant location for dissent is the nexus of national and provincial elites. Mass violence often escalates as these interests converge and declines as they diverge. De Waal argues that this is the pattern in Sudan and provides multiple examples of it. Bosnia also offers an illustration in the rift that grew between Serbia's Slobodan Milosević and the Bosnian Serb leadership – while separated by an international line after 1992, the Bosnian Serbs relationship to Milosević functioned as that of provincial and national elite. This pattern cautions us that elite decision making cannot explain all violence (Kalyvas 2006). However, the limits of such a focus cannot be improved by parallel isolation of intracommunal or microlevel factors. Rather, the overall path of mass atrocity violence, including endings – possibly distinct from other forms of violence – is determined by the convergence and divergence of incentives across these levels (Shaw 2013, pp. 154–155) in the context of the international environment.

Dissent is not necessarily a call to change a national political logic, and it may be more significant than reform in terms of ending discrete episodes of violence. Nonetheless, we have several examples of leaders with liberalizing agendas who played important roles in changing the longer-term dynamics – even if at times they also led governments that perpetrated such violence. From our cases, we note Indonesia and Burundi. In Indonesia, President Habibie led the government that committed mass atrocities in 1999, but his reformist agenda contributed to the accommodation that led to Timorese independence. Burundi, likewise, benefited from the actions of President Pierre Buyoya, who twice played a critical role in the peaceful transfer of power, despite also leading a government that deployed violence against civilians.

Perpetrators of mass atrocity are not cut from one cloth or destined to play only one role. It is important to understand the politics that animates their decisions to use mass violence. What causes perpetrators to re-evaluate the balance of their interests? We suggest three scenarios (Conley-Zilkic and de Waal 2014, pp. 60 – 61): first, perpetrators "succeed"; they meet their strategic goal, shift to policies intended to normalize the situation. Second, perpetrators are forced to abandon their goals by being defeated, in which case their long-term interests become irrelevant. However, while armed resistance and military pressure are important in several cases, none of our episodes ends with military defeat of the perpetrators. Third and most common, perpetrators modify their goal. This modification occurs in relation to a realignment of incentives, or, on a longer timeline, reformers champion a different approach. Across our cases, direct application of international pressure is never the sole factor for changing perception of long-term interests. However, as addressed in greater detail below, the geo-historical climate is significant and discrete policy measures can and do make an impact. Invariably, long-term interest is tied to a political dispensation; hence, national or regional level factors often are the most influential. Among the salient factors are internal dissent, resistance

(Conley-Zilkic and de Waal 2014), resource constraints, or other factors that increase the costs of pursuing mass atrocities (Krain 2014, p. 27).

Perpetrators recognize 'success' in highly variable terms, differing not only case by case, but episode by episode. Perhaps the most clear-cut of our examples is Guatemala, where the military developed a plan designating what degree of violence would be deployed against which areas, as well as when and where securitized development plans would be implemented. They then proceeded to carry out this plan as designed. In other cases, where the plan is less detailed in advance, nuanced shifts in capacity, organization, and the influence of various case-specific factors determine changes.

However, even when "success" was achieved through overwhelming military force, as occurred more frequently before the end of the Cold War, it was measured in relation to a goal of consolidating power. Endings were not mere expressions of overwhelming force, *per se*, but deployment of force toward a political goal. The goal in each case we document stopped short of total extermination of the target group. In Yugoslavia at the end of World War II, Burundi before 1993, Guatemala 1981–1983, Indonesia before 1999, and Iraq under Saddam Hussein, large-scale violence targeting civilians ended when the government decided it had sufficiently disabled resistance and dissent so that it could turn toward consolidating control and normalizing conditions. A particularly striking case was the amnesty memorandum issued by Saddam Hussein to end the Anfal campaign (Hiltermann 2008, p. 6). The Sudanese episodes chronicled by de Waal approximate this pattern, but the Southern rebels were never defeated to the extent witnessed in other cases mentioned here.

While overwhelming force is becoming rarer, we can better understand the logic behind this and other forms of endings through a political definition: perpetrators decide that their long-term interests are sufficiently secured and better served by other policies. In all of our cases, the decision moment is complicated by the way in which violence tends to take on its own logic, escalating in intensity, expanding geographic reach, enlisting agents, and activating diverse agendas, with endings occurring upon the dissolution or contraction of these factors. The manner of protecting long-term interests invariably will be determined by a country's specific political practices and embedded power structures. Even where significant political change occurs or is desired — including where there is a new regime in place – the changes align with and grow in relation to entrenched systems of how governance works. The distinct logic that governs episodes of violence forms the central focus of each chapter.

A story of historical–political change

The most significant historical–political change documented across the cases is the end of the Cold War. Hence, our analysis of endings resonates with efforts to theorize genocide within geo-political trends and international relations (Mann 2005, Levene 2013, Shaw 2013), adding details about how these trends impact both overall declines in the number of mass atrocity events, the lethality of such events, and endings in discrete instances. Rather than viewing the end of the Cold War as a fixed border, we suggest understanding it as a transition, after which overwhelming state force becomes a less notable trend and a wider range of factors contribute to atrocity endings.

Before and during the Cold War, geopolitics largely determined international responses to mass atrocities. Roddy Brett's chapter on Guatemala demonstrates this point in relation to the U.S. National Security Doctrine. Another example is Gary Bass's study of the Nixon administration's response to Pakistani offensives against civilians in Bangladesh in 1971, despite the concern expressed by U.S. embassy officials (Bass 2013). While none of our cases are drawn from the former Communist bloc and allies[5], mass atrocities in China, Ethiopia, Cambodia, and Afghanistan, for instance, all provide examples from this side of the geopolitical divide. Major powers interventions in local or regional conflicts tended to increase the overall death tolls, as well as civilian tolls (Lacina 2006).[6] In addition to how Cold War politics directly impacted specific policies, in general, atrocities were deemed tolerable; if they were even visible as an issue.

While endings during the Cold War tended to be pursued through overwhelming military force, given that all of our cases–bracketing Guatemala – experience mass atrocity events both during and after the conclusion of the Cold War, we must view the earlier 'endings' as incomplete. In this, our findings also align with some insights from conflict termination. For instance, Roy Licklider has presented data

[5] Guatemala, Iraq, and Indonesia were clear western allies throughout this period and all received significant support. Criticism of human abuses can potentially be understood as a mitigating factor in Guatemala, primarily from human rights organizations and U.S. Congress; nonetheless, the Reagan government actively defended the regime throughout the period of atrocities. In this case, international pressure may have impacted the Guatemalan government's perceived need to normalize quickly *after* having achieved their strategic aims. Yugoslavia was non-aligned. Sudan shifted camps, being pro-U.S. in the 1980s at the time when the southern Sudanese rebels were receiving aid from the pro-Soviet regime in Ethiopia under Mengistu, which of course inflicted mass atrocities on its own population. The Cold War was a less relevant factor in Burundi.

[6] One may argue that often these high death tolls were the result of airpower or other forms of heavy weaponry that render conflicts more lethal in general, and thereby attempt to differentiate these conflicts from those where there is more demonstrable "intent" to target civilians. This is the line of argument that accompanies studies of genocide and which we have abandoned in favor of trying to understand patterns of how civilians are killed in large numbers. Further, the argument can be unraveled on its own merits; after all, complete disregard for the affects of forms of fighting on civilian lives, particularly when easily anticipatable and repeated over place and time provides at best a very weak distinction between "intentional" destruction and "disregard" for human lives.

suggesting that military victories decrease the likelihood of identity wars recurring, but increase the odds of genocide (1998). And Jeffrey Dixon summarizes termination research by noting that between 1945-1990, no civil war that ended through negotiation produced a subsequent genocide (Dixon 2009, p. 129). In short, overwhelming military force is not as effective as negotiation for preventing future mass atrocities.

We further note that atrocity patterns warp over time. In Yugoslavia, Burundi, the Sudans, and Iraq, for instance, over multiple periods of atrocities, the identities of perpetrator and victim changed with important differences in scale. The deployment of overwhelming military force was not accompanied by political resolution, leaving toxic legacies for later periods.

Nonetheless, globally, and by a number of measures, mass atrocity events declined in number and scale after the Cold War. In terms of overall scale, the mid-twentieth century witnessed events of apocalyptic violence against civilians that makes contemporary cases, thankfully, pale: an estimated 20–30 million civilians killed in World War II, including 6 million Jews killed in the Holocaust; 20 million civilians killed under Stalin's regime; 40 million Chinese under the regime led by Mao Tse-tung. These numbers make even the horrific post–World War II events pale: with even low-end estimates of 300,000 people killed during the partition of India; tens to hundreds of thousands Algerians killed in the Algerian Revolution and similar numbers in the Nigerian Civil War, 500,000 killed during the war for Bangladeshi Independence; and over 1 million people under the Khmer Rouge in Cambodia.

By a range of measures, state-sponsored, widespread, and systematic violence against civilians began to decline toward the end of Cold War. Melander et al. (2009, p. 523) document this decline in the average level of violence targeting civilians in countries that have had at least one intrastate conflict in 1956–2004. Benjamin Valentino charts it in terms of both onsets of mass killing by governments as well as the scale of ongoing incidents (Valentino 2014, p. 100). The Minorities at Risk project documents that between 1991 and 2004, the number of minority groups being victimized by governments dropped from seventy-five to forty-one (quoted in Human Security Report 2010, p. 77). Scott Straus has drawn attention to the fact that in Africa, which experienced multiple Cold War-era high-civilian casualty wars and mass atrocities, there has also been an overall decline: "the peak of large-scale mass killing episodes in sub-Saharan Africa was the 1980s, with a decline in the 1990s and 2000s" (Straus 2012b, pp. 187–188).

The decrease cannot be solely attributed to the advent of policies designed specifically to address mass atrocities as the decline precedes the development of this work. Take, for example, the case of East Asia (HSR 2010; Bellamy 2013). During the first two-thirds of the twentieth century, the region was exceptionally bloody. The civilian tolls from civil war in China, World War II, the second phase of the Chinese Civil War, anti-colonial conflicts in Indochina, Mao's reign, the Korean War, the Vietnam War, the Khmer Rouge in Cambodia, among other conflicts arguably rendered the region the world's most dangerous location for civilians for decades. All of this began to change following the death of Mao, with further improvements in the mid- to late-1970s. The core international contribution to the change was arguably the end of major power interventions. As Melander et al. (2009) argue

> When the superpower rivalry ended, the main effect was not that previously restrained dogs of war were unleashed, but rather the opposite: some of the worst killer bands, in governments or fighting units, have since the end of the Cold War been reined in or dissolved (p. 531).

International military interventions declined, the wider region shifted toward priorities of stability, non-intervention, and economic development; Vietnam's 1978 invasion that ended mass atrocities committed by the Khmer Rouge in Cambodia is the exception that proves the rule. While the intervention installed an authoritarian government that repressed opposition, mass violence against civilians declined precipitously. The wider trend suggests the possibility that the trajectory for ending mass atrocities is not synonymous (or at least co-terminus) with advancing a human rights agenda.

The trend of decline in lethality of mass atrocity events finds a parallel fact in decline in the number and overall fatalities in conflicts as well, and a shift from interstate to intrastate armed conflict (Themnér and Wallensteen 2014). The number of wars, defined as conflicts with 1,000 or more deaths, has declined significantly over the last half century. When the increased number of states over time is taken into account, "the recent decline in armed conflict after the Cold War has now brought the probability of a country being in conflict to a level corresponding to the end of the 1950s and lower than at any later time during the Cold War" (Gleditsch et al. 2002, p. 621).[7] Given the above insights, it is unsurprising that an uneven but steady increase since 2005 in the intensity of conflicts (measured by battle deaths)–while insufficient to counter the historic decline–correlates with an increase in internationalized civil wars, that is, conflicts where international actors support one side or another (Pettersson and Wallensteen 2015, p. 536).

Regardless, the overall decline in atrocities is important and well-documented. Of the cases that sparked the anti-atrocity agenda from the 1990s and since, *only* the 1994 Rwandan genocide is anywhere near the scale of killing that marked the Cold War and earlier cases. The estimates of direct civilian fatalities in Bosnia-Herzegovina and Darfur, Sudan are, respectively: 36,684 and 40,000 civilians.

[7] There has been a recent increase in wars that produced more than 1,000 annual battledeaths, but it does as yet compare with Cold War era numbers.

Of the cases presented in this volume, only Iraq (2003–2015) surpasses the dismal mark of over 100,000 civilians killed, with a range estimated at 134,668–151,939 (Iraq Body Count 2015).

Another important shift that occurs around the end of the Cold War relates to perpetrators. Previously, authoritarian, strong states were the most likely perpetrators of genocide and mass atrocities. While governments remain responsible for the highest spikes in violence against civilians, increasingly the risk of mass violence against civilians is "highest for semi-authoritarian states near the middle of the democracy scale" (Melander et al 2009, p. 524). Several states in our studies that were previously considered strong, authoritarian regimes made the transition into the era of liberal peace as weakened, partially democratic, atrocity- (or violence) prone states: Yugoslavia, Iraq, Indonesia, Burundi, and Guatemala (if we include homicide rates into our discussion). Labeling a state "strong" or "weak" probably tells us more about the practice of labeling than the character of a society and its governance, but while the indices are problematic, there is an indubitably stronger set of challenges to state authority after the end of the Cold War. In several of our cases, financial, political, and, in the case of Iraq, military pressure eroded state capacity during the 1990s. While Sudan had suffered civil war and economic crisis that would challenge any definition of "strong state," its international fate would also fundamentally change in the early 1990s, when its decision to support Iraq in the Gulf War and become a haven for terrorists led to international isolation.

We also note that mass atrocities occurred while states exercised some form of democracy—if we measure by elections, for example, as occurred in Yugoslavia, Iraq, South Sudan, Sudan, and Burundi. We can add Indonesia in terms of the opportunity for popular vote on independence in East Timor. This is not to pretend that elections are a proxy for robust democracy, rather an indicator of some degree of a democratization process underway.

The backdrop of changes in the post-Cold War era is necessary for two questions about endings today. First, why do mass atrocities continue despite the global trend of decline? Second, how do geo-historical trends impact patterns of ending in specific cases, including the endings where the anti-atrocity toolbox is applied? Both questions are explored below. But before we move to these, we must delve deeper into analysis of the place of conflict vis-á-vis violence against civilians. In this question, we begin to catch a glimpse of how atrocities continue and why ending them today may entail new challenges.

A story of atrocity endings and conflict

The current consensus about mass atrocities is that they usually occur in the context of armed conflict (Midlarsky 2005; Shaw 2002) – particularly in counter-insurgency operations and close to the onset of instability (Valentino and Ulfelder

2008). Our cases confirm the correlation. However, most studies have been concerned with the how the correlation relates to when violence begins. In discussing endings, we ask, what happens once violence is underway? Two key issues then arise: timing and the role of armed resistance. We find great diversity in our cases on both points. Instructive is a third concern: military capacity.

The case that most closely adheres to consensus is Bosnia, where war and atrocities coincided within well-defined periods, with a sharp spike of several months duration close to onset. Nonetheless, another, more condensed escalation in civilian killing occurred late in the conflict (Srebrenica). In this case, however, the overall period of atrocities does track with the period of conflict.

This is not the case with our other country examples. Three countries experienced increased periods of assaults against civilians within a long-enduring armed conflict, and in none of them do conflict and atrocity termination coincide. Guatemala's civil war lasted for thirty years, with a concentrated two-year spike in atrocities in the second decade of the conflict. In this case, the heightened killing period both began and ended with military coup, an instability within the instability. Iraq, Sudan, and South Sudan appear to have established a stable political vocabulary of violence, such that it does not make sense to mark atrocities in relation to conflict as such, but rather in relation to any number of new incentives that arise–be they political, economic, or military. Atrocities are a ready-at-hand tool for managing contestation, usually unsuccessfully.

Completely upending any attempt to summarize the relationship between atrocity and conflict termination are Burundi and Indonesia, which both offer examples of mass atrocities (with large differences in scale) that fall within and outside periods of armed conflict. In Burundi, three episodes of atrocities occur during armed conflict (1972, 1993, 1994–2002), but another two take place during ostensible "peace" (1965, 1988). In Indonesia, both Papua and East Timor suffered sharp spikes of violence as they faced initial Indonesian invasion, but both also experienced spikes outside the dates of armed conflict: in East Timor, war lasted from 1997 to 1998, but atrocities spiked in 1999; and Papua experienced an increase in violence against civilians, although not all incidents would be characterized as mass atrocities by our definition and data are poor, from 1981 to 1985 and 1996, whereas as the last noted conflict date is 1984.

Turning to atrocity instances that occur within armed conflict, we find a similar degree of complication when analyzing the role of armed resistance. Fighting between combatants can increase or decrease individual spikes of violence, just as it can both contribute to fueling or ending periods of atrocities. A credible threat posed by rebel groups presaged overwhelming government violence against civilians in Guatemala; Darfur, Sudan; Iraq under Hussein during the Iran–Iraq war; and East Timor (1975). Mass violence did not work to suppress the guerillas under the Lucas Garcia regime in Guatemala or Burundi, but in both instances fed recruitment. However, in Guatemala and the other aforementioned cases, atrocities did ultimately subside once the government decided it had adequately suppressed the possibility for armed resistance. Demonstrating an entirely different pattern, in, for example, the Nuba Mountains, Bosnia, later Burundi, and Iraq (2007-2008), the ability of groups to hold ground against opposing forces helped protect civilians.

It is clear that the mere presence or absence of armed conflict does not help us understand the timing, scale, or pattern of ending mass atrocities. Of much greater significance is the relative capacity of armed groups, including how this changes over time. To explore this factor, we borrow a framework developed by Kalyvas and Balcels (2014) for analyzing conflicts in terms of capacity of conflict actors. We note, their insights derive from analysis of a large number of cases, we apply them to our limited set all of which are examples of mass atrocities. The three models are: irregular (asymmetric capacities), conventional (evenly matched, high capacity armed forces), or symmetrical non-conventional (evenly matched, low capacity armed forces). Violence against civilians tends to be highest in irregular conflicts, aligning with insights about the saliency of counterinsurgency. This model provides us the worst examples of "drain the sea" counterinsurgency, as witnessed in Guatemala, some Sudanese episodes, Burundi, and earlier Indonesian cases.

Conventional conflicts tend to be shorter with higher battlefield casualties, and lower civilian fatalities. Our cases indicate that these kind of conflicts can be intensively lethal for civilians under circumstances where the organizational capacity of the armed forces is applied in specific ways, either with great intent to kill, or as we note, when civilian centers are targeted. This helps explain why Iraq in March and April 2003 witnessed the highest monthly civilian death tolls thus far, even though later periods of violence were sustained over a longer period of time (Iraq Body Count 2015).

Symmetrical non-conventional conflicts, Kalyvas and Balcels argue, are increasing in number since the end of the Cold War. These conflicts tend to pit already weak states against rising insurgencies. With both sides composed of low-capacity forces, the impact of their direct violence is often more limited. While Kalyvas and Balcels argue that such conflicts are characterized by coercive pressure on civilians from rebels and are prone to end in compromise, our limited body of cases demonstrate that these conflicts can be characterized by targeting of civilians from both government and insurgent sides with significant civilian fatalities, as in Sudan, South Sudan and Iraq (which might better be described as asymmetrical conflict within which symmetrical non-conventional civil war occurs—combining the worst elements of both models). The fatalities do not tend to reach the heights of pre-1990 mass atrocity events, but they are costly.

Aligning with general trends as discussed above, our post-Cold War atrocity episodes witness fewer instances of states pursing policies of mass atrocities with impunity until their goals are met, although Darfur, Sudan provides one such example amongst our cases and Sri Lanka's offensive against the Tamil Tigers demonstrates another (and much more successful) case.

While it has been argued that non-state actors play increasingly prominent roles in the perpetration of violence, our cases refine this insight to argue that non-state perpetrators whether associated with the state or not, have long been an important component in the perpetration of violence against civilians in the former Yugoslavia, Sudan, Burundi and Indonesia. However, one difference in our contemporary examples in Bosnia, South Sudan, and Iraq is the decreased capacity of states relative to non-state actors. Contemporary Guatemala offers a variation on this theme of non-state actors, although ongoing violence there is generally categorized as criminal, related to transnational drug trafficking. Nonetheless, the murder rate, while not the highest in Central America, rivals civilian death rates in some war zones: for instance, in 2010, 5,960 people were murdered in Guatemala (Goldschein 2011); whereas civilian deaths in Afghanistan were recorded at 2,777 (UNAMA 2011) and in Darfur, Sudan at 2,321 (Agence France Presse 2011).

Further, the low capacity of both states and insurgents can result in highly contingent compromise endings that are not always sustainable. Agreements may be possible only at the convergence of multiple factors, therefore are temporary—what de Waal terms "turbulent" (2015) in the sense of conditions that are changeable and even chaotic over short spans of time, but retain their structure over longer periods. We find in Iraq, Sudan and South Sudan, for instance, where political expression is often violent, including atrocities, and fluctuates in scale as interests align and diverge.

Regardless of these changes, atrocity endings are still governed by the same logic as previously: perpetrators decide that they can better pursue their long-term interests through policies other than violence against civilians. However, given decreased capacity and international norm shifts, the pursuit of interests is increasingly subject to other forces. Perpetrators' vulnerability to multiple forces is without question directly related to the increasingly salient international consensus against mass atrocities. This is a clear historic shift that has saved lives. But how it works is not as straightforward as the current anti-atrocity framework suggests.

The story of international engagement and atrocity endings

In sum, mass atrocity endings in our cases, as noted earlier, tended to be defined by overwhelming military force during the Cold War. After this point, several important changes resulted in endings becoming subject to a wider array of forces. The changes include, as discussed, the importance of a decline in direct international engagement in conflicts (particularly before the global war on terror), and the increase in international condemnation of violence against civilians. Arguably, both have helped decrease the scale and number of mass atrocity events. These trends coincide with a rising number of democracies, but also increased vulnerability for mass atrocities within states that are somewhere between authoritarianism and democracy. The states that are most vulnerable for mass violence also tend to be very weak, with low capacity. In our cases, the low capacity is particularly relevant relative to the capacity to non-state armed groups.

Hence, the ability of states to impose an ending is more restricted, both for normative and capacity related reasons. It also means that endings are influenced by a wider range of factors, including military pressure, resistance, local alliance shifts, re-alignment of regional interests, and, international diplomatic, economic and military pressure. In our cases, the wider array of forces impacting endings can render endings more contingent upon the alignment of multiple factors. Consequently, endings are varied across cases, and, in weaker states, more difficult to impact through foreign interventions (of all sorts) and sustain.

This background now informs our discussion as we analyze the impact of specific policy mechanisms in the anti-atrocity toolbox.

The anti-atrocity toolbox model was developed as an extension of the liberal state building project, understood as international engagement with conflict-affected and post-authoritarian governments with strategies to promote peace through norm adherence and by encouraging policies of political and economic liberalization. Key among the norms is the delegitimization of the use of violence, both armed conflict and mass atrocities. Exceptions to the application of these new rules for state legitimacy remained at the discretion of major powers. Critically, the exception concerning legitimate use of force was reserved for response to mass atrocities, although within a decade it was eclipsed by the "Global War on Terror."[8]

The goal of the anti-atrocities toolbox was to sharpen the punitive edge of liberal state building mechanisms in order to stop mass atrocities. Policy approaches to mass atrocity prevention and response envision a continuum of increasingly coercive actions that international actors might deploy to hasten endings: investigations, denunciations, legal prosecution, economic or diplomatic sanctions, no-fly zones,

[8] Sri Lanka probably best illustrates this point. If viewed solely within the anti-atrocity lens, the government's use of overwhelming force against the Tamil population should have provoked significant international condemnation and exclusion of the government from legitimacy. However, given the profile of the Tamil Tigers, with dismal innovations like female suicide bombers, the case straddled two frameworks. Despite some condemnation, the government continued its offensive until it achieved "success," defined as military victory, along the lines of the dominant Cold War model of mass atrocities endings in our cases.

safe havens, consensual peacekeeping, limited air strikes, supporting armed forces already active on the ground, coercive international intervention to force perpetrators to adjust policies, or to overthrow a perpetrating regime.

The efficacy of these tools has only recently been rigorously evaluated and the results are complicated, particularly in relation to long-term changes versus short-term impact on mass atrocity campaigns. First and most successful is the expansion of the norm against mass atrocity campaigns. There is strong international consensus today that intentional, widespread, and systematic assaults against civilians are not excusable – they cannot be rationalized away by any political or geo-strategic goal. This was evidenced in 2005 at the World Summit when the principle of an international *Responsibility to Protect* (RtoP) was affirmed by world leaders. Precisely what this meant and how it would apply to specific cases, was an entirely different matter; but the shift was fundamental. Scrutinizing the cases where RtoP principles were invoked, Alex Bellamy has argued that the primary effect of the principle is not that it determines a course of action, but rather how it instills what he calls "habits of protection," that "mean that the Council gives consideration to RtoP-related issues as a matter of routine, but they do not determine particular courses of action" (Bellamy 2014, p. 3).

There is some evidence that converting this norm into practices of naming and shaming by non-governmental organizations, international organizations, and media produces a significant impact on reducing violence against civilians related to the most severe atrocities (Krain 2012). However, the impact of these responses does not appear to be the same for lower levels of violence (Hafner-Burton 2013, p. 3). We will return to this point.

The story about diplomatic or economic sanctions, as George Lopez has argued, is mixed. In order to impact perpetrator behavior, he argues, sanctions need to be multilateral, tied to clear policy goals and focused diplomacy, and in place for a significant amount of time (Lopez 2013). On the other hand, Matthew Krain argues that economic sanctions, whether applied alone, with other measures, targeted or otherwise have no effect whatsoever on the severity of genocide or politicide (Krain 2014).

The record for the impact of international armed interventions is likewise contested, but with increasing evidence that over the long term, neutral, peacekeeping interventions better protect civilians than do partial interventions. While Krain (2005) argued that within a year of anti-perpetrator coercive intervention atrocities decline, Kathman and Wood (2011) find that in the short term, third-party interventions, whether neutral or to aid victims, correlate with a spike in violence against civilians. However, they continue, over the long term, neutral interventions diminish violence, and they do so better than pro-government or pro-target interventions (p. 754). In a study analyzing peacekeeping missions in 1991–2008, including force level changes over the course of a mission and how these changes correlate with instances of violence against civilians, Lisa Hultman, Jacob Kathman and Megan Shannon (2013) found strong evidence that UN peacekeeping can play an important role in decreasing the level of violence against civilians, when forces were deployed at significant size and included strong policing capacity. While some debate remains about whether peacekeeping results in less decisive endings to conflicts – and how these types of endings may produce different sorts of subsequent challenges – the record of peacekeeping's contributions to lessening war resumption and likely hastening of endings is supported by cross-case data (Fortna 2003). As Hultman, Kathman, and Shannon (2013) conclude: "UN peacekeeping is seemingly better at reducing human suffering than more biased forms of intervention" (p. 15).

Our cases similarly reflect the uneven efficacy of specific international response mechanisms. Alex de Waal argues that the presence of international aid workers helped change the dynamics of targeting civilians during militia wars in southern Sudan in the 1980s, and that prescient planning and policy implementation by leading American officials at USAID made an enormous difference in stemming the dying in Darfur (2003–2004 particularly). Additionally, the negotiation of a ceasefire agreement and the deployment of a relatively small group of African Union ceasefire monitors impacted the de-escalation of violence in Darfur. The later deployment of a large, Chapter VII peacekeeping force did not coincide with a reduction of violence. Neither in Sudan nor in Bosnia did legal indictments against leaders correspond to reduction in civilian-targeted violence.

Claire Smith emphasizes three particularly significant actions by international actors in East Timor: the development of transnational advocacy networks; the presence of UN representatives on the ground in 1999; and the credible threat of Australian military intervention. However, Smith finds that none of these factors was relevant to patterns of violence in Papua. In Bosnia, Conley-Zilkic also credits humanitarian actors for providing life-saving aid, the 1995 NATO air campaign for ending the siege of Sarajevo, the decisions of international actors to stay with displaced people in Žepa (as comparison with Srebrenica), and intensive U.S.-led mediation. The presence of a UN peacekeeping force (which did not have a civilian protection mandate) may have stalled mass killing in Srebrenica and possibly elsewhere, but it was not a factor in the endings of mass atrocities. Likewise, in Burundi, Twagiramungu credits key international mediators with supporting the transition to a "transformative ending." In Iraq, leaving aside the question of onset of violence and observing only the trends in decline of violence, Haddad notes that changes in U.S. military strategy played a role in the temporary decrease in violence that began in 2008.

While the application of discrete anti-atrocity measures has mixed results, the toolbox also includes the entire suite of liberal state-building agenda, with the goal of preventing recurrence of mass atrocities and creating peaceful, democratic, law governed, economically liberal, stable states. Our studies demonstrate that the norm against atrocities is well-established within the international liberal agenda and has borne fruit in the reduction of instances and overall numbers of fatalities. States find it much more difficult today to pursue their interests through policies of mass atrocity and remain within the community of legitimate states. The Global War on Terror is complicating, but has not dislodged this norm. However, more important for ending instances of mass atrocity today is state capacity, not the liberalism of its orientation. The liberal state-building agenda assumes that atrocity prevention is synonymous with its agenda; our cases suggest that while they are related, they are not the same. Further, by shifting our focus from an analysis of liberal state building to a discussion of state capacity, a different story emerges.

When states are strong enough *to adopt the trappings of liberalism* and particularly in cases where the states rely on relationships with western allies, there is reduction in their use of widespread and systematic assaults against civilians.

However, what remains are a variety of forms of violence, oppression, and dysfunction. Leaders continue to test the limits of how much reform is necessary. Key power centers in the states' security and governance sectors adjust to the new rules of elections, prohibition on violence against civilians that surpasses a high threshold, cooperation with U.S. security strategy, and economic liberalization. They also adapt the rules by calibrating how much violence and oppression is tolerated against how much is needed to protect their ability to remain in power.

It would be false to read these transformations as qualitative. In many ways, for mass atrocities, unlike political rights or structural violence, it does not seem to matter. It is easier for those in power to remain under the mass atrocities radar and still dominate the political and economic scene than it is to adhere to other human rights or democratization tenets. In fact, Hafner-Burton, who documents increases in abuse of political rights following state ratification of the UN Covenant on Civil and Political Rights (Hafner-Burton 2013, p.27) argues that human rights abuse must be understood as an "insidious, system-level problem" (Hafner-Burton 2013, p.27), not easily altered. This is distinct from what we have noted in the occurrence of mass atrocities, which are not the norm in any context and rise and fall according to specific alignment or divergence of interest.

In Bosnia, Guatemala, and Indonesia, we find elites who have managed the transition from large-scale violence to the political arena and adopted enough liberal manners and vocabulary to protect their interests within the expectations of the liberal state system. Guatemala and Indonesia both managed their endings in relation to their powerful western allies; they had strong incentives to be seen as performing as liberal states. Thus, while the Guatemalan army crushed the guerilla movement, ravaged indigenous communities in the early 1980s; they nonetheless played the game by negotiating a peace agreement in 1995 – long after the war had ended for all practical purposes. Why negotiate at this point, let alone sign an agreement resplendent with cultural rights for indigenous populations, among many other liberal codices? Functionally, as Brett demonstrates, the Guatemalan peace agreement granted recognition for the state as a liberal actor without altering the political and economic structures instituted by violence.

Indonesia also learned the new rules of the international system quite quickly, as its allies threatened to impose them in East Timor. Nonetheless, Smith argues, the entrenched military and political elites set their own limits to these new rules: independence for ethnic minorities was firmly taken off the table after the establishment of Timor-Leste. In relation to other groups' political claims, Indonesian leaders alternated between reform, political opening, and repression. By re-calibrating the scale of violence – and notably its visibility – alongside efforts to buy the loyalty of local elites in Papua, they developed a sustainably violent governance model that is nonetheless internationally acceptable.

In the Yugoslav context, it is arguable that Serbia, Croatia, and possibly Kosovo (after the final phase of ethnic cleansing of the Serbian minority), emerged as states capable of playing by the new liberal state rules, but grudgingly so, resisting, prevaricating, or delaying wherever these terms seemed to clash with the affirmation of the ethno-nationalist states that triumphed in the wars. Bosnia provides a less clear end result. In Bosnia, political self-preservation is hard-coded into ethnic terms: access to power and economic benefits of the state are channeled through ethnically-defined, entrenched political parties and state structure. This works at odds with a functioning, liberally-defined central state, and against Bosnia's reality as a multi-ethnic society. Given its European context, one would hope that regional pressure and incentives would eventually provoke political reform rather than violence. However, the South Slav pattern, as Conley-Zilkic demonstrates, is long periods of peace between episodes of mass violence, typically catalyzed by geopolitical shifts – so it may be too early to say.

Burundi followed a distinct path. Because ethnic mass killing ended through the exceptional commitment to moderation exhibited by key political leaders, which, when added to overwhelming exhaustion with the stalemated conflict and ethnic logic that fueled violence, and sustained international mediation, arrived at a different sort of politics as the new terrain for contesting power. Twagiramungu presents a strong argument that large-scale, state-sponsored violence against civilians along an ethnic schism may have ended. However, given the historic saliency of violence as a tool for expressing political dissent and the self-protecting and self-perpetuating state as the governance model that has triumphed in the region, the country's politics will likely produce governments with oppressive tendencies.

On the question of recurrence, we must bracket Iraq, Sudan, and South Sudan as violence is ongoing as this volume is being published. In these cases, as de Waal and Haddad argue, politics is articulated through a "grammar" of violence. It is part of the expression of political contention and elite bargaining. Actual violence ebbs and flows in relation to new political realignments or shifts, but appears, for now, to be a persistent part of how the countries function.

In the 2000s, the Sudanese government aspired to international acceptability, in the form of normalized diplomatic relations with Washington and the lifting of international sanctions. It cooperated with the CIA on counter-terrorism, signed a peace deal with southern Sudan that involved democratic elections, accepted a UN mission in Darfur and in the end was ready to let South Sudan secede peacefully. None of these actions were sufficient to allow it readmission to the club of respectable states. Its continuing pariah status is symbolized by the International Criminal Court arrest warrant against President Omar al Bashir. The reason for this lies in the effectiveness of an American advocacy campaign with strong links to both Democrats and Republicans in Congress, which vetoes what it characterizes as any attempt to appease a criminal regime. The fact that the leaders of the independent Republic of South Sudan, who were indulged and supported by these same advocates over many years, have also inflicted mass atrocities, has not led the U.S. administration to reassess its stand. To the contrary, while Washington is condemning its former friends in South Sudan, it is even harder for it to lift any of its punitive measures against Khartoum. For Sudan's political leaders, de Waal argues, the lesson is simple: there is no reward for better behavior.

In South Sudan and Iraq, the governments are so poorly institutionalized that it makes little sense to describe their actions and capacities in terms of a state. In these countries, the calibration of violence in line with the rules of the "international community" simply is not possible. The state in both cases offers no decision-making apparatus to govern use of violence; which is not to say that decisions are not made, but that they are not made within the context of the state. Therefore, "endings" are not possible; only fluctuations as various factors align and break apart.

International condemnation of mass atrocities has significantly contributed to reductions in the number and scale of mass atrocity events, and specific policy measures have made an impact at times. Nonetheless, overall the insights that arise from assessment of the anti-atrocity toolbox are sobering. Even in higher capacity state contexts, the mechanisms that contribute to atrocity endings should not be confused with those that end other forms of injustice and oppression. In contexts of low capacity states, application of international pressure, no matter how robust, to counter perpetrator violence will not produce sustainable endings. This raises important questions about the need to engage states, even if and when they remain the greatest threats in terms of perpetrating mass atrocities.

CONCLUSION

The greatest challenge in atrocity prevention and response is foregrounding endings within the national politics of state-building, power contestation and capacity that determines both the possibility and sustainability of terminating atrocities.

The task of ending mass atrocities cannot be understood as primarily assertion of 'our' power. If we wish to hasten endings of mass atrocities, we cannot begin with the question: what should *we* do differently next time? While some of the answers to this question remain relevant and important, it forms the wrong framework from the beginning. In-depth study of actual endings suggests that two key questions should be central to any efforts to halt widespread and systematic violence against civilians: what factors influence how key leaders perceive the strategic value of violence against civilians? And how can their capacity be harnessed to terminate violence?

Posing these questions is a realist articulation of the idealist's proposal that mass atrocities need not be accepted as a permanent part of human existence. It proceeds in recognition that the factors that seem to contribute to decline do not readily translate into a policy playbook that applies evenly to all locations. Ultimately, there seems to be a limit to how much societies can absorb and integrate internationally defined change into their own practices, regardless of pressure, even in its most coercive forms. Change comes not in the form of tidy formulas for discrete actions, but rather when the alignment of political interests shifts.

Mass atrocity endings have changed over time. Before the 1990s, overwhelming military force was the primary mode of ending. States stopped inflicting mass atrocities when violence no longer served its purpose, however paranoid and irrational these goals appeared to others. Thereafter, endings became more varied and subject to multiple factors: internal dissent, military pressure, and international political pressure. They are also more contingent on the alignment of various factors to open a window of opportunity. However, while we do see that discrete anti-atrocity tools can make a difference, the more fundamental point is that the ending dynamic cannot be disarticulated into its component parts. Endings are possible when the preponderance of factors produce a realignment of interest. Thus, in terms of direct actions that international players might take – precisely the toolbox model that has dominated the anti-atrocities agenda – actual endings do not suggest a one-to-one relationship between international actions and atrocity endings.

Our understanding of how endings occur aligns with new studies of prevention, which reform or depart from the toolbox model in several ways. For instance, studies by Scott Straus (2015) and by Deborah Mayerson and Stephen McLoughlin (2011) explore negative cases, asking why places with comparable risk profiles do not manifest atrocities, emphasizing local agency and capacities.

They have argued for prevention models that assess how multiple historical, social, economic, and political factors interrelate over time to create risk or restraint, that is, atrocities-prone or resilient states.

Endings in the post-1990 landscape should not be understood within a salvation narrative. Rather, endings today occur when there is a fundamental change in the nature of contestation from high-level assaults against vulnerable groups to the political arena, and a subsequent adoption of the language and manners of liberal peace by a new or adjusted state formation, which nonetheless is oriented toward protecting power. Further, the capacity to achieve such an ending is not equally possible in our contexts. And, finally, even when it does occur, this shift does not herald, necessarily, a more just dispensation, rule of law, accountability, a triumph of human rights, a fully functional democratic state, or any of the other trappings of liberal peace and peace building. It is a more basic, yet nonetheless life-saving change.

WORKS CITED

Bass, Gary. 2013. *The Blood Telegram*. New York: Alfred A. Knopf.

Bellamy, Alex. 2013. "The Other Asian Miracle?: The Decline of Atrocities in East Asia" *Peace & Security* 26:1, 1–19.

2014. "R2P: Added Value or Hot Air?" *Cooperation and Conflict* 0: 1–25.

Boghossian, Paul. 2010. "The Concept of Genocide." *The Journal of Genocide Research* 12: 69–80.

Chandler, David. 2015. "Resilience and the 'Everyday': Beyond the Paradox of 'Liberal Peace'." *Review of International Studies* 41: 27–48.

Cunningham, David E. and Douglas Lemke (2014) "Beyond Civil War: A Quantitative Examination of Causes of Violence within Countries." *Civil Wars* 16:3, 328–345.

Conley-Zilkic, Bridget and Alex de Waal. 2014. "Setting the Agenda for Evidence-based Research on Ending Mass Atrocities." *Journal of Genocide Research* 16:1, 55–76.

Conley-Zilkic, Bridget. 2015. "The Pistol on the Wall: How Coercive Military Intervention Limits Atrocity Prevention Policies" In *Reconstructing Atrocity Prevention* edited by Sheri P. Rosenberg, Tiberiu Galis, and Alex Zucker, pp. 31–60. Cambridge: Cambridge University Press.

Cushman, Thomas. 2003. "Is Genocide Preventable? Some Theoretical Considerations." *Journal of Genocide Research* 5/4: 523–542.

DeWaal, Alex. *The Real Politics of the Horn of Africa: Money, War, and the Business of Power*. Cambridge: Polity Books (forthcoming).

Dixon, Jeffrey. 2009 "Emerging Consensus: Results from the Second Wave of Statistical Studies on Civil War Termination." *Civil Wars*. 11: 2, 121–136.

Fortna, Page. 2003. "Inside and Out: Peacekeeping and the Duration of Peace after Civil and Interstate Wars." *International Studies Review* 5:4, 97–114.

Gleditsch, Nils Petter, Peter Wallensteen, Mikael Eriksson, Margareta Sollenberg and Håvard Strand. 2002. "Armed Conflict 1946–2001: A New Dataset." *Journal of Peace Research* 39:5, 615–637.

Hafner-Burton, Emilie. 2013. *Making Human Rights a Reality*. Princeton, NJ: Princeton University Press.

Hiltermann, Joost R. 2008. "The 1988 Anfal Campaign in Iraqi Kurdistan, Online Encyclopedia of Mass Violence," published on February 3, 2008 Available at: www.massviolence.org/The-1988-Anfal-Campaign-in-Iraqi-Kurdistan. Accessed March 9, 2015.

Hultman, Lisa, Jacob D. Kathman and Megan Shannon. 2013. "United Nations Peacekeeping and Civilian Protection in Civil War." *American Journal of Political Science* 57: 875–891.

Human Security Report Project (HSR). 2010. *Human Security Report 2009/2010: The Causes of Peace and the Shrinking Costs of War*. New York: Oxford University.

Iraq Body Count. 2015. Available at: www.iraqbodycount.org/database/. Accessed March 11, 2015.

Kalyvas, Stathis N. 2006. *The Logic of Violence in Civil Wars*. Cambridge: Cambridge University Press.

Kalyvas and Balcels. 2014. "Does Warfare Matter?: Severity, Duration and Outcomes of Civil Wars." *Journal of Conflict Resolution* 58:8, 1390–1418.

Kathman and Wood. 2011."Managing Threat, Cost, and Incentive to Kill : The Short- and Long-Term Effects of Intervention in Mass Killings." *Journal of Conflict Resolution* 55: 735–760.

Krain, Matthew. 2014. "The Effects of Diplomatic Sanctions and Engagement on the Severity of Ongoing Genocides or Politicides." *Journal of Genocide Research* 16:1, 25–53.

2012. "*J'Accuse!* Does Naming and Shaming Perpetrators Reduce the Severity of Genocides or Politicides?" *International Studies Quarterly* 56: 574–589.

2005. "International Intervention and the Severity of Genocides and Politicides." *International Studies Quarterly* 49: 363–387.

Kraus, Keith. 2013. "Challenges to Counting and Classifying Victims of Violence in Conflict, Post-Conflict, and Non-Conflict Setting" In *Counting Civilian Casualties* edited by Taylor B. Seybolt, Jay D. Aronson, and Baruch Fischhoff, pp. 265–284. Oxford: Oxford University Press.

Lacina, Bethany. 2006. "Explaining the Severity of Civil Wars." *Journal of Conflict Resolution* 50:2, 276–289.

Lemkin, Raphael. 1944. *Axis Rule in Occupied Europe*. Washington, D.C.: Carnegie Endowment for International Peace.

Levene, Mark. 2013. *The Crisis of Genocide, Volumes I and II*. Oxford: Oxford University Press.

Licklider, Roy. 1998. "Early Returns: Results of the First Wave of Statistical Studies of Civil War Termination." *Civil Wars* 1:3, 121–32.

Lopez, George A. 2013. "Tools, Tasks and Tough Thinking: Sanctions and R2P." Policy Brief. Global Centre for the Responsibility to Protect. October 3. Available at: www.globalr2p.org/publications/263. Accessed March 11, 2015.

2000. "Economic Sanctions and Genocide: Too Little, Too Late, and Sometimes Too Much." In *Protection Against Genocide: Mission Impossible?* edited by Neal Riemer. Westport: Praeger, pp.67–84.

Mann, Michael. 2005. *The Dark Side of Democracy: Explaining Ethnic Cleansing*. Cambridge: Cambridge University Press.

Mayersen, Deborah and Stephen McLoughlin. 2011. "Risk and Resilience to Mass Atrocities in Africa: A Comparison of Rwanda and Botswana." *Journal of Genocide Research* 13:3, 247–269.

Melander, Erik, Magnus Öberg, and Jonathan Hall. 2009. "Are 'New Wars' More Atrocious? Battle Severity, Civilians Killed and Forced Migration Before and After the End of the Cold War." *European Journal of International Relations* 15:3, 505–536.
Pettersson, Therése and Peter, Wallensteen. 2015. "Armed conflicts, 1946–2014." *Journal of Peace Research*, 52:4, 536–550.
Shaw, Martin. 2013. *Genocide and International Relations*. Cambridge: Cambridge University Press.
Straus, Scott. 2012a. "'Destroy Them to Save Us': Theories of Genocide and the Logics of Political Violence." *Terrorism and Political Violence* 24:4, 544–560.
2012b. "Wars Do End! Changing Patterns of Political Violence in Sub-Saharan Africa." *African Affairs* 11: 443, 179–201.
2015. *Making and Unmaking Nations: War, Leadership, and Genocide in Modern Africa*. Ithaca: Cornell University Press.
Themnér, Lotta and Peter Wallensteen. 2014. "Armed Conflicts, 1946–2013." *Journal of Peace Research* 51:4, 541–554.
Tilly, Charles. *The Politics of Collective Violence*. Cambridge: Cambridge University Press.
Ulfelder, Jay and Benjamin Valentino. 2008. "Assessing Risks of State-Sponsored Mass Killing." Available at: http://ssrn.com/abstract=17033426. Accessed October 23, 2013.
Valentino, Benjamin. 2014. "Why We Kill: The Political Science of Political Violence Against Civilians." *Annual Review of Political Science* 17: 89–103.
2004. *Final Solutions: Mass Killing and Genocide in the Twentieth Century*. Ithaca and London: Cornell University Press.
Valentino, Benjamin, Paul Huth, and Dylan Balch-Lindsay. 2004. "'Draining the Sea": Mass Killing and Guerilla Warfare." *International Organization* 58: 375–407.

Guatemala

The persistence of genocidal logic beyond mass killing

Roddy Brett

INTRODUCTION

This chapter analyzes the complex array of factors that shaped the ending of mass atrocities perpetrated during the Guatemalan state's counterinsurgency campaign of the 1980s. Central to the military campaign and to the execution of mass atrocities was the strategic employment of public massacres in indigenous Maya communities accused of providing logistical and military support to the guerrilla army, the Guatemalan National Revolutionary Unity (URNG), in the country's western highlands. The United Nations–sponsored Historical Clarification Commission (CEH), one of a series of transitional justice mechanisms incorporated into the peace settlement negotiated between successive governments and the URNG, concluded in its final report that state agents had been responsible for *acts of genocide* committed in at least four regions of the country during counterinsurgency operations between 1981 and 1983 (CEH Vol. III 1999, pp. 423–424). Mass atrocities against noncombatant populations culminating in genocide represented a deliberate military strategy in Guatemala, as Valentino et al. (2004) and Kalyvas (2006) have identified for cases elsewhere.

Fuelled by deeply entrenched racism, by 1984, the massacres – whose objective was to eliminate the guerrilla's social base – ended, having precipitated the strategic defeat of the URNG and its withdrawal into Mexico by literally burning its support base off the map.[1] In the immediate aftermath of the massacres, indigenous survivors were confined within concentration camps, the so-called *model villages*, forced to participate in paramilitary Civil Defence Patrols, and subject to strict military control and indoctrination programs. These latter strategies were aimed at

[1] Significant academic scholarship has focused upon the genocidal nature of the counterinsurgency violence. See, for example, Black et al. (1984), Falla (1988), Jonas (2000), ODHAG (1998), Schirmer (1998), Taylor (1998), Sandford (2003), Brett (2007; 2016, forthcoming), and Casaus Arzú (2008).

isolating indigenous communities from the guerrilla and preventing political mobilization, whether armed or unarmed. Mass atrocities ultimately gave way to other forms of social control once the strategic goal of defeating the URNG had been achieved and indigenous communities had been successfully subject to military control.

Atrocities perpetrated during Guatemala's conflict represented a core component of counterinsurgency strategy, enabling the military to radicalize the state's killing machinery (Valentino et al. 2004, p. 376) and leading, in this case, to the effective disarticulation of the guerrilla's social base. Given that the episodes of mass killing represented an integral part of the national counterinsurgency campaign, determined, in itself, by a strict temporal, logistical, and geographical operational framework, the endings of mass atrocities were, in turn, contingent upon the successes of military strategy. As specific communities across the guerrilla heartland were effectively "cleansed" and pacified, mass killing within them stopped and a policy of confinement was implemented, leaving the military subsequently at liberty to extend and concentrate upon killing operations elsewhere. This chapter will argue that mass atrocities in Guatemala ended disjunctively, rather than abruptly and uniformly. Between 1981 and 1983, during the government of Lucas García and the regime of Ríos Montt, while specific instances of mass killing ended as bounded indigenous communities were eventually brought under military control – "recuperated" in military terminology – the overall strategic killing campaign only ended once the generalized guerrilla threat had been neutralized in 1984, during the regime of General Oscar Humerto Mejía Víctores.

With the strategic defeat of the URNG, the military orchestrated a political transition culminating with the gradual return to civilian rule, which signaled the closure of the atrocity campaign; on winning the first civilian elections after twenty years, President Vinicio Cerezo Arévalo assumed office in 1986. The return to civilian rule eventually led to a peace process concluded in 1996. What clearly differentiates the Guatemala case study is that while the policy of mass atrocities effectively came to an end in 1984, racism has animated the continuation of an eliminationist logic, wielding profound impact in the post-war era. The end to mass atrocities has not brought with it the end to genocide. Guatemala's past remains under contention and the country's nation-building project an ongoing site of struggle.

The investigation draws on empirical data gathered during prolonged periods of research in Guatemala, in particular in communities of genocide survivors in the highland department of El Quiché during 2002 and 2003; research carried out in Guatemala City in 2013; and archival research carried out over the past three years. The chapter is composed of five sections. First, a brief analysis of patterns of violence in Guatemala. Second, a brief exploration of the regional context in which the internal armed conflict was waged, leading to an analysis of the presidency of General Romeo Lucas García. Under the Lucas García administration, counterinsurgency operations came to be characterized by grave levels of violence and systematic human rights violations, particularly in urban areas, and, toward the second half of the administration, mass atrocities in rural Guatemala. The incapacity of the Lucas García government to defeat the guerrilla led to a coup d'état in March 1982 and the imposition of a military junta. With the subsequent assumption of Montt as de facto president, a gradual transformation of counterinsurgency strategy took place.

The third section addresses the Montt years, during which time rural violence escalated, spiking between 1982 and 1983. This phase was characterized by strategic planning that was developed in advance of and established the framework for the killing campaign. The atrocity campaigns during this period were the result of a conscious decision to commit mass atrocities and impose micro-level confinement over and control of the indigenous population. This section also explores the strategy of systematic massacres and the process of subjecting the indigenous population to military control. The fourth section discusses how mass atrocities ended in Guatemala, examining the strategic decisions made by the Montt regime and its successor, that of General Mejía Víctores. Key to this section is an enquiry into how the political transition that followed the strategic defeat of the guerrilla and the subsequent peace process shaped the ending of mass atrocities, if at all. The concluding section reflects upon the nature of endings and the broader legacy of genocide and mass atrocities within Guatemala's post-conflict context. It queries the relationship between the nature of the counterinsurgent violence and the complex historical formations of racism within the post-conflict scenario.

PART ONE: PATTERNS OF MASS ATROCITY VIOLENCE

The violence that characterized mass atrocities in Guatemala was highly complex and multidimensional, informing, to a degree, the nature of mass atrocity endings. A principal factor driving the instrumentalist violence was the counterinsurgency objective to *drain the sea to kill the fish*, as scholars such as Schirmer (1998) and Sanford (2003) have correctly observed. Counterinsurgency logics only partially explain the *objectives* behind mass atrocities in the Guatemala case, however, and are unable to elucidate clear understanding of the profoundly brutal and ritualistic *nature* of this violence. As a consequence, the counterinsurgency argument may also fall short in providing meaningful understanding of why, when, and how mass atrocities and genocide "end." While the perpetration of mass atrocities indeed terminated in 1984, sociopolitical, legal, and cultural formations in post-conflict Guatemala suggest important questions regarding the possible continuity of genocidal dynamics in the country. In this case, if we move away from the narrow legal definition of genocide and assume a broader definition, the ending of mass atrocities – defined in relation to killing campaigns – precedes and does not coincide with the ending of genocide.

In this respect, Raphael Lemkin's 1944 definition of genocide provides a stronger analytical framework than does the 1948 legal definition. Lemkin describes genocide as the intent to annihilate a group's national patterns and impose the oppressor's patterns upon said group. He introduces two processes of genocide, "one, destruction of the national pattern of the oppressed group; the other the imposition of the national pattern of the oppressor" (Lemkin 1944, p. 79). Diverse measures of oppression may be employed to achieve these ends, of which killing is only one: the objective is to eliminate a group's social power, cultural capacity, and symbolic or physical presence. As Martin Shaw has eloquently observed, while physical and biological extermination represents a key aspect of genocide, the phenomenon incorporates a further dimension of social and cultural destruction, "embodied in (a group's) ownership of land … (their) religious institutions, cultural and political organization, and all the other ways in which their presence in given social spaces and territories is manifested" (2007, p. 34). To understand the disjunction between mass atrocities and genocide in Guatemala, it is helpful to build on the critical insight of genocide scholars such as Midlarsky (2005), Shaw (2007), and Straus (2007), who have observed that attention should be paid to the structural and contextual aspects of genocide.

Entrenched historical racism against the indigenous Maya, reinforced by the opportunistic mobilization of an ideology of ethnic hatred by ethnic entrepreneurs within the state (Gurr and Harff 1994), gave profound meaning to mass, organized killing. Between 1981 and 1983, sequential cycles of mass atrocities were perpetrated by the Guatemalan military, a consolidated hierarchical organizational structure. Perpetrators' actions here were part of and subject to a broader system, were "concerted and systematic" and regulated by "division-of-labor principles" (Bloxham 2008, p. 205). As the threat to the Guatemalan state increased, the insurgency's social base, the historically vulnerable, stigmatized, and excluded indigenous population, was identified as the collective internal enemy through the operationalization of the National Security Doctrine. Moving beyond counterinsurgency logic, massacres were perpetrated initially by nonindigenous troops who believed their enemy was, effectively, *sub-human*. This essentialist violence against indigenous communities was deemed necessary to purify and build a consolidated whitened, homogeneous nation-state (Hale 2006; Semelin 2007). Driven by what Goldhagen (2009) has defined as an "eliminationist ideology," essentialist violence was orchestrated against the dehumanized deviant indigenous "other" (Campbell 2009, p. 151). The violence represented the extension of a nation-building project, and, partially, a state-building project, as Tilly (1996) has observed for the case of Europe. This convergence of instrumentalist and essentialist violence ultimately sculpted the idiosyncratic nature of Guatemala's mass atrocities.

Despite the perpetration of genocide, the ethnicized nature of the counterinsurgency violence was complex. Initially, mass atrocities were carried out by nonindigenous soldiers against indigenous Maya communities. The interethnic, macro-level killing campaign was executed by nonindigenous, or *ladino* soldiers, as articulated in the nationally orchestrated counterinsurgency strategy planned by the military high command. However, mass atrocities were not exclusively interethnically driven. Over time, and once paramilitary units were consolidated in indigenous communities by the military, macro-level violence affected local-level community dynamics, in turn, hastening systematic episodes of egregious political violence within and between indigenous communities. As Kalyvas (2006) has cogently documented in the context of Greece, local politics and political economies also played a crucial role in shaping the political violence within indigenous communities in Guatemala. In Guatemala, there was a productive relationship between macro- and micro-level violence in contexts, leading to a "cumulative radicalisation" (Kalyvas 2006; Finkel and Strauss 2012). As the research evidences, as the dynamics and logics of violence evolved, macro-level killing precipitated micro-level violence, and, in turn, local-level politics moulded the trajectory of the counterinsurgency. Not all community-level violence was *political*.

PART TWO: THE CONTEXT OF GUATEMALA'S INTERNAL ARMED CONFLICT

Geopolitical Context

Guatemala's internal armed conflict was not waged in a political vacuum; it was shaped by the security, military, political, and ideological logic of the Cold War. The country's conflict was decisively determined by the specific revolutionary-counterrevolutionary dynamics of Latin America's long and violent Cold War, as Joseph and Grandin (2010) have eloquently detailed, a period during which the region experienced profound and painful processes of social, political, cultural, and economic change (Kruijt and Koonings 1999). Azpuru (2012) further disaggregates the Latin American encounter, arguing that the region underwent differentiated experiences of conflict/civil war and authoritarianism from the 1960s onward. In this respect, Latin America confronted a "heightened period" of state terror and resistance, in both the Southern Cone and Central America (Grandin 2010), as guerrilla and social movements and state responses to them violently disputed the region's destiny. From the 1970s, the "terms of history" changed for Latin Americans, as states became omnipresent counterinsurgency structures, ushering in continuing waves of political violence and terror that would intimately sculpt all aspects of everyday life (Grandin 2004).

Latin America's Cold War experience was effectively borne out of the violence that emerged from challenges seeking to incorporate the masses into the political system, a process that began as far back as the 1930s (Kruijt and Koonings 1999). The process implied direct challenges to the region's diverse and multiple oligarchic orders, and, as the Cold War became embedded, social conflict became politicized and ideologically charged, leading to violence waged within ideological and doctrinal paradigms. This phenomenon ultimately culminated in internal conflict, state terrorism, and dirty war, as states crafted unprecedentedly sophisticated counterrevolutionary apparatuses.

Counterrevolutionary violence sought to impede the capacity of insurgencies to wield an enduring and effective impact upon Latin American states and societies, as had been the case in Cuba (Broder and Lambek 1988; Grandin 2004). In the aftermath of the Cuban revolution, across the region, guerrilla movements mobilized to challenge the closure of political systems and patterns of socioeconomic exclusion and inequality (Dunkerley 1989; Dunkerley 1993). Latin America's Cold War confrontation was shaped by the clash of worldviews, interests, and ideologies; the contingent possibility of and hope for change that progressive actors felt; and the dread that change would not bring sufficient transformation (Grandin 2010). In countries such as Colombia, these conditions were exacerbated by a profound lack of *state-ness*, the absence of state monopoly over use of force and its inability to uphold a legal order, precipitating system-wide mobilizations, and, ultimately, diverse and protracted insurgencies.

Counterrevolutionary violence principally triumphed in almost all cases, however, because it was uncompromisingly decisive in its brutality (Grandin 2010); the Guatemalan case was no exception. In this context, Latin American militaries vehemently defended the interests of the economic and political elite. Military institutions gradually moulded themselves as the arbiters of national order, stability, and progress (Kruijt and Kooning 1999), resulting in the consolidation of "spaces of death and cultures of terror" (Grandin 2010). In this regard, and as the Guatemala case of mass atrocity perpetration evidences, Latin America has played a pioneering role in the institutionalization of modern state terrorism, one of the "modern state's constitutive modes of operation" (Wilson 2013, p. 15). As we shall see later, in the wake of the revolutionary victory of the Sandinistas in Nicaragua in 1979, the Guatemalan state and the country's economic elites would unleash their demons: Guatemala would not fall as Nicaragua had done. Central American states and societies would ultimately pay a high price for the Sandinista victory; for Guatemala, this price was manifest in mass atrocities shaped by profound racism.

In this context, the United States within the framework of the U.S. National Security Doctrine (NSD), provided the principal assistance to right-wing Latin American militaries, delivering economic and military aid, military training through the School of the Americas and U.S. Southern Command, and, in certain cases, directly through its embassies (Broder and Lambek 1988; Schirmer 1998). International support, particularly from North America, directly contributed to the perpetration of mass atrocities in Guatemala. Nevertheless, impelled by their own demographic conditions, historical trajectories and logistical objectives, Latin American security forces and the Guatemalan military *par excellence* developed their own capacity for barbarous acts of counterrevolutionary violence, becoming innovators and experts in the field (Grandin 2004). The Guatemala case will evidence how this logic became key to the success of the genocidal counter-insurgency strategy.

The Lucas García Government and Onset of the Counterinsurgency

The administration of General Lucas García (1978–1982) represents one of the darkest chapters in Guatemala's history, with the logic of violence evolving as Lucas García attempted to ward off chaos and consolidate control by subordinating the state to militarized security and deploying violence against all opponents. As the state shifted from a racist post-colonial state to a racist, securitized counterinsurgency state, the practice of mass-killing campaigns emerged under Lucas García, who became the president in 1978 at the height of "the most severe economic and political crisis of the century" (Bulmer-Thomas 1995, pp. 364–372). At the end of the 1970s, Guatemala's economy was characterized by capital flight, spiraling annual inflation rates, and national debt, in a context in which the private sector had effectively derogated confidence in the country's economy. As the crisis worsened, through manifestly fraudulent elections, and with only 15% of the registered votes, Lucas García was elected.

From the beginning of his mandate, Lucas García faced a series of simultaneous challenges, including the economic crisis, and containing both his political and military opponents (from both extremes of the ideological spectrum) and the security situation (Kemp, unpublished, p. 87).[2] Despite the defeat of the first insurgency in 1960, the revolutionary threat was rekindled with the formation of the Guerrilla Army of the Poor (EGP) in 1975,[3] and its subsequent increasingly public acts of defiance in the indigenous highlands. By the middle of Lucas García's term, the political crisis escalated, a direct consequence of the government's hapless counterinsurgency offensive between 1978 and 1980 that led many to question if the URNG might actually possess the capacity to overthrow the state, particularly in the wake of the 1979 Sandinista guerilla victory in Nicaragua.

By the late 1970s, the EGP and another insurgent faction, the Revolutionary Organisation of People in Arms (ORPA), were building their social bases within indigenous populations in the highlands, claiming that they represented these communities politically and militarily and would act on behalf of their collective grievances and interests. Initially, this was not the case. Guatemala's conflict was not a conventional ethnic conflict as such, arising from direct conflict between mobilized ethnic groups; nor was the EGP an exclusively indigenous faction (Brett 2013). However, as greater numbers of indigenous communities across the western highlands voluntarily supported or became incorporated into the ranks of the

2 See also Gramajo (1995, p. 156).

3 See Gleijeses (1992), Brett (2007), and Kruijt (2008) for a detailed analysis of this period.

guerrilla – a consequence of military repression against these communities – so the insurgency, in turn, extended and consolidated its social base (Stoll 1993; Valentino 2004; Brett 2007).

As the political crisis worsened, the Guatemalan military, political, and business elite began to demonstrate frustration toward the Lucas García administration, exacerbating the international isolation it was facing as a result of the U.S. President Jimmy Carter government's condemnation of its human rights record.[4] In response, the Lucas García government extended the operational framework of the NSD – applied since the early 1960s in Guatemala – identifying a broad group as internal enemy. The goal of this strategic shift was to tighten control over civil and political society by imposing military ideology and doctrine as the key organizing principle of the state.[5] The military aimed to embed itself into the administrative, political, and juridical foundations of the state as the sole institution within the country (Schirmer 1998, p. 9), an objective that would ultimately be achieved under the Montt dictatorship. Over the subsequent years, a series of bureaucratic military structures were consolidated, serving key functions in the counterinsurgency and, specifically, to eliminate the guerrilla's support base. The Army Intelligence Directorate (D-2) and the Military Intelligence Section (G-2) conducted extensive espionage operations and engaged directly in the murder, torture, and disappearance of "subversives" (Schirmer 1998). The DIC (Criminal Investigations Department), the PMA (Mobile Military Police), and, from 1982, the Army Section for Civilian Affairs (S-5) also assumed a central role in the counterinsurgency.

Between 1979 and 1981, hyper-securitization precipitated approximately 7,000 murders, disappearances, and politically motivated kidnappings, as the military and death squads supported by the private sector operated freely (Black et al. 1984; Schirmer 1998; Sanford 2003; Brett, forthcoming, 2016). Ferocious repression, particularly in urban areas, was deployed against all political opposition, including political parties, social movements, and trade unions, with the objective of eliminating subversion. Initially, the administration unleashed a strategy of selective repression and killing, targeting politicians, trade union organizations, and the Committee for Peasant Unity (CUC). Urban violence was the most visible pattern of state violence until, on May 29, 1978, the military perpetrated the massacre of approximately 150 rural indigenous Maya K'ekchi's in Panzós, Alta Verapaz, in response to local political mobilization.[6] While not part of a centrally planned

[4] Shortly after Ríos Montt came to power, the Reagan administration removed Guatemala from its "black list" of countries responsible for human rights violations and reinitiated official military an economic assistance (Black et al. 1984, pp. 119–130; Ball et al. 1999).

[5] See Cardoso (1979) and Shelton and Carozza (2012) for an in-depth discussion on the theme of NSD.

[6] See Sanford (2001) and Grandin (2004) for an eloquent and detailed discussion of the significance of the massacre of Panzós.

strategy, the Panzós massacre represented the first instance of rural massacre that would later become the central tenet of the mass atrocity campaign.

The state demonstrated the lengths to which it was willing to go to silence opposition, demonstrating blatant disregard for national and international law when it stormed the Spanish Embassy on January 31, 1980, in the "defining event" of the armed conflict (Arias 2007, p. 161). A group of displaced K'iche' and Ixil peasant farmers, some of whom had links to the CUC, had occupied the embassy to protest against acts of violence carried out by the military in the department of K'iche'. On executive order, the armed forces attacked the embassy, setting it on fire and preventing those inside from exiting, an intentional act resulting in the deaths of thirty-six people, including embassy officials.

The albeit reactionary policy of mass killings, homicides, disappearances, and torture under Lucas García was institutionalized by January 1980. As the CEH stated in its final report, state terror served a dual purpose "of physically eliminating some dissidents while dissuading others from getting involved" (Rothenberg 2012, p. 12). The Guatemala case evidences how deliberate state-sponsored violence possesses a productive and ordering function, as it seeks to dissuade, to spread fear, and to weaken, punish, and eliminate enemies of the state. The case study then contests the proposition that violence is irrational, and lacks order, rules, and objectives, as Kalyvas (2006) and Leiby (2009) have also cogently evidenced.

The Limits of Mass Violence

In the months leading up to the summer of 1981, state-sponsored political violence in urban areas spiraled out of control, as the regime followed a killing strategy that sought to subject 100 percent of political opponents to fatal violence. A counterinsurgency killing campaign in rural Guatemala followed: the strategy, such as it was, sought to eliminate the insurgency and its supporters and the regime's political adversaries. Despite the escalation in the use of mass violence during the Lucas García administration, however, the strategy ultimately failed to contain the guerrilla and pushed indigenous communities toward the URNG. The extreme visibility of the killings "allegedly generated a degree of contention within the political establishment and the regime itself, as officials, at least in private, opposed the sheer unguided brutality with which the regime acted" (Brett 2013, interview with Juan Francisco Forno in Guatamala City). Ultimately, perhaps the most effective component of the Lucas García strategy was not mass killing, but rather the militarization of the countryside through the imposition of paramilitary Civil Defence Patrols. The Lucas García period then raises questions regarding under what conditions mass atrocities may fail to achieve their goal.

Counterinsurgency operations evolved under Lucas García, intensifying in mid-1981 during a six-week military campaign in Guatemala City, which precipitated the escalation of violence in urban areas. In July and August, and with the support of Argentine specialists in urban counterinsurgency strategy, the Guatemalan military raided "safe houses" belonging to the EGP and ORPA in Guatemala City. The offensive, combined with intelligence operations occurring simultaneously across the country, brought a transformation in the dynamics of the counterinsurgency campaign. Intelligence appeared to evidence a massive level of support for the guerrilla in the indigenous highlands, confirming the regime's most acute fears. The military estimated between 100,000 and 250,000 members of the insurgents' support base (Brett 2007). The guerrilla strategy of "prolonged popular war" had been effective across highland departments in constructing an increasingly extensive social base. The EGP had generated political structures necessary for mass insurrection – the Clandestine Local Committees (CCL) – as well as armed local defence committees – the Irregular Local Forces (FIL) – and Mobile and Permanent Military Forces (UMP) (Dunkerley 1989; Brett 2007, chapter 2).

The increasing guerrilla threat emerged at a time when the Lucas García regime appeared to be losing both its legitimacy and its grip on political power. As Midlarsky has observed, "Any process that simultaneously increases both threat to the state and its vulnerability, as well as the vulnerability of a targeted civilian population, also increases the probability of genocide" (2005, p. 4).[7] Arguably, the perception of a possible guerrilla triumph, apparently supported widely by the (vulnerable) indigenous population, increased the likelihood that the state would resort to mass atrocities against indigenous communities. The military's response was in this regard to broaden the strategy of selective repression previously implemented in urban and rural areas between 1978 and 1979, toward deliberate acts of mass murder aimed at eradicating the insurgency. To this end, the military identified the indigenous population as the *internal enemy*, within the operational framework of the NSD.[8]

The large-scale rural military counteroffensive, the so-called scorched earth campaign, *Operation Ashes*, was officially launched on October 1, 1981 (Ball et al. 1999). The campaign was executed utilising a series of mobile Task Forces, drawing strategically upon approximately 15,000 troops from broader military brigades, which systematically attacked the civilian population. The campaign was undergirded by a series of mutually reinforcing objectives: to identify and subsequently pacify those zones of major guerrilla activity; to isolate the insurgency from its social base; to prevent the development of subversion; and to eliminate it where it already existed. The military identified so-called areas of operation within which Task Forces would operate, saturating the areas with "overwhelming military force"

[7] Bloxham similarly argues that genocide and mass violence is likely to occur where victims "had previously been the subject of suspicion, stereotype, or persecution" (2008, p. 208).

[8] The NSD proposed that a "state may legitimately employ military force against an ideological threat within the national territory with the aim of protecting national security" (Kemp, unpublished, p. 107).

with the purpose of controlling the population. Military actions aimed at "cleansing the areas of subversive activities" were launched against military and nonmilitary targets, emphatically the guerrilla's indigenous social base (Kemp, unpublished, pp. 86–89).

Significantly, integral to the campaign was the strategy to control the surviving civilian population. The military revived the feared historical figure of Military Commissioner throughout the country, an individual within communities mandated to coordinate with the military. Often under threat of death, survivors were forced to establish paramilitary Civil Defence Patrols (PACs). Designed to "pacify" predominantly indigenous highland communities, the PACs were composed obligatorily of all male peasants between 16 and 65 years. Their role was to "protect" indigenous communities from the guerrilla, oftentimes accompanying military operations. The PACs were also used deliberately to draw the civilian population into the conflict, militarizing rural communities, while extending the reach of military intelligence.[9]

In many cases, PAC commanders and members severely abused their position of power for material gain, plunder, political power, and sexual gratification. In certain cases, PACs evolved into brutal killing machines, perpetrating egregious intra-ethnic violence, as was the case in the massacre of Rio Negro in 1982, evidencing the link between macro- and micro-level violence observed by Kalyvas (2006) elsewhere. As Kalyvas has argued, the Guatemala case evidenced how macro-level violence played into and shaped micro-level violence: "civil war violence often privatizes politics. Insofar as it reflects local conflicts and personal disputes, the intimate nature of violence in civil war can be seen as the dark face of social capital" (2006, 14). Not all violence was political, as individuals and groups took advantage of the chaos of armed conflict; "in the aftermath of mass atrocities perpetrated by the military, the PACs continued to exert power and employ violence" (Brett 2013, interview with Rodrigo Salvadó in Guatemala City).[10]

Beginning in the department of Chimaltenango, the Guatemalan armed forces blockaded the Pan-American Highway and razed several nearby villages, carrying out mass public killings. The severity and scale of massacres perpetrated by the army largely depended on the extent to which a given community was believed to be collaborating with the insurgency. The army left a trail of blood and destruction throughout the highland departments of Chimaltenango, Sololá, Quiché, and Huehuetenango, massacring civilian inhabitants, razing villages to the ground, burning food and crops, allegedly to starve out the guerrilla, and butchering

[9] See Robert Kennedy Centre (1994) and Sáenz de Tejada (2004) for a detailed discussion of the PAC.

[10] This information was corroborated by Hector Rosada, who stated in an interview, "The brutal counerinsurgency generated the context for other forms of violence... the fact that this structure was there opens the way for other types of violence, of killing" (Guatemala City, June 13, 2013).

animals. It has been estimated that the killing campaign caused approximately 11,000 deaths (ODHAG 1998). The campaign was guided by two principal objectives: to permanently block the guerrilla's strategic transit route through the central highlands, impeding access to the capital city, and to decimate the insurgency's support base.[11] The military indiscriminately targeted indigenous communities classified as the "internal enemy" and, by the first months of 1982, the campaign in the western highlands had succeeded in stabilising those zones of manifest guerrilla influence, permitting the army to achieve a degree of military supremacy. Although insurgent forces had not been entirely eradicated, the military felt confident enough to extend the killing campaign to the northwest region, to the Verapaces, where the insurgents had also crafted their social base.

As zones were neutralized, the initial wave of mass atrocities came to a temporary pause. Significantly, however, as the military stabilized the western highlands, so the EGP dug in. The massacres, furthermore, pushed indigenous communities toward the guerrilla for protection, consolidating and extending its social base in indigenous regions (Stoll 1993; Brett 2007). Consequently, the EGP's extensive presence across the country and its increasingly daring military strategy, particularly of attacking military bases in Quiché and Huehuetenango, continued to represent a genuine threat: mass atrocities had failed to achieve their goal.

Toward a More Radical Solution: The Coup D'état

The decisive and ferocious violence of Lucas García's campaign did not contain the insurgency, nor did it unify the military and political establishment, instead leading to further fractures within it. Sectors within the military considered that the counterinsurgency's focus upon systematic terror did not extinguish the root causes of revolution and thus would be unlikely to impede it in the long term. Political and economic elites, moreover, viewed Lucas García's administration as corrupt and inept, concerned only with protecting its own interests.[12] The rifts in the establishment gradually became irreconcilable, leading powerful sectors within the military, political elite, and private sector to oppose the regime vehemently. Military officials rejected political and economic mismanagement by the government, expressing doubts over whether a plan existed regarding the institution's future trajectory. In certain cases, officials felt excluded from the material benefits of political power and corruption bestowed by the regime upon its close supporters. In this context, two groups emerged within the military, the hardline sector committed to the strategy of Lucas García, and the institutionalist line, more open to the possibility of constructing longer term, transformative strategies within the institution, which Montt allegedly came to represent (Kemp, unpublished, pp. 156–166).

[11] See Schirmer (1998, p. 43) for a similar argument.

[12] See McCleary (1997, 1999) and Kemp (unpublished document) for a detailed analysis of the fragmentation within the establishment.

On March 23, 1982, Lucas García was deposed through a military coup staged by high-ranking *institutionalist* officers, allegedly precipitating the beginning of the political transition, as the military orchestrated a process through which to return the country gradually to civilian rule.[13] The junta comprised of General Efraín Ríos Montt, General Horacio Egberto Maldonado Schaad (Commander of the Guard of Honour), and Colonel Fernando Gordillo (former commander of the Brigades of Izabal and Quetzaltenango), linked to the extreme right-wing party, the Movement of National Liberation (MLN), and thus to the urban death squads. The junta declared it would confront corruption, strengthen the counterinsurgency offensive, and modernize public administration, while generating greater confidence within the private sector. Less than two weeks later, the Army Special Staff presented the National Plan for Security and Development, a strategy that would intensify counterinsurgency tactics and institutionalize mass atrocities, thus defining the outcome of the conflict.

The coup consolidated the military as the sole institutional power, embedding counterinsurgency strategy across and militarizing all aspects of political, social, and legal life. The change in regime precipitated an immediate decrease in urban violence, as the junta sought internationally to project an image of the rule of law and human rights guarantees. However, rural killings continued and the policy of mass atrocities crafted under Lucas García would soon escalate.

Montt soon declared himself de facto president, and introduced legislation to strengthen counterinsurgency operations, while seemingly concerned with crafting a legal framework for the counterinsurgency violence and improving its international image. In April, the junta had banned all media coverage of political violence, while in June a nationwide amnesty was offered for political crimes, giving insurgents thirty days to surrender. The amnesty provided Montt with the "legal and moral justification for subsequently storming communities where the guerrilla still operated or whose inhabitants were resistant to government authority" (Kobrak 1997, p. 21). However, it was largely unsuccessful, leading to the surrender of only 1,936 individuals (Sanford 2003, pp. 21–22). Simultaneously, the regime intensified rural militarization and decreed a state of emergency, formally suspending the constitution.

PART THREE: AN ANALYSIS OF MASS ATROCITIES IN THE GUATEMALAN CASE

Operation Victory 82

Under Montt, the strategy was highly centralized, coordinated as it was by the military command structure with the aim of intensifying the killing campaign. The

[13] The military proposed that the transition began in 1982, with the assumption of Montt, an approach shared by certain scholars (Schirmer 1998; Jonas 2000). The perspective taken in this research is that the transition began after the end of the killing campaign in 1983.

strategy did not represent a radical departure from the Lucas García years insofar as it demonstrated two clear aspects of continuity with the preceding strategy: the use of Task Forces and the identification of the indigenous population as internal enemy (Kemp, unpublished, p. 418). Massacres were systematic and were driven by clear and integrated objectives. The Montt strategy developed, however, a series of distinct priorities: (i) the urgency to control the population in the wake of military operations; (ii) engagement with the ideological roots of the conflict, in particular through indoctrination programs (Kemp, unpublished, pp. 417–420); and (iii) a shift from the 100 percent kill strategy to 30 percent "total kill" and 70 percent "soft pacification" in the zones of conflict (Garrard-Burnett 2010, p. 87).

The pacification strategy was undergirded by development programmes and psychological operations, a shift in strategic planning that differentiated the Montt counterinsurgency from its predecessor. The model villages eroded indigenous culture, continuing the genocidal impact of the massacres. Sanford (2003) contests the proposition that the number of massacres and massacre victims decreased under Montt, arguing that the number of victims per massacre in fact increased from an average of 37–45 victims, an 18 percent increase in the number of victims per massacre. Sanford further disaggregates her analysis, focusing upon massacres perpetrated during the final 3 months under Lucas García and the initial 3 months under Montt, evidencing a total of 775 victims and 1,057 victims, respectively (2003). It is within this framework then that scholars have identified the immediate spike in killing under the Montt regime (see Figure 1.1).

Within this framework, in July 1982, Montt inaugurated the most intensive phase of the counterinsurgency campaign, with the launch of *Operation Victory* 82, which involved the mobilization of more than 60 percent of the armed forces with the objective of exterminating thousands within indigenous communities (Schirmer 1998, p. 45). The plan, designed by Montt and his military strategists, sought the total elimination of armed subversion and its roots, as well as of its so-called parallel organizations. The plan proposed the implementation of three strategies: (i) to rescue the civilian population; (ii) to recover members of the FIL; and (iii) to annihilate the CCL and the UMP (Guatemalan Army 1982; cited in ODHAG 1998, Vol. 3, p. 164).

Victory 82 institutionalized the annihilation of the insurgency's principally indigenous social base, either "rescuing" or executing suspected collaborators through the mass-killing campaign. The strategy identified the entire indigenous civilian population as a collective enemy to be physically eliminated, what Valentino has termed "collective punishment" (2004, p. 201). Ultimately, the army engaged in both regular and irregular warfare, operations accompanied by sophisticated psychological operations, with the support of state institutions, with the goal of winning the hearts and minds of the surviving population. As part of the strategy, in 1982, the Department of Civil Affairs (S-5) was established, with special divisions in each military zone tasked with indoctrinating "recuperated" members of the

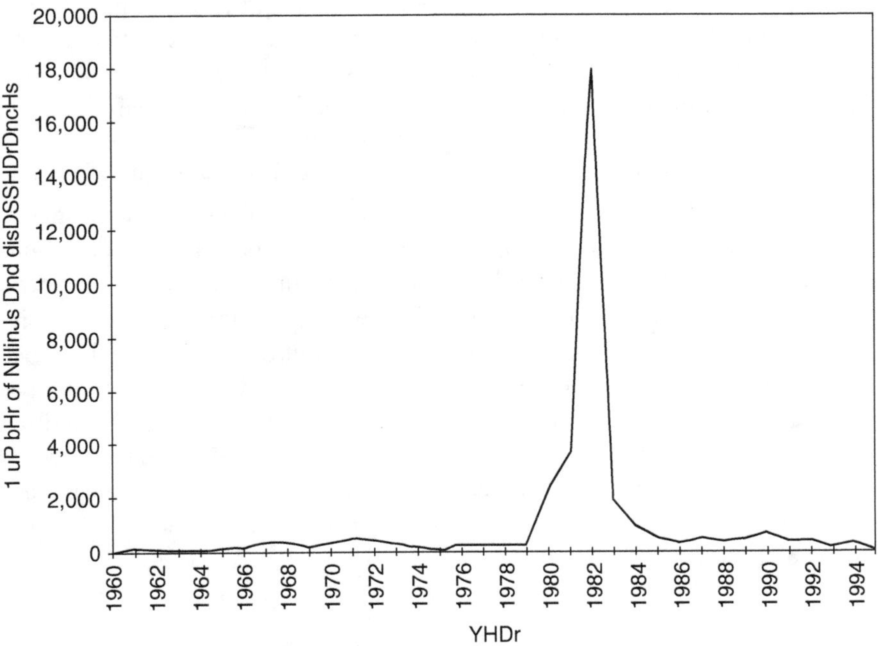

FIGURE 1.1: The escalation of violence as a result of Victoria 82 and Operation Sofía. Source: *State Violence in Guatemala, 1960–1996: A Quantitative Reflection*. American Association for the Advancement of Science

population. Although S-5 staff included soldiers with training in "social services, psychological techniques, and ideological indoctrination" (ODHAG 1998, Vol. 2, p. 83), psychologists and anthropologists were also contracted, methods later used by the U.S. counterinsurgency efforts in Afghanistan and Iraq.

On July 1, 1982, the massacres commenced, characterized by brutal performative cruelty, and included torture, forced cannibalism, and systematic sexual violence. The state of emergency had given the military the power to expand the armed forces by enlisting former soldiers under the age of thirty years and ordering the transfer of military reserves to the regular armed forces.[14] In the following months, massacres were carried out once more in the western and northwestern highlands in those zones that continued to represent a perceived guerrilla threat, continuing the decimation initiated under Lucas García. A total of 660 villages were literally razed to the ground. Military operations were executed by the newly

[14] Kemp cites the International Institute for Strategic Studies' estimation that, in 1982, the Guatemalan Armed Forces was composed of 18,550 individuals. Schirmer estimates that during Ríos Montt's regime, this was increased to a total of 36,000 (Kemp, unpublished, p. 407). For the latter, military bases throughout the country, including highland, central, northern, and coastal Guatemala, were utilized; the military was mandated to coordinate with the National Police.

created Task Forces, with the support of reservists, strategists, paratroopers, special forces (Kaibiles), the Guard of Honour, and members of the Guatemalan Air Force. From the middle of 1982, the military experimented with the inclusion of a low number of indigenous recruits in its units; the majority of troops, however, were ladino.

The execution of mass atrocities was planned and perpetrated within the framework of Plan Sofía, a plan designed from within the military high command. Imposed through the "routinisation of terror" (Green 1999, p. 60), Plan Sofía demonstrated the meticulous level of planning behind the killing campaign, the "scientifically precise" and "intentional" systematic annihilation of "subversive elements" utilizing such tactics as burning communities to the ground; perpetration of massacres, generally on Sundays or holidays, when there would be more individuals in the communities targeted[15]; mass public rape; forced sterilization; and destruction of food supplies. Operations also intentionally targeted and destroyed ancestral ceremonial sites (Grandin 2004, p. 3; Brett 2007). In the wake of mass atrocities, once communities had been "cleansed," came the imposition of military control.

The First Stage of Mass Atrocity Ending: From Collective Killing to Population Control

In the aftermath of the massacres, the so-called development poles were built near or upon the ashes of towns that had been razed through Plan Sofía, representing a central component of the army's "Action Plan for Conflict Zones" after 1982. The PACs, intensified under Victory 82 (Manz 1989; Manz 2004, p. 158), and the so-called model villages were imposed with the objective of extending the reach of military control over potential subversive elements and "integrating" and indoctrinating indigenous people to "conform to the dominant cultural mold" (Hale 2006, p. 51). Forms of mass pacification restricted population movement and transmitted "the army's nationalist discourse" (Wilson 1995, p. 230). The concentration and control of indigenous survivors formed Montt's second phase of the "beans and bullets" strategy: an attempt to win the hearts and minds of the indigenous people through a counterinsurgency as development logic.

In the wake of the violence, the programme was designed to restructure the foundations of rural life with the objective of guaranteeing and perpetuating military supremacy. The army imposed a new form of social organization upon the rural population, a population still regarded as a potential support base for the guerrilla.[16] Indigenous survivors were obliged to inhabit model villages, some of

15 The CEH documented a total of 626 cases of massacres committed by the Guatemalan Army, security forces, and paramilitary structures (1999, p. 46).

16 According to REMHI, between 50,000 and 60,000 indigenous peoples populated the model villages in the Ixil region alone (ODHAG 1998, Vol. 2., p. 141).

which boasted electricity and running water. The villages were shaped by a "developmentalist philosophy that combined military action with [limited] economic growth activities" (Rothenberg 2012, p. 39). The villages were monitored through permanent military presence and male residents were forced to join the PACs. Residents were obliged to sign up for "civic work" programmes, including "Roofs, Work and Tortillas," which involved rebuilding areas previously destroyed by the military, and the construction of roads and bridges.

Over and above the strategic objective of control, an explicit goal of the model villages was to destroy indigenous culture, extending the impact of the mass atrocities. Indigenous people were prohibited from speaking their own languages (Spanish was the lingua franca) or practising their ancestral religion and traditional customs (Taylor 1998, p. 37). Subjugation to the military brought the disappearance of indigenous authorities and historical mechanisms of conflict resolution, precipitating a systematic rupture with mechanisms of communal self-government, while embedding the total militarization of civilian life.

Indoctrination programmes by the S-5 were designed to assimilate indigenous Maya into the predominant ladino culture, representing "a programme of ideological warfare...designed to brainwash the population, with the explicit aim of eroding ethnic identity" (Editorial Praxis 1988, p. 175). In this regard, the counterinsurgency aimed to impose a new sociocultural identity upon the indigenous, as Hale has termed it, to "whiten" the nation, so engineering the construction of an "authorized" or "permitted Indian" (Hale 2006, p. 16). The villages simultaneously guaranteed that indigenous survivors depended upon the military, while fostering intra-communal surveillance, which further broke down social capital within indigenous communities (Grandin 2004, p. 130). Ultimately then, the counterinsurgency sought to destroy both the physical infrastructure of indigenous communities (massacre strategy) as well as the social relations within them (model villages) (Green 1999, p. 32), ultimately colonizing "the spaces, symbols, and social relations analysts believed to be outside of state control" (Grandin 2004, p. 129).

The Second Stage of Mass Atrocity Ending: The Strategic Defeat of the Guerrilla

The initial stage of mass atrocity ending commenced in the final months of 1982, once the killing campaign had begun effectively to "cleanse" indigenous communities in the western and northwestern highlands and the military had subsequently confined the surviving population in model villages and isolated it from the insurgency. By 1983, the military launched Plan Firmness 1983, a continuation of Victory 1982, although with a strategic focus less emphatically dependent upon mass atrocities and more upon concentrating the surviving population within development poles. As had been the case with Victory 82, Firmness 83 was signed by General Héctor Mario López Fuentes, the chief of the Army General Staff, the entity mandated with the formulation of army policy and general strategy. However, both plans were "prepared, emitted and implemented" under the orders of Montt, the general commander of the armed forces, under whose responsibility the chief of the Army General Staff directly lay (Kemp, unpublished, p. 728).

As the killing campaign moved through the country in an arc, from Chimaltenango near the capital city to the northern reaches of el Quiché, the Petén, and the Verapaces, it precipitated a disjunctive end to the massacres. The military advanced its operational focus from one zone to another as the specific situational guerrilla threat was neutralized. As the campaign achieved its objective, mass atrocities in specific communities ceased. The strategy logically affected different regions of the country in a differentiated manner, according to their demographic context, the antecedents of conflict there, and the velocity with which atrocities achieved their objective.

For example, in March 1982, massacres had been initially perpetrated in Chimaltenango. PACs and model villages were subsequently imposed upon rural communities there, although the zone was only neutralized by October, when the last vestiges of the killing campaign subsided. The dual strategy of massacres and population control forced the EGP and another armed group, the Rebel Armed Forces (FAR), out of the zone and into neighboring el Quiché by November. However, the killing campaign had begun in el Quiché as early as April 1982: operations began in the departmental capital, Santa Cruz, and gradually moved to the Ixil region in the north of the department. Under Victory 82, massacres in the Ixil region of el Quiché began in August 1982, building upon mass atrocities that were previously perpetrated under Lucas García. Many strategic villages in Ixil, including San Francisco Javier and Vivitz, were massacred between August and September. However, according to interviews, the military continued to carry out massacres and other forms of political violence, while persecuting the displaced population through bombing campaigns and ground operations, until August 8, 1983, when Montt was overthrown in a coup.

The case of the Ixcán is also of significant importance, given that this region was perhaps one of the last to experience mass atrocities and systematic violence. Between 1975 and 1981 the population of the Ixcán were subjected to a process of selective repression; from 1976 onward, this process was accompanied by military actions of a "civic" nature (including the construction of health clinics and schools). During the early phase of the counterinsurgency, the armed forces employed a strategy of low-intensity repression (selective murders and kidnappings) (Falla 1992, p. 219). In 1981, initial attempts to disarticulate the insurgency through selective repression failed, and, to the military's dismay, guerrilla presence in the region increased (Falla 1988; Falla 1992, p. 46). With the exception of Playa Grande, the army abandoned its military detachments and barracks in the Ixcán on November 17, 1981, withdrawing its troops in preparation for the "scorched earth" campaign.

The first mass atrocity campaign was subsequently implemented in the Ixcán in February 1982. The second mass-killing campaign, a campaign of particular brutality, took place in April 1982, within the framework of Victory 82, as the military sought to wipe out what it perceived to have been a particularly persistent insurgent threat in the region. According to one survivor from Pueblo Nuevo:

> When my father returned to our house, the army was there. They shot him several times, tortured him and then hung him from a tree, with his hands tied behind his back; maybe he remained alive during the night because the rope had been twisted around several times as though he had struggled to free himself. It's not easy to die like that.
>
> (Brett 2007, interview with survivor in Pueblo Nuevo)

There was no respite for the population of the Ixcán, even in the aftermath of the Montt regime in August 1983. In fact, the situation escalated toward the end of October 1983, even after the national massacre strategy had come to an end. The first model village was created as a base for carrying out search-and-destroy missions against civilians hiding in the mountains in 1983. During this period "many families were captured, there were murders, machine gun attacks and aerial bombings, mortar strikes, crop destruction, and induced intoxication and famine" (Falla 1992, p. 217).

Between February 1982 and 1984, the Ixcán remained a virtual ghost town; villages lay abandoned, with the exception of the "model" villages. Only in 1984 did the army conclude that the region could finally be repopulated, given that the dangers represented by the EGP were minimal. In interviews, survivors of the massacres in the Ixil and Ixcán regions testified that the armed forces remained in the area beyond August 1983, and that, although systematic massacres drew to a close by August, political violence against the civilian population persisted up until the middle of 1984, the date at which the military achieved strategic supremacy in the region and mass atrocities ended.

The Third Stage of Mass Atrocity Ending: The Political Transition

On August 8, 1983, Montt was deposed in a military coup by General Mejía Víctores, his defence minister, precipitating the beginning of the political transition. The causes of the coup are complex. Allegations were made that Montt was straying from his original mandate to consolidate the institutionalist line and guarantee counterinsurgency victory, succumbing to religious fanaticism and steeped in corruption (Gramajo 1995; Schirmer 1998). It is, however, likely that the objective of the coup was to oust Montt – under whom the "dirty war" had achieved its key goal of neutralizing the guerrilla threat and detaching the insurgency from its civilian support base – and clean the military's national and international image. By 1984, the military had, moreover, imposed control over all political institutions, militarized all aspects of society, and eradicated any potential subversive threat. The political transition was, initially, elite-led and "authoritarian" (Jonas 2000, p. 105), a transition likely pacted between the military and the private sector, yet emphatically controlled by the military, leaving minimal space for civilian participation or oversight, as was the case in the South America's Southern Cone.

The assumption of Mejía consolidated the institutionalist line, although the regime continued to follow counterinsurgency logic with the aim of pacifying the population and embedding national security doctrine within civilian affairs. Despite the neutralization of the immediate insurgent threat, ongoing political and economic instability meant domestic reorganization remained a key priority. Under the knowledge that it remained firmly in control of the country, the military proposed the return to civilian rule by 1986, largely as a means of guaranteeing institutional survival, regaining international legitimacy, reconciling the military and private sector, and generating the conditions for the insertion of the country into the global economy (Schirmer 1998, pp. 31–34). However, while the transition brought the definitive end to rural mass killing, levels of urban violence, including extrajudicial executions, disappearances, and political kidnappings, once again increased, as the government sought to eradicate the seeds of political opposition. The military remained the sole arbiter of the political transition and decisively determined its scope and terms. The return to civilian government, a condition achieved as a result of mass-killing strategy, would not permit meaningful challenge to military power, nor aperture for subversion.

In June 1984, a National Constituent Assembly (ANC) was called with the aim of stabilizing the transition from military to civilian rule through constitutional reform. The ANC drafted the 1985 constitution, which came to effect in May, and subsequently became a key mechanism in the oversight of elections later that year. For the first time in twenty years, a civilian candidate, Vinicio Arévalo Cerezo, was elected president in 1985, taking up office in January 1986. However, "the military never relinquished power, maintaining strict control from behind the scenes" (Brett 2004, interview with Hector Rosada in Guatemala City).[17] Nevertheless, the 1985 constitution and the return to civilian rule precipitated a partial political opening in which organizations of victims of the armed conflict mobilized (Brett 2008).

Between 1986 and 1987, Central American presidents, including Cerezo and Costa Rican president and subsequent Nobel Peace Prize winner, Oscar Arias, pushed forward the regional peace process that sought a "firm and lasting peace" in Central America, eventually leading to the signing of the Esquipulas II Accord in 1987. As the process gained ground, and civil society began to wield important leverage, the political transition shifted away from the "authoritarian," civilian-led

[17] See Brett and Delgado (2005) for a detailed analysis of the process of constitutional reform.

politics of counterinsurgency that defined the Mejía administration toward a more broadly "democratic transition" (Jonas, 2000, p. 105; Brett 2008, chapter 2). After 1987, with the imminent end of the Cold War, and the gradual achievements of Esquipulas II, the peace process in Guatemala gained impetus, and the international community began to pressure for a role in the negotiations. The commencement of mass atrocities, not their ending, had been facilitated by international support, particularly by the United States. However, the international community subsequently became a key player in the peace process that led to the end of formal hostilities.

PART FOUR: THE PEACE PROCESS: THE ELUSIVE END TO GENOCIDE?

In the aftermath of the Cold War, with the support of the Contadora Group (Colombia, Mexico, Panama, and Venezuela) and Guatemalan civil society organizations, and due to pressure from Europe and North America, the Esquipulas process established the conditions for an increasingly irreversible peace process within Guatemala. From 1986, moreover, both the profoundly weakened URNG and the victorious military demonstrated open political will to negotiate. The URNG had little to lose and everything to gain, while the military, under pressure from the international community, believed that the peace process would permit it to consolidate its position and attain international legitimacy, assumptions that were both ultimately correct.[18]

The Esquipulas process ultimately laid the foundations for the Oslo Accord, signed in 1990, which, in turn, opened the door for the formal peace process to begin in Guatemala in 1994 (Jonas 2000). The peace process began in earnest with the signing of the Framework Agreement in January 1994, establishing The United Nations Verification Mission for Guatemala (MINUGUA) and the Group of Friendly Countries (Colombia, Spain, the United States of America, Mexico, Norway, and Venezuela).[19] Between 1994 and 1996, seventeen accords were signed, with the aim of bringing a definitive end to the causes and consequences of the armed conflict. The negotiations closely followed the paradigm of a post–Cold War, United Nations-mediated Liberal Peace intervention, projecting political democratization and economic neoliberalism as the most adequate responses to the causes and consequences of the armed conflict.[20] The accords included

[18] As a result of both licit and illicit dealings, the military had become a relatively autonomous economic actor by the end of the conflict.

[19] Azpuru (1999) argues that the peace process followed two phases: indirect negotiations (1987–1990) and direct negotiations (1991–1996). See also Jonas (2000) and Brett (2008; 2014) for a discussion of the international context and the role of the UN Agenda for Peace.

[20] Richmond (2005) and MacGinty (2011; 2012) define as the "Liberal Peace" paradigm, a conceptualization of peace as linked intimately to (western) liberal values, institutions, norms, and practices. See also Paris (2004) and Brett (2013).

unprecedented measures to redress the historical discrimination and sociopolitical and cultural exclusion suffered by the indigenous population, address military and civilian power, and transform state institutions. However, the accords did not directly address the genocide, nor establish meaningful transitional justice mechanisms through which to seek justice for past human rights violations. While limited implementation severely restricted the impact of the accords,[21] it was principally the design of the peace process that led to its failure to precipitate structural transformation, particularly with respect to the conditions faced by indigenous peoples. Guatemalan elites opposed broad, transformative accords that would have consecrated commitments that challenged their historical economic interests: the objective of the mass-killing campaign had been precisely to prevent changing the terms of history in this respect. Consequently, the negotiation of the causal factors of the armed conflict – including horizontal inequality and land distribution and control – was sacrificed, in part, in order to lower the resistance of the parties to negotiate and prevent spoiling actions. Guatemala's peace truly represented a "victor's peace" (Brett 2013).

The peace process, while consolidating the end to mass atrocities and formalizing the closure of hostilities, impeded the meaningful possibility of generating minimal conditions for preventing future conflict. In Guatemala's *negative peace*, conditions of structural violence profoundly affecting the indigenous population – including extreme poverty, regional famines, maternal mortality, and chronic infant malnutrition – have escalated, as has resource extraction in indigenous communities, precipitating the systematic violation of indigenous peoples' fundamental right to autonomy.

PART FIVE: CONCLUSIONS

On May 10, 2013, after a trial that lasted only 53 days, General Ríos Montt was found guilty in a domestic court of law of genocide and crimes against humanity and sentenced by the judges to eighty years imprisonment. The sentence appeared to bring juridical closure to the cycle of mass atrocities and acts of violence that, in this specific case, had been perpetrated under Montt's dictatorship in the Ixil region of Guatemala. However, ten days later, as a result of the pressure exerted by economic, political, and military elites, in whose name the genocide had been waged, and despite international protestations to the contrary, the Constitutional Court annulled the trial on highly dubious grounds. The judges were obliged to step down and the case was pushed back into Guatemala's notoriously slow legal system.[22] The trial eventually began again on January 5, 2015, with the 88-year-old

[21] See scholars such as Jonas (2000), Caumartin (2004), Stewart (2005), and Arnson and Azpuru (2012).

[22] See Kemp (2014) for a detailed analysis of the trial.

Montt being wheeled in to the courtroom on a stretcher bed. The verdict and the annulment of the trial evidenced the fragile and polarized nature of Guatemala's post-conflict peace and the continuing traumatic legacy of the violence for indigenous peoples, as they struggle for the guarantees to their fundamental rights, to write themselves into history, and to assert their political subjectivity. As Hayden has argued, "rights claims remain politically irrelevant or ineffective if they are unheard and unseen by others who do not recognize the claimant as sufficiently human" (2012, p. 576).

The research presented in this chapter has argued that mass atrocities ended disjunctively in Guatemala. Under Lucas García, mass killing did not achieve its goal, leading to the intensification of the counterinsurgency under Montt. Montt's campaign precipitated the strategic defeat of the insurgency, a result of the effective killing and confinement campaign embodied by Victory 82 and Firmness 83. Mass atrocities remained a strategic option until 1984, and only finally came to an end that year, under the Mejía regime, when the insurgency had been chronically weakened and its social base decimated. International pressure played no role in the decision to wind down mass atrocities. On the contrary, it was counterinsurgency logic, not international intervention – either military or otherwise – that persuaded the military to stop the killing. The few "external appeals, exhortations, and pressures" lodged against the Guatemalan military, principally by international NGOs such as Amnesty International, did not "dissuade determined elites from their abusive courses," a proposition made by Lake and Rothchild (1996, p. 47) for other cases. However, the decision made by the Mejía regime and the military to return the country rapidly to civilian rule once the insurgency had been neutralized was indeed shaped by foreign policy calculations and was likely reinforced by international pressure. In the wake of the political transition, the country's Liberal Peace settlement did not respond adequately to the underlying structural causes of armed conflict, nor permit challenge to the economic and political status quo.

Neoliberal policy interventions came to represent the cornerstone of the peace process and post-conflict polity, subjecting the indigenous population to acute levels of structural violence, and precipitating processes of social and cultural destruction. Guatemala's post-conflict genocide is not the consequence of mass atrocities, as it had been during the Cold War, but rather the modern, "murderous cleansing," the "dark side of democracy," as Mann (2005) has posited. As Guatemala becomes increasingly incorporated into the global economy and as neoliberal economic policies force the expropriation of their lands, indigenous peoples face seemingly irreversible pressures to eliminate their own culture, to "ladinise," as Guatemalans have termed it. The consequences of so-called development policies today seem almost indistinguishable to those of the model villages and development poles of the Cold War. Bolstered by profound racism, indigenous communities in post-conflict Guatemala remain quarry to the "imposition of the national pattern of the oppressor." Two decades after the peace process, while the operative means of extermination has ended, the destruction of indigenous social power, cultural capacity, and symbolic or physical presence continues. The end to mass atrocities has not coincided with or brought about an end to genocide. The struggle for indigenous Guatemalans is no longer to guarantee the end to mass atrocities; it is to prevent the ongoing, invisible genocide caused by the egregious and dehumanizing racism and structural violence to which they are subject.

WORKS CITED

Arias, Arturo. 2007. *Taking Their Word: Literature and the Signs of Central America.* Minnesota: University of Minnesota Press.

AVANCSO (Association for the Advancement of the Social Sciences). 1990. *Assistance and Control: Policies Toward Internally Displaced Population in Guatemala.* Washington, D.C.: Georgetown University.

Azpuru, Dinorah. 2012. "Democracy and Governance in Conflict and Postwar Latin America: A Quantitative Assessment." In *In the Wake of War: Democratization and Internal Armed Conflict in Latin America*, edited by C. Arnson, pp. 35–70. Stanford: Stanford University Press and Washington, D.C.: Woodrow Wilson Center Press.

1999. "Peace and Democratisation in Guatemala: Two Parallel Processes." In *Comparative Peace Processes in Latin America*, edited by C. Arnson. Stanford: Stanford University Press and Washington, D.C.: Woodrow Wilson Center Press.

Ball, Patrick, Paul Kobrak, and Herbert F. Spirer. 1999. *State Violence in Guatemala, 1960–1996: A Quantitative Reflection.* Washington, D.C.: American Association for the Advancement of Science.

Black, George, con Milton Jamail, and Norma Stoltz Chinchilla. 1984. *Garrison Guatemala.* New York: Monthly Review Press.

Bloxham, Donald. 2008. "Organized Mass Murder: Structure, Participation, and Motivation in Comparative Perspective." *Holocaust and Genocide Studies* 22:2:203–245.

Brett, Roddy. Forthcoming (2016). *The Post-Conflict Legacy of Genocide: Political Violence in Guatemala.* London: Palgrave MacMillan.

2014. *Local Level Peacebuilding in Colombia.* Bogota: UNDP.

2013."Peace Stillborn? Guatemala's Liberal Peace and the Indigenous Movement." *Peacebuilding* 1:2: 222–238.

2008. *Social Movements, Indigenous Politics, and Democratisation in Guatemala, 1985–1996.* Leiden: Brill Academic Publishers/CEDLA.

2007. *Una Guerra sin Batallas: del Odio, la Violencia y el Miedo en el Ixil y el Icxán, 1972–1983.* Guatemala: F&G Editoriales.

Brett, Roddy and Antonio Delgado. 2005. *Guatemala's Constitution-Building Process.* Sweden: International IDEA.

Broder, Tanya and Bernard Lambek. 1988. "Military Aid to Guatemala: The Failure of U.S. Human Rights Legislation." *Yale Journal of International Law* 13:5:111–145.

Bulmer-Thomas, Victor. 1995. *The Economic History of Latin America Since Independence.* Cambridge: Cambridge University Press.

Campbell, Bradley. 2009. "Genocide as Social Control." *Sociological Theory* 27, 2:150–172.

Cardoso, Fernando Henrique. 1979. "On the Characterization of Authoritarian Regimes in Latin America." In *The New Authoritarianism in Latin America*, edited by David Collier, pp. 33–60. Princeton: Princeton University Press.

Casaus Arzú, Marta. 2008. *Genocidio ¿La máxima expresión del racismo en Guatemala?* Guatemala: F & G Editores.

Caumartin, Corinne. 2004. *Racism, Violence and Inequality: An Overview of the Guatemalan Case*. Oxford: CRISE Working Paper No. 11.

CEH (Comisión del Esclarecimiento Histórico). 1999. *Guatemala: Memoria del Silencio. Tomo III. Las Violaciones de los Derechos Humanos y los Hechos de Violencia*. Guatemala: CEH.

Conley-Zilkic, Bridget. 2012. "A Challenge to Those Working in the Field of Genocide Prevention and Response." *Revista Sur* 9, 16.

Dunkerley, James. 1993. *The Pacification of Central America*. London: University of London.

1989. *Power in the Isthmus, a Political History of Modern Central America*. London: Verso.

Editorial Praxis. 1988. *Guatemala: Polos de Desarrollo. El Caso de la Desestructuración de las Comunidades Indígenas*. Vol. I. Praxis, M.C.: Guatemala.

Falla, Ricardo. 1992. *Masacres de la selva: Ixcán, Guatemala, 1975–1982*. Guatemala: Editorial Universitaria.

1988. "Struggle for Survival in the Mountains: Hunger and Other Privations Inflicted on the Internal Refugees from the Central Highlands." In *Harvest of Violence: The Mayan Indians the Guatemalan Crisis*, edited by Robert M. Carmack, pp. 235–255. Oklahoma: University of Oklahoma Press.

Finkel, Evgeny and Scott Strauss. 2012. "Macro, Meso, and Micro Research on Genocide: Gains, Shortcomings, and Future Areas of Inquiry." *Genocide Studies and Prevention* 7:1:56–67.

Garrard-Burnett, Virginia. 2010. *Terror in the Land of the Holy Spirit: Guatemala Under General Efraín Ríos Montt, 1982–1983*. New York, Oxford: Oxford University Press.

Gleijeises, Piero. 1991. *Shattered Hope, The Guatemalan Revolution and the United States 1944–1954*. Princeton, N.J.: Princeton University Press.

Goldhagen, Daniel Jonah. 2009. *Worse than War: Genocide, eliminationism, and the ongoing assault on humanity*. New York: Public Affairs

Gramajo, Hector. 1995. *De la Guerra a la Guerra, la Dificil Transición en Guatemala*. Guatemala: Fondo de Cultura.

Grandin, Greg. 2010. "Living in Revolutionary Time: Coming to Terms with the Violence of Latin America's Long Cold War." In *A Century of Revolution: Insurgent and Counterinsurgent Violence During Latin America's Long Cold War*, edited by Greg Grandin and Gilbert Joseph. Duke University Press.

2004. *The Last Colonial Massacre: Latin America in the Cold War*. Chicago: University of Chicago Press.

Grandin, Greg and Gilbert Joseph. 2010. *A Century of Revolution: Insurgent and Counterinsurgent Violence During Latin America's Long Cold War*. Duke University Press.

Green, Linda. 1999. *Fear as a Way of Life: Mayan Windows in Rural Guatemala*. New York: Columbia University Press.

Gurr, Ted Robert and Barbara Harff. 1994. *Ethnic Conflict in World Politics. Boulder,* Colorado: Westview Press.

Hale, Charles. 2006. *Más Que Un Indio: Racial Ambivalence and Neoliberal Multiculturalism in Guatemala*. Santa Fe: School of American Research Press.

Hayden, Patrick. 2012. "The human right to health and the struggle for recognition." *Review of International Studies*, 38, 3:569–588.

Jonas, Susanne. 2000. *Of Centaurs and Doves: Guatemala's Peace Process*. Boulder, Colorado: Westview Press.

Kalyvas, Stathis. 2006. *The Logic of Violence in Civil War*. New York and Cambridge: Cambridge University Press.
Kemp, Susan. 2014. "Guatemala Prosecutes Former President Ríos Montt: New Perspectives on Genocide and Domestic Criminal Justice." *Journal of International Criminal Justice* 12:133–156.
Unpublished document. *La Cadena de Mando del Ejército de Guatemala*.
Kobrak, Paul. 1997. *Village Troubles: The Civil Patrols in Aguacatán, Guatemala*. Unpublished PhD dissertation, Department of Sociology, University of Michigan.
Kruijt, Dirk. 2008. *Guerrillas: War and Peace in Central America*. London: Zed Books.
Kruijt, Dirk and Kees, Koonings. 1999. "Violence and Fear in Latin America." In *Societies of Fear: The Legacy of Civil War, Violence and Terror in Latin America*, edited by Dirk Kruijt and Kees Koonings, pp. 1–30. London: Zed Books.
Lake, David A. and Donald Rothchild. 1996. "Containing Fear: The Origins and Management of Ethnic Conflict." *International Security* 21, 2:41–75.
Leiby, Michele. 2009. "Wartime Sexual Violence in Guatemala and Peru." *International Studies Quarterly* 53,2: 445–468.
Lemkin, Raphael. 1944. *Axis Rule in Occupied Europe: Laws of Occupation, Analysis of Government, Proposals for Redress*. 2nd edn (2008). London: Clark, The Lawbook Exchange.
McCleary, Rachel M. 1999. *Dictating Democracy: Guatemala and the End of Violent Revolution*. Gainesville: University Press of Florida.
1997. "Guatemala's Postwar Prospects." *Journal of Democracy* 8, 2:129–143.
MacGinty, Roger. 2012. "Against Stabilisation." *Stability: International Journal of Security and Development* 1, 1: 20–30.
2011. *International Peacebuilding and Local Resistance: Hybrid Forms of Peace*. London: Palgrave MacMillan.
Mann, Michael. 2005. *The Dark Side of Democracy: Explaining Ethnic Cleansing*. Cambridge: Cambridge University Press.
Manz, Beatriz. 2004. *Paradise in Ashes: A Guatemalan Journey of Courage, Terror, and Hope*. Berkeley: University of California Press.
1989. *Refugees of a Hidden War: The Aftermath of Counterinsurgency in Guatemala*. Albany: SUNY Press.
Midlarsky, Manus. 2005. *The Killing Trap: Genocide in the Twentieth Century*. Cambridge: Cambridge University Press.
Oficina de Derechos Humanos del Arzobispado de Guatemala (ODHAG). 1998. *Guatemala: Nunca Mas. Informe del Projecto La Recuperación de la Memoria Histórica (REMHI)*. Guatemala: ODHAG.
Paris, Roland. 2004. *At War's End: Building Peace After Civil Conflict*. Cambridge: Cambridge University Press.
Pécaut, Daniel. 1999. "From the Banality of Violence to Real Terror: The case of Colombia." In *Societies of Fear: The Legacy of Civil War, Violence and Terror in Latin America*, edited by Dirk Kruijt and Kees Koonings, pp. 141–168. London: Zed Books.
Popkin, Margaret. 1996. *Civil Patrols and their Legacy: Overcoming Militarization and Polarization in the Guatemalan Countryside*. Washington, D.C.: The Robert F. Kennedy Memorial Centre for Human Rights.
Richmond, Oliver. 2005. *The Transformation of Peace*. London: Palgrave MacMillan.
Robert F. Kennedy Memorial Centre for Human Rights. 1994. *Institutional Violence: Civil Patrols in Guatemala, 1993–1994*. Washington, D.C.: The Robert F. Kennedy.

Rothenberg, Daniel. 2012. *Memory of Silence: The Guatemalan Truth Commission Report*. New York: Palgrave Macmillan.
Sáenz de Tejada Rojas, Ricardo. 2004. *Víctimas o Vencedores? Una Aproximación al Movimiento de los Ex-PAC*. Guatemala: FLACSO.
Sanford, Victoria. 2003. *Violencia y Genocidio en Guatemala*. Guatemala: F & G Editores.
2001. *La Masacre De Panzós: Etnicidad, Tierra y Violencia en Guatemala*. Guatemala: F & G Editores.
Schirmer, J. (1998). *The Guatemalan Military Project: A Violence Called Democracy*. Philadelphia: University of Pennsylvania Press.
Semelin, J. (2009). *Purify and Destroy: The Political Uses of Massacre and Genocide*. New York: Columbia University Press.
Shaw, Martin. 2007. *What is Genocide?* Cambridge: Polity Press.
Shelton, Dinah and Paolo G. Carozza. 2012. *Regional Protection of Human Rights*. Oxford: Oxford University Press.
Stewart, Frances. 2005. *Policies towards Horizontal Inequalities in Post-Conflict Reconstruction*. Centre for Research on Equality, Human Security and Ethnicity, University of Oxford, CRISE Working Paper 7.
Stoll, David. 1993. *Between Two Armies in the Ixil Towns of Guatemala*. New York: Columbia University Press.
Straus, Scott. 2007. "Second-Generation Comparative Research on Genocide." *World Politics* 59, 3:476–501.
Taylor, Clark. 1998. *Return of Guatemala's Refugees: Reweaving the Torn*. Philadelphia: Temple University Press.
Tilly, Charles. 1996. *Citizenship, Identity and Social History*. Cambridge: Cambridge University Press.
Valentino, Benjamin. 2004. *Final Solutions: Mass Killing and Genocide in the 20th Century*. Ithaca, NY: Cornell University Press.
Valentino, Benjamin, Paul Huth, and Dylan Balch-Lindsay. 2004. "Draining the Sea: Mass Killing and Guerrilla Warfare." *International Organization* 58:375–407.
Wilson, Richard. 1995. *Maya Resurgence in Guatemala: Q'eqchi' Experiences*. Norman: University of Oklahoma Press.
Wilson, Tim. 2013. "State Terrorism and Human Rights: International Responses Since the End of the Cold War." In *State Terrorism and Human Rights*, edited by Gillian Duncan, Orla Lynch, Gilbert Ramsay, and Alison M.S. Watson, pp. 14–31. London: Routledge.

Burundi

The anatomy of mass violence endgames

Noel Twagiramungu

The rainstorm had ended and the gray mist and clouds had been swept away in the night by the wind.

– Frances H. Burnett, *The Secret Garden* (1911, p. 239)

INTRODUCTION

Two decades ago, Burundi was seen as a hopeless case: a "society gravid with premonitions of genocidal slaughter," pitting two social groups, the Hutu and the Tutsi, against one another (Lemarchand 1995, p. xi). The resulting horrors were unspeakable:

> Nowhere else in Africa has so much violence killed so many people on so many occasions in so small a space as in Burundi during the years following independence. [. . .]. Behind . . . faceless statistics lies a human tragedy of monumental proportions, the scale of which evokes genocide. (Lemarchand 1995, p. xxv)

For a while, the situation seemed so endemic that a U.S. diplomat prescribed a radical solution:

> To prevent further ethnic blood-baths, both communities must be separated. My diplomatic experience in Burundi leads me to conclude that . . . [s]eparation is the only solution that will prevent further ethnic slaughter. (Melady 1988)[1]

Today, while Burundi is no paradise, Hutu and Tutsi live side by side from the highest spheres of power to the darkest valleys of poverty, and ethnic bloodbaths are no longer a routine occurrence in the country. To be sure, political violence

[1] For a forceful counterargument, see Nyankanzi (1988).

is still a major feature of the Burundian landscapes. What has changed, however, is that the ethnic factor has become less salient, with the once-rigid Hutu-Tutsi ethnic rifts showing remarkable signs of closing. More remarkable still, boundaries between the two communities have been loosened in a rather ironic way. On the one hand, the current Hutu-dominated ruling party, CNDD-FDD, and the former Tutsi-dominated ruling party, UPRONA, have come together to form a governing coalition. On the other hand, the former Hutu-dominated parties including Ndadaye's FRODEBU and the once Hutu supremacist FNL-PALIPEHUTU have joined forces with a number of Tutsi parties to form an opposition coalition known as ADC-Ikibiri.

Against this backdrop, this chapter documents and explains how Burundi reversed the trends, and, in defiance of primordialist prognostics and separatist prescriptions, embarked on a path of recovery from the abyss of mass atrocities. The analysis is composed of four sections. Part one begins with a background to ethnic antagonism in Burundi. Part two examines the dynamics of ethnic violence with a focus on major episodes, a discussion of the data on fatalities, and presentation of the core pattern of endings. Part three addresses the empirical puzzle of how to define an ending. As most incidents of mass atrocities in Burundi do not end with definitive changes, but steady normalization, endings are treated as narratives with contested meanings. Part four sheds light on the causal mechanisms governing the overall endgame of identity-based violence as a social construct.

The overall picture shows that mass violence in Burundi consistently began with a flash, evolved through a sequence of silent antagonism and episodes of acute violence – some of which reached genocidal proportions – and eventually ended with the changes in domestic and international purposeful engagement to advance a viable political accommodation. This endgame became possible through a combination of factors: the dynamics of agency, and a number of contingencies including domestic exhaustion – a true "mutually hurting stalemate" in the sense of Zartman (1989) – caused by the cycles of violence as well as external incentives and pressures, all of which interacted to create a moment of possibility for a transformational ending.

PART ONE: BACKGROUND TO ETHNIC VIOLENCE

Located south of the equator in the heart of Africa, Burundi is an overpopulated country (with 10,745 square miles for a population of 10 million people), landlocked between Rwanda in the north, Democratic Republic of Congo (DRC) in the west, and Tanzania in the east. Founded in the early seventeenth century by King Ntare Rushatsi, whose Ganwa dynasty dominated the political scene until 1966, Burundi, like its neighboring Rwanda, belongs to one of Africa's rare "ancient political zones that were real potential nations, comparable to European states in the early nineteenth century" (Chrétien 2003, p. 291).

Conquered by the Germans in 1897 by virtue of the 1894–1895 Berlin Conference, it became a Belgian colony following the German defeat in the wake of the First World War in 1917. It recovered its independence on July 1, 1962, only to experience "some highly violent episodes of ethnic relations" over the next three decades (Fearon and Laitin 2000, p. 845). The coming into ending of these episodes of violence, some of which reached genocidal proportions, is the focus of this chapter.

To begin with, like any other "imagined community" in the tradition of Anderson (1983), the people who identify themselves as Barundi have multiple and overlapping social and political identities that have changed over time. The most problematic juncture in this process began with John Hanning Speke, an English scholar, who had spent four-and-a-half months at the court of King Muteesa of Buganda in 1856 before visiting Burundi in 1858. In his famous 1863 *Journal of the Discovery of the Source of the Nile*, Speke claimed the existence of an aristocratic race, assumed to belong to "a small residue of the original European stock," which ruled over the African Negroes in the Buganda and other neighboring kingdoms including Rwanda and Burundi (Speke 1863, p. 248). A half-century later, Speke's theory found fertile ground in Rwanda and Burundi, where Belgian colonizers used pseudo-scientific measurements to validate the alleged biological evidence pertaining to Tutsi and Hutu as different races. The former were associated with a Caucasian appearance assumed to be taller, with thin lips and pointed noses, whereas the latter were seen as true Negroes portrayed as shorter, with broader lips and flat noses (for insightful critique, see Sanders 1969, pp. 521–532).

Later on, Father Pagès added a divine dimension to Speke's theory by portraying the Tutsi as distant descendants of Ham, the biblical son of Noah, and therefore the founders of the highly civilized "Hamitic kingdom" of Rwanda to rule over the savage Hutu Negroes and Twa pygmies (Pagès 1933, p. 8). "Apart from relatively late Semitic influence," claims one proponent of the Hamitic theory, "the civilizations of Africa are the civilizations of the Hamites" (Seligman quoted in Sanders 1969, p. 521). This racist position echoes Hegel's view of Sub-Saharan Africa as "the land of childhood, ... lying beyond the day of history, ... [and] enveloped in the dark mantle of night" (Hegel 1956, p. 91).

In line with this thinking, the colonial administration concentrated all the privileges of power in the hands of educated youth selected from the royal families and their associates assumed to be of Caucasian descent. In the process, all the chiefs believed to be associated with the commoners from then onward collectively referred to as Hutu were evicted, forced into exile, or even killed. For instance, one colonial account suggests that the number of Hutu chiefs in Burundi fell from 20% in 1929 to 7% in 1933, 2% in 1937, and 0% in 1945 (Gahama 2001, p. 116).

This process of "slow assassination" (Botte 1985) was in line with the recommendation by Mgr. Léon Classe, then Bishop of Rwanda, to "work mainly with" the Batutsi whom he assumed to be "the ones best suited to understand progress and the ones the population likes the best" (Classe quoted in Prunier 1995, p. 26). It followed that a zealous "Tutsi" elite in the colony of Ruanda-Urundi trained and appointed by the colonial administration pursued an aggressive implementation of the unpopular policies of *igikoloni* [colonialism], from forced labor and excessive taxations to corporal punishments and forced migration. The result was a "dual colonialism" (Newbury 1988, p. 53) led by the colonial administration and their protégés, the youth Tutsi elite, at the expense of the oppressed masses. The ensuing "cohesion of oppression" (Newbury 1988, pp. 53–72) prevailed until the late 1950s, when a combination of the post–World War II consequences and the emergence of a United Nations-led world order paved the way for the struggles for independence.

In Burundi, a prince called Louis Rwagasore distanced himself from the elite trained by the colonial administration and joined forces with people from different backgrounds and social categories to found a nationalist political party, UPRONA (Union pour le Progrés National). Much to the dismay of the colonial administration, UPRONA went on to win the legislative elections in 1961 and to lead Burundi to independence on July 1, 1962. Rwagasore, however, was assassinated on October 13, 1961. The ensuing competition for succession caused UPRONA to split into two rival factions, known as MONROVIA and CASABLANCA.[2] Roughly, the ruling elites split across the power base lines of two rival leaders: Paul Mirerekano, a community organizer from modest origins whose power base was rural Burundi; and André Muhirwa, an aristocrat from the Ganwa dynasty of the Batare faction whose power base was the urban and educated elites.

For the next three years, the rift between the two factions took an increasingly pronounced ethnic coloration, with Muhirwa's CASABLANCA now being seen as a Tutsi bloc and Mirerekano's MONROVIA as a Hutu bloc. In the end, the rift turned bloody in January 1965 when Pierre Ngendandumwe, a Hutu who had just taken the oath of office as prime minister, was assassinated by a Tutsi refugee from Rwanda. This assassination plunged the country into a state of crisis from which a CASABLANCA-leaning military group emerged as the new center of power. For the next four decades, this military elite whose influential members hailed from the hitherto obscure Hima clan from the province of Bururi dominated the political scene, first under Captain Michel Micombero (1965–1976), then his cousin Colonel Jean Baptiste Bagaza (1976–1987), and finally another cousin, Major Pierre Buyoya (1987–1993 and 1996–2002).

The "Bururi lobby's" grip on power, however, met resistance and, in response, engineered state-sponsored campaigns of purges and repression. The dawn of a new

[2] This language was borrowed from two opinionated factions that emerged within the Organization of African Union in the early 1960s: The leftist Casablanca faction led by Kwame Nkrumah advocated immediate political federation of all African countries; the pro-West Monrovia bloc led by Senghor of Senegal advocated a gradual process of unification through economic cooperation. In Burundi, CASABLANCA leaders considered themselves nationalist and their rivals as the puppet of the former colonial masters.

era began with the presidency of Major Pierre Buyoya, who initiated a wave of sweeping reforms at the outset of which, ironically, he lost the 1993 elections to his Hutu opponent, Melchior Ndadaye. Angered by the electoral outcomes, the Tutsi-controlled army assassinated the new president along with a dozen of his collaborators in October 1993. The result was a decade-long civil war from which the country is now recovering.

PART TWO: MAPPING ETHNIC VIOLENCE IN BURUNDI

This section illuminates the history of five major periods of mass atrocities in Burundi's post-colonial period. Before turning to the details of each period, it is important to discuss and review the significant gaps in data about these periods. As of today, rigorous accounting for the number of the victims from Burundi's multiple incidents of mass atrocities has received scant attention from researchers. With the notable exception of the 1988 events, deliberate efforts by the government to suppress evidence about the atrocities committed by the army have made it impossible for independent sources to collect meaningful evidence to inform their estimates. The result is a huge gap between the official accounts and the data provided by the sources close to survivors. Unfortunately, the mechanism of the Truth and Reconciliation Commission provided for by the Arusha Peace Agreement to deal with this issue has yet to be operational. With this caution in mind, the following is a tentative comparative picture with the sole purpose of providing a sense of why some episodes captured more international attention than others. The victims of violence per episode are divided into three major categories (Table 2.1): killed, refugees, and internally displaced persons (IDPs).

According to this figure, several issues pertaining to the dynamics of ending are worth noting. For instance, the 1972 episode of mass violence appears by far the most fatal, followed by the civil war. To this date, there is no reliable account of fatalities for the army and the rebels during the civil war. What is certain is that the toll of civilian fatalities is far higher: "We are victims every day," observed one civilian, "We are truly the forgotten ones" (Human Rights Watch 2003, p. 1). The toll of refugees reached its peak during the civil war. For instance, according

TABLE 2.1: *Big picture of the number of victims of mass violence per episode*

Period	Killed	Refugees	IDPs
October–December 1965	7,500	15,000	40,000
April–August 1972	100,000	150,000	2,000,000
August 14–24, 1988	12,000	60,000	25,000
October–November 1993	50,000	75,000	200,000
1994–2005	150,000	1,200,000	4,000,000

to a 2003 comprehensive account, while some 100,000 refugees returned from Tanzania from March 2002 to November 2003, another 500,000 reportedly remained in Tanzania (Human Rights Watch 2003, p. 42). Most of the refugees who fled Burundi since 1965 remained in exile for decades. The notable exception is some 60,000 refugees who fled to Rwanda in August 1988, the vast majority of whom returned back to Burundi in December 1988 (Chrétien, Guichaoua, and Le Jeune 1989, p. 141).

For all periods, the number of IDPs is greater than the number of refugees. The high figure of IDPs suggests that, at some points, the quasi-totality of the populations in some areas left their homes to seek refuge in IDPs camps (the case of Tutsi for the periods 1993 and 1994–2005) or to hide in forests and marshes (the case of Hutu). To fathom the patterns of ending, one has to pay attention to evidence about changes in the dynamics of killing as well as in the movements of refugees and IDPs.

1965 *Events: Failed plot, counter-coup, and large-scale repression*

By all accounts, the year 1965 embodied the first instance of mass violence with ethnic coloration in the history of Burundi. Like most of Burundi's subsequent periods of mass atrocities, the beginning of this first instance of ethnic atrocities can be clearly marked: January 15, 1965, when a newly appointed Hutu prime minister was assassinated by a Tutsi refugee from Rwanda. This assassination became a rallying cry for the Hutu faction during the May legislative elections in which it won 23 of the 33 seats. In response to pressures from the Tutsi faction to contain the syndrome of "the Hutu demographic tyranny à la Rwandaise,"[3] the king chose a noble Ganwa, Léopold Biha, to form a government of "national unity."

Far from calming the situation, the royal choice sparked a wave of ethnic clashes especially in the capital Bujumbura and in the northern part of the country near the Rwandan border. The ensuing unrest culminated in a failed military coup, staged by a group of Hutu officers on October 19, and easily crushed by a counter-coup led by a young Tutsi officer, Captain Michel Micombero. On October 20, thirty-four Hutu soldiers including seven officers were arrested; they were shot dead on October 22, after a martial court found them guilty of participation in a failed plot to establish a Hutu republic (Ngayimpenda 2005, p. 260). On October 26, another nine Hutu officers were arrested and summarily executed. The next day, ten Hutu political leaders were sentenced to death by the martial court and executed. For the next two months, Micombero's junta launched a slaughter

[3] Following the "1959 Hutu Revolution," which abolished a four-century-old kingship and forced the then king, Kigeri Ndahindurwa, along with thousands of his followers into exile, the new all-Hutu ruling elite framed its hold on power in the language of "democracy = rule of the majority" on the grounds of the colonization-era demographic census: 85% Hutu, 14% Tutsi, and 1% Twa.

campaign in the countryside that left more than 5,000 Hutu people dead and tens of thousands forced into exile. In some regions, the pogroms became so widespread that as early as October 7, the World Labor Confederation was calling for a UN-led international intervention to "stop the genocide against ethnic Hutu" (Ngayimpenda 2005, p. 260).

The most widely known of these pogroms took place on December 25, 1965 in Muramvya, the provincial home of most of the alleged Hutu conspirators.[4] "It was Christmas," recalls one eyewitness, then a teenager, who counted his "father among several hundreds of men arrested and embarked in 8 military jeeps by a Tutsi officer named Mandi" (Twagiramungu, interview with a 55-year-old male, Muramvya, 2014). The repression in Muramvya was particularly severe because it followed the massacre of about 500 civilian Tutsi in the communes of Bukeye and Busangana, a carnage attributed to the followers of the alleged mastermind of the Hutu plot, Major Serukwavu, on his way to Rwanda where he found refuge.

By New Year's Day, the repressive machine had ceased. The military junta then turned its attention to counterattacking international condemnation of the violence. This resulted in diplomatic expulsions like the one of January 10, 1965 against U.S. Ambassador Donald Dumont and two of his colleagues, Thomas Buchanan and Nicholas Milroy (Le Monde 1966). For the following years, while most of the Hutu leaders considered sympathetic to the MONROVIA faction were purged from strategic positions, a fair number of Hutu civilian and military cadres served in the post-putsch government. This lasted until September 1969, when rumors of a coup allegedly engineered from Rwanda served as an excuse for the military junta to sack several dozens of Hutu cadres including a former prime minister, six ministers, three top military commanders, and several university students; some were summarily executed and others left to die in prison.

1972: *Peripheral insurgency followed by state-sponsored pogroms*

For Burundi's ruling elite, 1972 was a year of all kinds of dangers: rumor spread that Hutu refugees were plotting an invasion from exile; several Tutsi leaders, notably those from the north of the country, "Banyaruguru," were increasingly expressing discontent with the Bururi lobby's nepotism; and Western powers, including Belgium and the USA, were suspected of helping the ousted king, Ntare III Ndizeye, in a bid to return to power in Bujumbura. To meet the threats head-on, the regime abducted former King Ndizeye from Uganda on March 30, 1972, and ordered his execution on April 29. This fateful execution divided the government, which was dismissed by Micombero the same day. As the rumors of regime collapse and regicide spread, a Hutu insurgency, made of the elements who had

4 They include former Prime Minister Bamina, Paul Mirerekano, Governor Etienne Miburo, and a local mayor named Nzobaza.

fled to Tanzania in the wake of the 1965 killings and 1969 purges, judged the situation ripe for an all-out revolt (Twagiramungu, interviews in Bururi, 2014).

They launched deadly attacks in the southern part of Burundi. Throughout their attacks from the Nyanza-lac and Rumonge in the south to Bujumbura in the west and Cankuzo in the east, "the insurgents proceeded to slaughter every Tutsi in sight, as well as a number of Hutu who refused to join the rebellion" (Lemarchand 1995, p. 91). Within a matter of three days, the insurgents proclaimed a "people's republic" headquartered in the Vugizo commune (Bururi). By the end of April, when the army began to crush the insurgents, and thus bringing the short-lived Hutu republic to an end, up to 3,000 people, most of them Tutsi, had perished.

On April 30, 1972, President Micombero dismissed the civilian governors and replaced them with military commanders. The following day, he declared a state of emergency, restricting freedom of movement and assembly. Over the next weeks, the army carried out a systematic, methodic, and brutal pogrom meant to "decapitate the Hutu leadership" (Twagiramungu, interview with two former soldiers, Bujumbura, 2014) throughout the country. The resulting mass violence marks 1972 as the darkest year in the history of Burundi.[5] One scholar sums up the unfolding horrors, stating:

> On May 30, while vigorous counterattacks were being launched against the insurgents, elements of the armed forces and the JRR [Jeunesse Républicaine Rwagasore] began to coordinate their efforts to exterminate all Hutu suspected to have taken part in the rebellion. Martial law was proclaimed throughout the country, and a dawn-to-dusk curfew was enforced. Within Zairian paratroopers holding the airport, the Burundi army then moved into the countryside. What followed was not so much a repression as a hideous slaughter of Hutu populations. The carnage continued unabated until August. By then, almost every educated Hutu was either dead or in exile. (Lemarchand 1995, p. 91)

On July 14, 1972, a new government was sworn in and tasked to "restore order." In early August 1972, the newly appointed prime minister, Albert Nyamoya, along with several members of his government toured the country, "spreading the message of peace, national reconstruction, and unity" (Twagiramungu, interview with a former minister, Bujumbura, 2014). On August 22, 1972, the emergency decrees were abrogated and the military governors replaced by the civilian ones (Mukuri 2013, p. 38).

On August 31, 1972, the Catholic Bishops of Burundi met with the prime minister to discuss "the ways and means of putting the country back on its feet" (Twagiramungu, interview with a 69-year-old clergyman, Ngozi, 2014). "After the two parties harmonized their views on a number of issues including order and security in the countryside; justice; emergency aid to widows and orphans; and the problem of IDPs and refugees," reveals one priest who attended the

5 For Hutu refugees' accounts, see Malkki (1995).

meeting, "the church spread out the good news that 'the nightmare was over'" (Twagiramungu, interview with a 69-year-old clergyman, Ngozi, 2014). For the next 16 years, life returned to normalcy, albeit in a quasi-apartheid regime dominated by Tutsi army officers from Bururi and in which the Hutu populations were considered second-class citizens.

1988 Events: Peasants' uprising followed by army's reprisals

Given existing tensions and distrust between communities in Burundi, even local disputes contained the potential to spark violence that killed thousands. The events of 1988 clearly illustrate the security dilemma that fed violence in Burundi throughout its post-colonial existence. In the summer of 1988, rumors that began in Burundian refugees camps in Rwanda spread into northern Burundi: the army was about to massacre the Hutu populations. Seeking to defuse the rumors, Burundian national leaders toured the area – a much-applauded initiative but which, in the end, yielded meager result because of what one observer called "the perceived distance between promise and performance [of] . . . an impending detente in Hutu-Tutsi relations" (Lemarchand 1995, p. 117). It was in this ambivalent context that a dispute between Hutu peasants and a wealthy Tutsi, Reverien Harushingoro, turned violent on August 14, 1988. Reverien used his firearm to disperse his alleged aggressors. Once people in the neighborhood heard the gun sounds, rumors spread that ". . . the Tutsi army is back again to wipe out the Hutu people" (Twagiramungu, several interviews with peasants, Kirundo, 2014).

In response, hundreds of Hutu peasants armed with machetes and spears attacked Tutsi, starting with a number of Tutsi soldiers who happened to be on leave. Violence erupted first in Ntega and, two days later, reached Marangara in the neighboring province of Ngozi. Government armed forces intervened in Ntega in the evening of August 16 and in Marangara on the morning of August 17. Thus a campaign of "pacification" began that left some 10,000 Hutu dead and several thousand others forced to seek refuge in Rwanda. One observer summed up the incident: "Fear bred fear. In Burundi, premonitions of 'another 1972' panicked local Hutu populations, in turn causing government troops to unleash a savage retaliation" (Lemarchand 1995, p. 118).

President Buyoya signaled the end of army reprisals with an address on August 24, 1988 and, more importantly, a visit to Ntega and Marangara on September 9 (Chrétien et al. 1989, p. 35). However, it was only after the formation of a new cabinet on October 19 (Mukuri 2013, p. 314) that the vast majority of the refugees returned home from Rwanda (Chrétien et al. 1989, p. 142). For the next five years, Buyoya's regime embarked on sweeping political reform that culminated in the June 1993 democratic elections won by his Hutu opponent, Melchior Ndadaye. While Buyoya candidly conceded defeat and handed power over to his opponent on July 9, 1993, in the end, "the military veto prevailed over the popular vote."[6] The result was a deadly military coup attempt that plunged the country into an extreme crisis.

1993: *Military coup, popular resistance, and army reprisals*

On October 21, 1993, President Ndadaye along with several top leaders of his party, FRODEBU, was assassinated by the army as part of a military putsch. As the news of the coup spread, a spontaneous uprising of the Hutu populations emerged throughout the country. Between October 21 and October 25, Hutu uprising movements left several thousands of Tutsi slaughtered, particularly in the central and northeast part of the country. On its way to "restore order," the army killed several thousands of Hutu and forced others into exile, while rounding up Tutsi civilians in IDP camps. As one mission of inquiry found out, "the army and the police used Tutsi and Twa civilians, both adults and students, to extend the reach of their attack" (HRW et al. 1993, p. 1).

Eventually, the scale of domestic counter-coup efforts and international pressure forced the army to surrender power to a civilian government by November 9, 1993. By then, reliable estimates put the fatalities at 200,000, of whom at least 40,000 were Tutsi. It thus came as no surprise that the surviving civilian government, whose most powerful members had been assassinated alongside President Ndadaye, proved too weak to restore order, and more so in the countryside where the military reprisals served as a much-needed rallying cry for Hutu activists to form an armed rebellion devoted to "defending democracy."[7]

1994–2005: *Civil war*

The already bad situation got worse, when in April 1994, the newly appointed Hutu president of Burundi was killed in a plane crash alongside his Rwandan counterpart. This fatal incident sparked genocide in Rwanda, and affected Burundi in two ways. On the one hand, the shocking images of Tutsi slaughtered by their Hutu neighbors in Rwanda served as a post hoc justification of the October coup, and Tutsi armed gangs emerged spontaneously in Bujumbura with a self-imposed mandate of preventing "another Rwanda" in Burundi. On the other hand, after the Rwandan Patriotic Front (RPF) defeated and forced into exile the Hutu army in July 1994, a former aide to Ndadaye, Leonard Nyangoma, used the human and logistic resources of the defeated Rwandan army to form a Hutu rebellion in Burundi called Conseil National pour la Defense de la Democracy (CNDD).

[6] I thank French scholar André Guichoua for this insightful observation.

[7] Note that the resulting armed group called itself "National Council for the Defense of Démocracy."

This time, the Hutu rebellion could not be easily crushed. Instead, the civil war stagnated into a dangerous deadlock, with the casualties on both sides so high that cross-ethnic voices were calling for negotiated solutions. Later on, a combination of complex factors (see Part Four: Accounting for the Endgame, later) created favorable conditions for a negotiated settlement that culminated in the 2005 elections.

Patterns in endings

Seen from a comparative perspective, the previous episodes show a number of recurrent patterns about how violence unfolds and ends. While each episode embodies complex, nonlinear, dynamics, three major patterns can be singled out: hit-and-run, dead-end, and bushfire scenarios. A textbook example of the hit-and-run scenario is the 1972 Hutu-led insurgency, which invaded the country, slaughtered every Tutsi in sight, and ran away once overwhelmed by military intervention. The same scenario unfolded in Ntega and Marangara for two or three days in August 1988 before the army's intervention. The latter scenario, however, can be better conceived of as a dead-end scheme because, unlike the 1972 and 1993 respective scenarios, the boundaries of both the Hutu peasants' mob violence and the army's interventions were geographically and, to some extent, temporally limited.

The bushfire scheme is best illustrated by the army's interventions in 1972 and 1993. In 1972, after the army defeated the Hutu-led insurgency in the southern and western parts of the country, it launched a relentless and countrywide witch hunt targeting educated and/or influential Hutu people. In 1993, what begun as a military coup ended up plunging the country into a ten-year civil war.

In terms of ending, a comparative reading of various episodes suggests four major scenarios: mission accomplished; aborted plot; stalemate; and transformational accommodation. The phrase "mission accomplished" is the catchphrase used by a great many eyewitnesses of the 1972 atrocities committed by the army against, to use one elderly Burundian wiseman's metaphor, "the shining flowers of the Hutu garden." In fact, strong evidence shows that the atrocities came to an end only when the perpetrators' mission was fulfilled, namely, to eradicate "the Hutu peril" – that is, the threat of Hutu domination à la Rwandaise.

Regarding most of the Hutu uprisings in the episodes under consideration, they can be best described as an aborted plot, that is, a move to wipe out the Tutsi population that lasts for a couple of days, subject to the time it takes for the army to intervene (3 days in Nyanza-lac in 1972; 1 day in Ntega in 1988; 5 days in Karuzi in 1993). This scenario can also apply to the army reprisals in Ntega and Marangara in 1988 that came to an end within a couple of days, on the explicit orders of President Pierre Buyoya.

Contrariwise, the outcomes of the 1993 events are a paradigmatic example of the stalemate scenario – a situation when the conflicting parties have neither the upper hand on their adversary nor the ability to secure safe haven for their protégés. The transformational scenario describes the way Burundian parties defied the prescription of ethnic separation and found a common ground upon which to form a bi-ethnic army and government.

Across these different modalities of endings, one common thread repeats. There are no dramatic events that mark the "end." In each case, the ending is a transition out of mass atrocities as the situation normalizes. This raises the question: How, empirically, are endings recognized?

PART THREE: DOCUMENTING ENDINGS: A QUESTION OF EVIDENCE AND INDICATORS

"When I came out, there were no birds," said one survivor who had hidden throughout the genocide. "There was sunshine and the stench of death."

(des Forges 2009, p. 1)

This account by a Rwandan genocide survivor is consistent with the dominant narrative of how genocidal violence ends: A military force (the Allied Forces in 1945 Germany, or the RPF in 1994 Rwanda) defeats the genocidal forces and rescues the survivors. The day of "liberation" can be recorded with precision for the rescued survivors, whose main challenge now is to recount what happened to them and to recover from the unspeakable horrors they have gone through. In contrast to this standard narrative, however, in Burundi regime change did not enter the ending equation. In this context, when asked about how, when, and why they knew violence was over, Burundians' responses vary sharply depending on the narrator's position vis-a-vis the atrocities, then and now. This section begins with a few narratives, underscoring the notion of ending as a contested terrain before shedding light on core pieces of evidence or indicators about the nature and extent of endings.

Ending as a contested terrain

There is no question that each instance of violence has multiple endings, and each ending, when there is one, is likely to mean different things to different people. Three examples underscore this point (Boxes 2.1–2.3).

Taken together, these three accounts hint at how the legacies and outcomes of violence shape the views of people on the nature and extent of endings. These legacies take the form of social scripts in the psychological sense, that is, a sequence of expected behaviors that people "internalize through day-to-day interaction with other people, and which influence their presupposition, and hence their way of communication" (Meng 2008, p. 1). In this regard, distinction needs to be made between ad hoc endings of specific episodes of violence and the true endgame of the continuum of violence.

Box 2.1: "Home for the survivors"

Iwabo-nabasigaye [Home for the survivors] is a popular bar settled in the heart of Bujumbura, the capital city of Burundi. The bar belongs to a former rebel military commander and now a powerful general in the CNDD-FDD administration. When I visited the bar in March 2014 and asked a military officer who is very close to the bar's owner what the name stood for, he didn't bother to shout as loudly as proudly: "The nightmare is over! So is the Tutsi domination![...]. For us the survivors, time has come to [enjoy] life."

Box 2.2: "Who told you these atrocities ever ended?"

Manchester, New Hampshire, July 2013. I was talking with a group of Burundian refugees settled in New Hampshire about their experience with the 1972 events. One of my interlocutors was a 60-year-old woman who didn't leave her hometown until 1995, when she joined her son in exile in Tanzania before being relocated in the United States in 2007. To my question, "back in 1972, how did you come to realize that violence was over," she looked me in the eyes and asked, "Who told you that these atrocities ever ended?" For much of the next two hours, most of my interlocutors insisted that I was wrong to assume that the nightmare was over in Burundi. "You don't get it, Mister," observed one old man in his early 70, "the truth is: the Tutsi is still in control; he is the master, and the Hutu puppets do nothing more than sucking up to a new face of the old Tutsi domination."

Box 2.3: "Our killers are still there"

Gitega, March 2014. When I visited Gitega in the central of Burundi, I was surprised to find myself in an IDP settlement hosting several dozens of the Tutsi families who were forced to abandon their properties in 1993. Asked why they were still living in IDP camps, one of my interviewees stated, "Our killers are still there, ready to finish their work if we return back to them!"

The language of increase and decrease in violence

In their day-to-day language, Burundians hint at various degrees of severity and stages in the gradual process of violence from escalation to de-escalation. Key revealing terms recorded throughout my interviews can be grouped into three pairs of Kirundi verbs corresponding to three stages in the life of an episode of violence as shown in Table 2.2:

"Gutangura" refers to the first day of violence outbreak, which is generally well documented: October 19, 1965, when a failed Hutu plot sparked a wave of counter-coup reprisals; April 29, 1972, when a gang of Hutu insurgents invaded south Burundi, slaughtering every Tutsi in sight; August 14, 1988, when Hutu peasants attacked an armed wealthy Tutsi in northern Burundi; October 21, 1993, when the army assassinated President Ndadaye along with his close aides. The phase of "Gukara" or increase in violence is relatively short: In 1972, it lasted from

TABLE 2.2: *Core terminology of mass violence escalation and de-escalation*

State of violence	Escalation	De-escalation
First stage	Gutangura (to start)	Guhwama (to decrease/diminish)
Advanced stage	Gukara (to increase)	Guhagarara (to stop)
Final stage	Kwimonogoza (to endure/expand)	Guhera (to end/disappear)

May 3 to 30; in 1988, the duration was from August 16 to 22; and in 1993, it lasted only two days, October 23–25.

As to the phase of "Kwimonogoza" or enduring process of violence, the dynamics vary greatly. In 1965, as well as in 1972, the army's counterattacks were followed by a bloody "witch hunt" that lasted up to three months. In 1993, "Kwimonogoza" became the law of the land as the short-lived calm that followed the army's return to barracks exploded into civil war largely fueled by the Rwandan genocide.

The notion of Guhagarara, "halt" or "stop," implies a sudden or abrupt ending, generally as a result of an external intervention. The ending patterns of Hutu-led massacres against Tutsi in 1965, 1972, and 1988 fall in this category: Hutu insurgents attacked Tutsi civilians, and within the next two to five days, the Tutsi army intervened to "liberate the victims." The notable exception was 1993, when the perpetrators were strategic enough to destroy bridges and barred the main roads to minimize the risk of military interventions. Interestingly, few among my interviewees used the term Guhera, and when they did, it was generally to emphasize how far they have come from: byaraheze [it's over]! This emphasis underscores the idea of empirical distinction between episodic endings or, rather, halts in the continuum of violence and the true ending that augurs the dawn of an era of non-repetition.

Assessing the damage

Seen from a victim's perspective, endings are synonymous with the last day of violence-related harms. As in many other cases, fatalities rank high on the list of harms. A Hutu survivor of the 1972 bloodbath recalls:

> It was the third Sunday of May. Soldiers attacked our village and rounded up all the men in sight and then Pa! Pa! Pa! Pa! Pa! Pa! ... When the guns fell silent, all were dead ... all, but me and two or three others. [...]. We only survived because we were the first to fall down and therefore thought dead under the pile of dead bodies. [...]. I then went into hiding but never heard any gun sound until our priest toured the region to tell the hiders that peace had been restored.

A Tutsi survivor of the October 24, 1993 massacres in Gitega describes a different scenario in which the sound of guns was a game changer: "We were hiding in the house of a good Hutu. When our killers heard the sound of gunshots approaching, they run away in panic shouting, 'mwopfa abasoda!' [mind the soldiers]. Tutsi who panicked and followed the killers were the ones who lost their lives."

Besides fatalities, Burundians invoke other recurring forms of harm, notably, acts of looting and displacement. Generally, acts of sacking, plundering, and pillaging tend to intensify in the aftermath of large-scale atrocities. For many of the incidents I documented, especially with regard to violence in 1965, 1972, and 1993, very few fatalities were registered after the perpetrators embraced the campaign of looting.

Regarding refugees and IDPs, the official and unofficial records about the period when the host facilities register the last clients give a sense of the endings of violence. For instance, converging sources show that Burundian refugees crossed en masse into Rwanda and Tanzania during the period of October–November 1965, May 1972, August 18–24, 1988, and October–November 1993. Data from IDP facilities in Burundi corroborate the same patterns, with one major difference: from 1972 onward, the army tended to round up the Tutsi in IDP camps before launching large-scale massacres against Hutu populations. As many eyewitnesses in different parts of Burundi told me, paying attention to this pattern saved many lives of the Hutu populations throughout the 1994–2000 civil war period, because "whenever the army arrived in a region and created [IDP] camps, Hutu peasants knew it was high time to flee." In short, the decrease in refugees and IDPs' movements augurs the dawn of return to normalcy.

Narratives of return to normalcy

In describing the signs of endings, eyewitnesses invoke a number of recurring events, behaviors, and attitudes. One of the key factors that augur decrease in violence is the return to law and order. This notion may sound contradictory in the context of state-sponsored violence. However, evidence suggests that a key factor in mass violence is the reign of arbitrary, parallel, and generally informal structures of power. It is only after the official hierarchical centers of power begin to recover their full authority that the rest of the population feel safe enough to approach the victims, and more importantly, to confront the troublemakers. This period generally coincides with remarkable change in the behavior of the perpetrators toward the survivors. A survivor of the 1972 in Ngozi confided to me her chilling encounter with the man who had killed her father a few days ago: "When he found me hidden under the bed of his own mother, he told me: don't be afraid, I am sorry for what happened to your dad." The fate of a Hutu leader that President Micombero appointed in the July 1972 government is even more revealing: "Shortly after I was appointed [as a cabinet member]," he stated, "the same military commander who had vowed to kill me and chased me in vain for weeks was the first one to come congratulate me and offered to help recover some of my belongings pillaged" (Twagiramungu, interview with a former minister, Bujumbura, 2014).

Freedom of movement is another key indicator of the ending of violence: "When I saw the sun again and breathe fresh air," states a Tutsi survivor of the 1993 massacre in Ngozi, "I just sat down and cried for joy" (Twagiramungu, interview with a 62-year-old female, Ngozi, 2014). Above all, however, return to normalcy becomes evident the day survivors embrace daily activities such as farming, attending school for students, and going to church. These are followed by social manifestations, including beer-sharing gatherings, weddings, and other festivities.

Another important testament to "life after violence" (Uvin 2009) is the social reintegration of the victims, notably IDPs and refugees. In a limited number of cases, some victims invoke mechanisms of accountability and reparation as "the true sign that authorities really care about the survivors and impunity is no longer the law of the land" (Twagiramungu, interview with a human rights activist and anti-Tutsi pogroms survivor, Bujumbura, 2014). However, numerous accounts suggest that the rare perpetrators to have so far been held accountable were Hutu who committed atrocities against Tutsi in 1965, 1972, 1988, and 1993, whereas justice is still slow in coming for other horrendous atrocities, including the crimes of genocide and war crimes committed during the civil war period.

To sum up, the notion of ending means different things to different people, depending on one's position vis-a-vis the outcomes and enduring consequences of violence. Nevertheless, evidence shows a number of factors that augur the dawn of a post-violence era. The kind of endings experienced since the 1965 massacres until the 2000 signature of the Arusha Peace Agreement can be only seen in retrospect as partial endings, or precisely episodic "halts" along the continuum of violence. In the aftermath of each episode, the ruling elite vowed to restore "peace and unity" only to be proven wrong by a new wave of bloodbath – a fate that calls to mind Gramsci's words: "The old is dying and the new cannot be born; in this interregnum there arises a great diversity of morbid symptoms" (Gramsci 1999, p. 74). What makes Burundi a case of great interest, however, is its empirical experience in rising from the "morbid symptoms" to foreclose the hitherto prevailing drivers of antagonism, and thus embrace a new era of ethnic cooperation born from the ashes of the old world where ethnic separation seemed the only viable way out. For the purpose of this study, the paradigm of "endgame" is used to name this important shift in the dynamics of ethnic violence – a short closure to a sequence of episodic incidences. This notion along with the dynamics underlying it begs the question: How did Burundi foreclose its four-decade history of violent antagonism?

PART FOUR: ACCOUNTING FOR THE ENDGAME

When asked what it took for Burundi to forge a way out from mass violence, Burundians invoke several factors revolving around the complex interaction between individual agency and shifting contingencies.

Individual agency

A fair number of Burundians interviewed for the purpose of this chapter are convinced that Buyoya made all the difference (author interviews). Born in south Burundi in 1949 and trained in various military academies in Belgium, France, and Germany, Major Pierre Buyoya entered the political scene in 1979, when he was elected to the central committee of the ruling party, UPRONA. When he led a bloodless coup against President Bagaza in September 1987, he pledged to "heal the Hutu-Tutsi rift" – a pledge that then seemed unthinkable. As one analyst observed, "when Buyoya took over, three-quarters of the cabinet and National Assembly, about two-thirds of all university students, 13 out of 15 provincial governors, all army officers, and 96 percent of all enlisted soldiers and police were Tutsi" (Eggers 2006, p. 21). In the wake of the 1988 massacres of Ntega and Marangara, which tested his good faith, Buyoya radically reshuffled his administration. He appointed a new cabinet led by a Hutu prime minister, and created a consultative commission with twelve Hutu and twelve Tutsi members tasked to find the ways and means of restoring and maintaining national unity. In February 1991, a charter of national unity was adopted as the supreme law of the land. In line with the charter, the government ratified a new constitution along with new laws that legalized and regulated the multiparty system.

All along the way, Buyoya championed the politics of moderation at a time when the conservative Tutsi deemed political openness "suicide," whereas the radical Hutu dreamed of a Hutu revolution à la Rwandaise as the only viable solution. To his supporters' dismay, however, Buyoya's politics of "ethnic parity" between Hutu and Tutsi, along with massive recruitment of influential Hutu figures to fill strategic positions in both the government and the UPRONA party, did not prevent him from losing the 1993 elections. Gracious in defeat, he handed over power to his Hutu opponent, Melchior Ndadaye.

After the army assassinated Ndadaye in October 1993, Buyoya adopted a low profile while remaining fully supportive of the constitutional order. At the end of the day, however, Buyoya resurfaced again in July 1996 at a time when the country was on the verge of anarchy caused by, on the one hand, a deadlock between the Tutsi-dominated army and the Hutu-dominated government, and on the other hand, the horrors of civil war. After restructuring the army and silencing Tutsi hardliners, Buyoya went on to form a new cabinet that eventually became a key player in the Arusha peace process.

Other sources insist that the Burundi success story has many fathers. Place of pride goes particularly to former Tanzanian President Julius Nyerere, who is credited for having patiently and relentlessly convinced the Burundian warring parties that "a negotiated peace was the only viable best option for all of them" (Twagiramungu, interview with a former vice president of the National Assembly, Bujumbura, 2014). Nyerere's credit is shared by former South African President

Nelson Mandela, who took over from Nyerere and proved instrumental in using the South African model to broker a deal between the Tutsi-dominated army and the main Hutu rebel group, CNDD-FDD – the latter having been until then sidelined by Nyerere, whose focus was on political forces at the expense of armed groups. Among other external actors, most of the credit is given to Howard Wolpe, a former U.S. special envoy to the Great Lakes of Africa who committed much of his efforts to Burundi throughout the crisis and beyond (Wolpe 2011).

Regarding local actors, Melchior Ndadaye is credited for having set the tone for a new era within the Hutu community by breaking up with the PALIPEHUTU ethnist ideology when he returned to Burundi from exile and formed a moderate party, FRODEBU, whose non-sectarian stance attracted a number of prominent Tutsi.[8] Ndadaye's power-sharing commitment informed the Arusha peace process and was manifest in his allocation of one-third of the cabinet seats to Tutsi figures including the position of prime minister held by Sylvie Kinigi, a Tutsi woman from UPRONA. Many other observers also emphasize the unique role played by current president, Pierre Nkurunziza, whose low profile, conciliatory attitude, and Christian devotion won his CNDD-FDD exuberant support among ordinary people in the countryside, whereas his political moderation and negotiation skills proved instrumental in winning the Tutsi-dominated army's trust. Many more others still invoke the name of the father of Burundi's independence, prince Louis Rwagasore, seen by all as "the rock of Barundi unbreakable unity," and therefore, the source of inspiration for all peace seekers.

While the endgame of violence in Burundi cannot be limited to the efficacy of purposeful actors, the role of individuals was crucial. The process of ending rose from a set of few steps taken by key actors like Buyoya and Ndadaye before growing into a web of mass actions undertaken by thousands of followers and facilitators at different levels. Translated in the language of causality, this view concurs with the logic of agentic approaches[9] according to which social phenomena "typically arise in the backwash of intentionality, through the oversights and miscalculations of purposive agents engaged in projects of their own" (Goodin 1996, p. 25).

Limits to the individual agency for change

While individual actions (and inactions) matter as rationalist theories may rightly suggest, strong evidence shows that the ending of mass violence in Burundi did seldom unfold according to a preordained master plan. For instance, upon his return to power in 1996, Buyoya's plan was to incorporate "moderate Hutu groups" in his administration (as he had done on the eve of the 1993 elections) while

8 Notable among of them were vice president of the National Assembly, Gilles Bimazubute and Jean-Marie Ngendahayo, minister of foreign affairs.

9 On the notions of "human agency" and "agentic perspective," see particularly Bandura (2000) and Bandura (2001).

marginalizing "the genocidal forces" (République du Burundi 1998, para. 186) – a label then used to name a variety of Hutu actors including the perpetrators of the 1993 anti-Tutsi massacres. He could not control the armed groups who took up arms against the army, and Hutu exiles who opposed his regime. This co-optation strategy proved counterproductive, however, as his "Hutu of hire" were seen as too opportunistic to win the hearts and minds of the wider Hutu population.

By the same token, Buyoya's administration along with many in the Tutsi elite in Bujumbura hoped to capitalize on "the genocide card" to win sympathy and support from the newly installed Tutsi-dominated regime in Rwanda, which endorsed calls for negotiations. Moreover, Buyoya agreed to negotiate at a time when the facilitator, Nyerere, was forcing a ceasefire on the armed groups as a precondition for peace talks. However, upon Nyerere's death in 1999, his successor, Mandela, reversed the strategy and recommended to include all the excluded forces, notably the armed groups and political prisoners. In this regard, the endgame is best understood as an outcome of complex contingent factors, including individuals but also notably, (i) the Rwanda factor, (ii) military stalemate, (iii) internal dissent toward moderation functions, and (iv) external pressure and incentives.

The Rwanda factor

Events in Rwanda had a strong impact on Burundi in many respects. First, a combination of the horrors of the 1994 genocide and the failure of the international community to intervene made the neighboring Burundi a world's laboratory for new strategies to "save face." This obsession translated into a new agenda beautifully summed up in a catchphrase coined by a U.S. special envoy, "Making Peace After Genocide" (Wolpe 2011), and which eventually became the cornerstone of the Arusha peace process.

Second, while the coming into power of the Tutsi-dominated Rwandan Patriotic Front in Kigali was warmly welcomed by the Burundian Tutsi elite, the ensuing dynamics defied all expectations. On the one hand, the defeat of the Hutu Rwandan army provided the newly created Burundian Hutu rebel movement with massive weapons and soldiers necessary to bring to fruition a viable strategy of violent struggle. It thus comes as no surprise that the CNDD was born in Bukavu in the summer of 1994, in the Panzi refugee camp, and then the headquarters of the former Rwandan armed forces (ex-Forces Armees Rwandaises, ex-FARs) in exile. On the other hand, when Pierre Buyoya returned to power in July 1996, Rwandan forces along with their Ugandan allies were busy building a regional military coalition to invade Zaire. "Had Kagame openly welcome Buyoya's coup," one former Rwandan diplomat stated, "extremist Hutu propaganda about a regional Tutsi plot could be damaging to our cause." It was in this context that Rwanda and Uganda were prompted to back Tanzania's efforts to use economic sanctions to force Buyoya's regime negotiate with his opponents. In short, the

Rwandan decision to pursue war in Congo also helped determine its approach in Burundi, toward negotiations.

Third, when Burundi's warring parties agreed to join the table of negotiations and Arusha was chosen as the ideal venue, the lessons learned from the collapse of the donor-backed Arusha peace negotiations between the Rwandan government and the Rwandan Patriotic Front under the auspices of Tanzania served as hallmark against which new strategies were devised to minimize the risks of a new failure.

Military stalemate

The endgame in Burundi is also an outcome of a typical "mutually hurting stalemate" (Zartman 1989). This is particularly evident when one is reminded of the 1965, 1972, and 1988 scenarios when the army literally crushed Hutu uprisings and imposed the law of the strongest. Contrariwise, in the aftermath of President Ndadaye's assassination in 1993, Hutu uprising in the countryside was so massive and far better organized that it forced the Tutsi-dominated army to abandon some remote areas in the hands of insurgent Hutu activists and to contend itself with controlling major urban areas and strategic areas such as schools and IDP camps. At the end of the day, however, as causalities on both sides escalated, calls for negotiated solutions could be increasingly heard. The stalemate delegitimized the hard-liners, and shifted momentum to the compromise-seeking factions.

Intra-party realignment toward moderation

One cannot stress enough how the enduring legacies of the 1965, 1972, 1988, and 1993 massacres along with the social scripts of violence associated with them politically empowered extremists on both sides of the ethnic divide. The story of Burundi's transformative ending is one whereby moderate leaders could expand their influence and demonstrate the benefits of accommodation in parallel with a realignment of political positions. For example, in the Tutsi camp, Major Pierre Buyoya, as noted earlier, emerged from the Bururi lobby and committed himself to bridge the Hutu-Tutsi rift in 1987. Despite challenges (noted previously), he negotiated the Arusha peace agreement in the name of which he presided over the first half of the transition and retired in 2003. In the process, his party, UPRONA, split into rival factions, some of which were led by hard-line Tutsi interest groups, led by people like former President Jean-Baptiste Bagaza. The other side was, "Buyoya's Tutsi" – a label referring to the UPRONA faction close to Buyoya along with the former army who embraced the logic of bi-ethnic power-sharing and remain, as this chapter is written, part of the new regime.

When Buyoya launched the democratization process in the late 1980s, the Hutu elite also split into two factions: A Hutu supremacist group called PALIPEHUTU opted for violent confrontation, and a moderate faction led by Ndadaye, who adopted a low-profile approach, compromised with the regime and eventually led his FRODEBU party to victory in 1993. In the wake of Ndadaye's assassination, the surviving FRODEBU split into two major factions, one opting for compromising with putschist army, the other opting for violent means to "defend democracy." The latter faction, CNDD, was led by a hard-liner revolutionary, Leonard Nyangoma, whose power rested largely on military and logistic resources he was receiving from the ex-FARs, and then based in Zaire, now DRC. However, after the RPF troops and their allies invaded Zaire and destroyed the Hutu refugees camps, Nyangoma's influence declined and the CNDD split into several factions. Eventually, a faction led by a young generation of officers around Nkurunziza emerged as the most powerful. By the time this faction, the CNDD-FDD, was able to pursue its interests through the terms of the Arusha Peace Agreement and joined the transitional government in 2003. In the course of this period, it learned how to advance its goals by winning both the hearts and minds of millions of Hutu people and the Tutsi army's trust, two key factors that paved the way for its landslide and unchallenged victory in the 2005 legislative and presidential elections. All along the way, the PALIPEHUTU, which had made it its credo to never compromise with the Tutsi and thus boycotted both the peace negotiations and the 2005 elections, went on to lose the ground and split into a mosaic of small factions, some of which are still fighting the government as of today.[10]

External incentives and pressures

A negotiated path became particularly inescapable as the international community, notably the UN (UN General Assembly 1996, para. 48), major donor countries, and a Tanzania-led coalition of the neighboring countries, committed efforts to prevent Burundi from becoming "another Rwanda." This unusually shared commitment was embedded in the predicament that "The conflict between Tutsi and Hutu in Burundi ... is at the heart of Central African regional instability, producing massive refugee flows, insurgencies, and cross-border violence" (Wolpe 2011, p. 1). Thus, on October 24, 1993, only three days after the coup, the UN secretary-general sent his special envoy, Under-Secretary-General James Jonah, on a mission of good offices to Burundi. In addition to condemning the coup and publicly expressing UN support for the civilian government then in hiding, Jonah discussed the possibility of sending of a military UN presence – an idea the government welcomed but the army rejected. On November 16, the UN secretary-general appointed a special representative for Burundi (UN Security

[10] For a compelling contrast between the CNDD-FDD and the PALIPEHUTU, see Uvin and Bayer (2013), p. 274.

Council 1993), former Mauritanian Ambassador Ahmedou Ould-Abdullah, who took up his duties on November 25, 1993.

Through his envoy, the UN secretary-general vowed (i) to restore the democratic institutions overthrown by the abortive coup, (ii) to facilitate dialogue between the parties to the crisis, (iii) to establish a commission of inquiry into the events of October and the massacres that followed, and (iv) to work in close collaboration with the Organisation of African Unity (Ould-Abdallah 2000, p. 38). By the same token, both the European Union and the United States of America appointed their own envoys, whose combined efforts proved instrumental in bringing the warring parties to a negotiated settlement and in providing various resources including peace-keeping forces, technical expertise, and millions of dollars, all of which combined to foster peace.

To sum up, the endgame of violence in Burundi is a complex transformational process going back and forth between individual actions, power dynamics within and between rival factions, and other contingencies including external pressures and incentives, all of which culminated in the signature of the Arusha Peace Agreement in August 2000.

The question at the heart of this essay – what did it take to end mass violence in Burundi? – implies a straightforward explanatory pathway along which a causal factor of interest (aka independent variable) is strongly associated with an outcome (aka dependent variable), holding other factors constant (Gerring 2007, p. 233). However, this model of simplistic causality fails to render justice to the complex trajectories between the onset of ethnic violence and its closure. Instead, the issues discussed earlier plead for the causal logic of "configuration" understood as "a specific combination of factors (or stimuli, causal variables, ingredients, determinants, etc [...] that produces a given outcome of interest" (Rhioux and Ragin 2009, p. xix).

The search for causal factors behind the endgame of mass violence stems from a predicament that two leading comparativists have defined as "one widespread view holding that [causal] mechanisms lead to deterministic outcomes" (Falleti and Lynch 2009, p. 1151). However, as Elster reminds us, causal mechanisms are generally "triggered under generally unknown conditions or with indeterminate consequences" (Elster 1998, p. 45). This view, which underscores the role of "accidents" and "unintended consequences" in shaping the course of human choices and actions, hints at the open-ended nature inherent to mass violence along with the antagonistic forces that fuel it.

The process of making and unmaking ethnic walls in Burundi seems to have followed the logic of path dependence according to which, "once a country or region has started down a track, the costs of reversal are very high" (Levi 1997, p. 45). "There will be other choice points," adds Levi, "but the entrenchments of certain institutional arrangements obstruct an easy reversal of the initial choice" (Levi 1997, p. 45).

It is in this view that we can understand the defining momentum of the 2000 Arusha peace process. Once this step was reached, both the signatory and non-signatory parties felt obliged to comply with it and those who did not were doomed to pay a high cost. The cost of defying this historic agreement proved particularly high after it became the cornerstone of political and military arrangements on the basis of which the transitional government organized the 2005 elections from which emerged the consociational scheme of power-sharing that has prevailed as of today.

CONCLUSION

At this moment in history, when we have the sense of a world dying and another coming to birth ... we must seize and size up the dying system to understand what is being born.
Max Lerner, *The Age of Overkill* (1962, p. 19)

Twenty-six years ago, a former U.S. ambassador to Bujumbura prescribed ethnic separation as the only viable solution to end the longstanding bloody Hutu–Tutsi conflict that characterized much of political life in Burundi since independence. As of today however, despite the on-going crisis associated with the recent controversial elections, the ethnic factor seems less salient in political life to the extent that the cost of cementing intra-group breaches seems far higher than the one of expanding trans-group and cross-boundary ties. How did Burundi get there?

This chapter concludes that the prevailing endgame of violence, like the motives behind it, defies simple explanations. It is in part the result of complex power dynamics, the latter being understood as the interaction between contending purposeful actors, each pursuing specific interests and goals. It is also an outcome of complex contingent factors, some of which are beyond the control and/or reach of idiosyncratic forces.

Strong evidence also shows that neither the Burundi endgame developed overnight, nor did it unfold according to a preordained master plan. It is rather best understood as a process during which, under the right conditions, several efforts converge to "produce a situation in which one part of action becomes far more attractive or far less costly than another, and thus can define preferences by creating overwhelming incentives for decision-makers to choose (or to avoid) a specific set of policies" (Coppedge 1999, p. 474). It is in this perspective that one can understand better how and why, when the civil war became extremely violent with no sight of victory for either side, domestic and international pressures for a negotiated settlement became irresistible.

For nearly four decades, the violent path prevailed until a combination of factors brought about a new "critical juncture," that is, one of those defining moments in political life that "establish certain directions of change and foreclose others in a way that shape development over long periods of time" (Mahoney 2000, p. 504). The signature of the Arusha Peace Agreement in August 2000 proved to be such a juncture.

So far, the ruling elites from both communities have understood the basic principle of institutional reform that "the distribution of political power in society is the key determinant of [institutional] evolution" (Acemoglu and Robinson 2010, p. 1). In doing so, they have proved right the prophetic motto of their national anthem: "O blessed Burundi! . . . Wounded and bruised, you have remained master of yourself; When the hour came, you arose."

Whether the accommodative scheme of power distribution that helped to foreclose the drivers of ethnic violence will prevail beyond the on-going election-related crisis is another question. Nevertheless, without pretending to know what the future holds in store for Burundi, it is my hope that by continuing to "seize and size up the dying system to understand what is being born" (Lerner 1962, p. 19) – as I have strived to do throughout this chapter – Burundians and other concerned actors can understand better what it takes to anticipate and meet head-on the challenges ahead in the shared endeavor of fostering lasting peace.

WORKS CITED

Acemoglu, Daron and James Robinson. 2010. "The Role of Institutions in Growth and Development." *Review of Economics and Institutions* 1:2, 1–33.

Anderson, Benedict. 1983. *Imagined Communities: Reflections on the Origin and Spread of Nationalism*. London: Verso.

Bandura, Albert. 2000. "Exercise of Human Agency through Collective Efficacy." *Current Directions in Psychological Science* 9, 75–78.

Bandura, A. 2001. "Social Cognitive Theory: An Agentic Perspective." *Annual Review of Psychology* 52, 1–26.

Botte, Robert. 1985. "Rwanda and Burundi, 1889–1930: Chronology of a Slow Assassination." *International Journal of African Historical Studies* 18:1, 53–91 (Part 1) & 18:2, 289–314 (Part 2).

Burnett, Frances H. 1911. *The Secret Garden*. New York: F. A. Stokes Company,

Buyoya, Pierre. 1998. *Mission Possible: Construire une paix durable au Burundi*. Paris: L'Harmattan.

Chrétien, Jean-Pierre. 2003. *The Great Lakes of Africa: Two Thousand Years of History*. New York: Zone Books.

Chrétien, Jean-Pierre, André Guichaoua, Gabriel Le Jeune. 1989. "La Crise d'août 1988 au Burundi." *Cahiers du CRA* no. 6. Paris: Karthala.

Coppedge, Michael. 1999. "Thickening Thin Concepts and Theories: Combining Large N and Small in Comparative Politics." *Comparative Politics* 31:4, 465–476.

des Forges, Alison Liebhafsky. 2009. *Leave None to Tell the Story: Genocide in Rwanda*. New York: Human Rights Watch.

Eggers, Ellen K. 2006. *Historical Dictionary of Burundi*. Plymouth: Scarecrow Press, Inc.

Elster, Jon. 1998. "A Plea for Mechanism." In *Social Mechanisms: An Analytical Approach to Social Theory*, edited by P. Hedstrom and R Swedberg, 45–73. Cambridge: Cambridge University Press.
Falleti, Tulia and Julia Lynch. 2009. "Context and Causal Mechanisms in Political Analysis." *Comparative Political Studies* 42:9, 1143–1166.
Fearon, James D. and David D. Laitin. 2000. "Violence and the Social Construction of Ethnic Identity." *International Organization*, 54:4, 845–877.
Gahama, Joseph. 2001. *Le Burundi sous administration belge*. Paris: Karthala.
Gerring, John. 2007. "Is There a (Viable) Crucial-Case Method?" *Comparative Political Studies* 40:3, 231–253.
Goodin, Robert E. 1996. "Institutions and Their Design." In *The Theory of Institutional Design*, edited by Robert E. Goodin, 24–27. Cambridge: Cambridge University Press.
Gramsci, Antonio. 1999. *Prison Notebooks*, edited and translated by Quentin Hoare and Geoffrey Nowell Smith. London: The Electric Book Company.
Hegel, G.W.F. 1956. *The Philosophy of History*, translated by J. Sibree. New York: Dover Publications.
Human Rights Watch. 2003. *Everyday Victims: Civilians in the Burundian War*. New York: Human Rights Watch.
HRW, FIDH, LDGL, OMCT, CNCD, NCOS, and NOVIB, 1993. *The International Commission of Inquiry into Human Rights Violations* in Burundi Since October 21, 1993. Final Report. Amsterdam: Novib.
Lemarchand, René. 1995. *Burundi: Ethnic Conflict and Genocide*. Cambridge: Cambridge University Press.
Le Monde. 1966. "Les États-Unis Expulsent l'Ambassadeur du Burundi." January 13. Available at: www.lemonde.fr/archives/article/1966/01/13/les-etats-unis-expulsent-l-ambassadeur-du-burundi_2702566_1819218.html#Xuoxt5JROCDe3WzC.99. Accessed February 17, 2015.
Lerner, Max. 1962. *The Age of Overkill: A Preface to World Politics*. New York: Simon & Schuster.
Levi, Margaret. 1997. "A Model, a Method, and a Map: Rational Choice in Comparative and Historical Analysis." In *Comparative Politics: Rationality, Culture, and Structure*, edited by Mark I. Lichbach and Alan S. Zuckerman, 19–41. Cambridge: Cambridge University Press.
Mahoney, James. 2000. "Path Dependence in Historical Sociology." *Theory and Society* 29:4, 507–548.
Malkki, Liisa. 1995. *Purity and Exile: Violence, Memory, and National Cosmology among Hutu Refugees in Tanzania*. Chicago: Chicago University Press.
Melady, Thomas Patrick. 1988. "To Stop the Killing, Partition Burundi." *The New York Times*, September 1.
Meng, Hongdang. 2008. "Social Script Theory and Cross-Cultural Communication." *Intercultural Communication Studies* XVII:1, 132–138.
Mukuri, Melchior. 2013. *Dictiomnaire Chronologique du Burundi. Volume 2: 1966–1993* L'Ere des coups d'Etats. Bujumbura: Université du Burundi.
Newbury, Catharine. 1988. *The Cohesion of Oppression Clientship and Ethnicity in Rwanda 1860–1960*. New York: Columbia University Press.
Ngayimpenda, Evariste. 2005. *Histoire du conflit politico-ethnique burundais: les premières marches du calvaire (1960–1973)*. Bujumbura: Editions de la Renaissance.
Nyankanzi, Edward. 1988. "Partition of Tiny Burundi Is Not the Answer." *The New York Times*, October 15.

Ould-Abdallah, Almedou. 2000. *Burundi on the Brink 1993–1995: A UN Special Envoy Reflects on Preventative Diplomacy*. Washington: United States Institute for Peace Press.
Pagès, Alexandre. 1933. *Un royaume hamite au centre de l'Afrique: Au Ruanda sur les bords du lac Kivu (Congo belge)*. Bruxelles: Académie Royale des Sciences d'Outre-mer.
Prunier, Gérard. 1995. *The Rwanda Crisis: History of a Genocide*. New York: Columbia University Press.
République du Burundi. 1998. *Plan d'Action du gouvernement pour la lutte contre le génocide*. Bujumbura: Ministère des Droits de la Personne humaine, des Réformes institutionnelles et des Relations avec l'Assemblée nationale.
Rihoux, Benoit and Charles Ragin (Eds.). 2009. "Introduction." In *Configurational Comparative Methods: Qualitative Comparative Analysis (QCA) and Related Techniques*, xvii–xxv. Thousand Oaks: SAGE Publications, Inc.
Sanders, Edith R. 1969. The Hamitic Hypothesis: Its Origin and Functions in Time Perspective." *The Journal of African History* 10:4, 521–532.
Speke, John Hanning. 1863. *Journal of the Discovery of the Source of the Nile*. Edinburgh and London: William Blackwood and Sons.
UN General Assembly. 1996. "Interim Report on the Human Rights Situation in Burundi Submitted by the Special Rapporteur of the Commission on Human Rights." UN Doc. A/51/459. 7 October 7.
UN Security Council. 1993. "Note by the President of the Security Council." UN Doc. S/26757. November 16.
Uvin, Peter. 2009. *Life after Violence: A people's story of Burundi*. London: Zed Books.
Uvin, Peter and Leanne Bayer. 2013. "The Political Economy of Statebuilding in Burundi." In *Political Economy of Statebuilding: Power after Peace*, edited by Mats Berdal and Dominik Zaum, pp. 263–277. Abingdon and New York: Routledge.
Wolpe, Howard. 2011. "Making Peace After Genocide: Anatomy of the Burundi Process." Peaceworks No. 70. Washington: United States Institute of Peace.
Zartman, William I. 1989. *Ripe for Resolution*. New York: Oxford University Press.

AUTHOR INTERVIEWS

Interview with a 55-year-old male who witnessed and survived the 1972 anti-Hutu pogroms in Muramvya, March 2014. Interviewee requested anonymity.

Interview in Bururi, 2014. Interviewees requested anonymity.

Interview with two former soldiers, Bujumbura, 2014. Interviewees requested anonymity.

Interview with a former minister, Bujumbura, 2014. Interviewee requested anonymity.

Interview with a 69-year-old clergyman, Ngozi, 2014. Interviewee requested anonymity.

Interviews with peasants, Kirundo, 2014. Interviewee requested anonymity.

Interview with a 62-year-old female, Ngozi, 2014. Interviewee requested anonymity.

Interview with a former vice president of the National Assembly, Bujumbura, 2014. Interviewee requested anonymity.

Interview, Muramvya, March 2014. Interviewee requested anonymity.

Interview with a former member of the invading insurgency, Bujumbura, March 2014. Interviewee requested anonymity.

Interview, direct participants, Bujumbura, March 2014. Interviewee requested anonymity.

Interview, former cabinet member, Bujumbura, March 2014. Interviewee requested anonymity.

Interview, Bujumbura, March 2014. Interviewee requested anonymity.

Interview, Ngozi, March 2014. Interviewee requested anonymity.

Interview, Muyinga, July 2011. Interviewee requested anonymity.

Interview with a 45-year-old male, human rights activist, and survivor of the 1993 anti-Tutsi pogroms, Bujumbura, March 14, 2014. Interviewee requested anonymity.

Indonesia

Two similar civil wars; two different endings

Claire Q. Smith

It was the best of times, it was the worst of times ... it was the season of Light, it was the season of Darkness, it was the spring of hope, it was the winter of despair, we had everything before us, we had nothing before us, we were all going to Heaven, we were all going direct the other way.

Charles Dickens, *A Tale of Two Cities*

INTRODUCTION

During its early years as an independent republic, with multiple rebellions at play, the Indonesian population witnessed an unfortunate wealth of mass atrocities. But under the New Order regime that followed the early republic (1965–1998), mass atrocity events hit new heights. It is difficult to underestimate the impact of these multiple atrocities, an not just in terms of the massive numbers of people killed. The ongoing social, political, and cultural impacts of these mass atrocities continued to affect Indonesia fifty years after their ending. The first decade of Suharto's New Order regime was grounded in mass violence by the state against its civilian population: from the massacres of an estimated half to one million Communist Party members, between 1965 and 1966, to the subsequent annexation of Papua in 1969, to the invasion of East Timor in 1975.

By 1998, the New Order regime was in freefall. Indonesia's economy had imploded during the East Asian financial crisis of 1997, triggering mass public uprisings against the regime. Suharto stepped down in 1998 at the height of the *reformasi* political movement, under great pressure from both within and outside the regime to resign. As politics shifted dramatically at the center, secessionist movements on the periphery reignited. Following the anticommunist massacres of the mid-1960s, the regime's worst atrocities took place during the long-running civil wars in Aceh, Papua, and East Timor. It was in these three regions that the demand for secession was loudest. In this chapter, I explore two of these sites of mass atrocity – Papua and East Timor. I contrast how mass atrocities ended there, in the late twentieth century, when Suharto stepped down; but I also account for the reasons why these two civil wars, and related atrocities, ended so differently.

Despite their different political pasts – East Timor was never legally recognized internationally as a formal part of Indonesia, unlike Papua, which was – the two regions experienced very similar annexations into the Indonesian nation-state. Both suffered Indonesian occupation during Suharto's first decade in power, occupations which were accompanied by similar patterns of mass atrocities. Both the Papuan and Timorese annexations were conducted at the high point of the Cold War, when U.S. support for the Suharto regime – including support for the regime's two occupations – was at its strongest point. In both regions, mass atrocities formed a core part of the government's political and military counterinsurgency strategy: to divide and control the local population, intimidate civilian political opposition, and eliminate organized armed groups. But there are striking differences in how these two parallel cases of civil war – and their associated mass atrocities – eventually ended in the late twentieth century. Following Suharto's resignation, and the onset of democratization, both regions sought independence via civilian and armed means. Both regions also experienced a spike in massacres during the transition to democracy, from 1998 to 1999, as independence activists made public demands for secession, and the Indonesian military, police and pro-Indonesian militia elements responded. But despite these similar national and structural conditions affecting both regions, it was only East Timor that was able to negotiate an ending to civil war via Indonesian military withdrawal and secession.

Following Suharto's resignation in 1998, and the flowering of democracy nationwide, both regions entered the final phases of their respective civil wars. It is common in contested territories in large democratizing states, that when the stakes over national political control rise, so too does the use of state and state-sponsored violence as means of control over the population. But only East Timor experienced a successfully *negotiated* ending to this final phase of civil war and its related mass atrocities. There, the internationally mediated settlement over East Timor's future territorial status led to the withdrawal of Indonesian security forces, and the Indonesian parliament's final acceptance of East Timor's secession from the nation-state in late 1999. In contrast, in Papua, the civil war ended via a combined national strategy of continued military occupation, a rise in security force repression, a "divide and rule" governance policy, and the extension of limited political and economic reforms under the guise of "special autonomy." International negotiators were never involved, and mass atrocities were never explicitly addressed.

Given these different endings to both civil war and mass atrocity, the central puzzle I pose in this chapter is as follows. Why, despite similar overarching structural conditions within the same national space, could only East Timor achieve a negotiated ending to civil war and its associated mass atrocities? Why, in contrast, did the "ending" to mass atrocities in Papua come via a return to militarized rule and a suppression of resistance? Many have argued that the differences between the two regions – in colonial, international legal, cultural, and/or economic terms – explain these two different endings. But at the time of democratization, hopes for independence were great in both regions. The reasons why Papua subsequently remained an internationally legal part of Indonesia after the transition, while East Timor was able to declare formal independence in 2002, are nuanced and inter-connected.

In this chapter, I outline the two regions' parallel annexation and occupation by Indonesia, considering the associated waves of mass atrocity perpetrated by the same regime, during the same timeframe, at the height of the Cold War. From the perspective of both the regime and the resistance in both locations, there are parallel grounds for the civil wars in both regions. The central government during Suharto's rule perceived the two regions similarly, and that perception continued to influence government policy during the democratic transition, and beyond. This point is important, as it explains why massacres peaked in *both* East Timor and Papua during the transition, as Jakarta resisted secessionism across the country. East Timor's negotiated ending to civil war was fragile and contingent *at the time* – it was not pre-ordained. The Indonesian military withdrawal was far from inevitable at that moment. East Timor's negotiated secession and an internationally imposed military withdrawal was dependent on a unique combination of political factors operating at multiple levels. These factors converged in particular ways, at a very particular moment, for East Timor. Lacking any single one of those factors, the outcome for East Timor might have been very different.

The comparison I make here between two parallel and historically similar cases of mass atrocity with such different endings within the same nation state highlights two points. One, it contests the dominant narrative that international military intervention *alone* brought about an ending to mass atrocities in East Timor. Two, it challenges the oft-repeated story of Papua's "exceptionalism," used to explain the lack of an internationally negotiated settlement to end its civil war and associated atrocities. By examining the endings to mass atrocities in both regions, when so many other structural variables at the national level can be held constant, I show which precise factors, and at which political levels of analysis, enabled a negotiated ending in East Timor. I also show how and why an ending to mass atrocities was eventually reached in Papua – not via agreement, but instead via increased military and political repression, the related defeat of the resistance, and in the context of international indifference to these events and policies. Indonesia in democratic transition was a place and time of great hope for change, for both the East Timorese and the Papuans. But these two cases demonstrate how democratization alone is an insufficient condition to generate sustained political change: three other factors were critical.

The first factor to consider is the national dynamic of internal regime cohesion, or dissent. Dissent within the new post-Suharto government over how it should respond to the rising East Timor crisis between 1998 and 1999 enabled a political window to open. The Timorese civilian and military resistance, along with a combined effort by the international diplomatic and civil society community, then forced this window ajar. In contrast, over Papua, the regime did not suffer significant internal dissent, only brief disagreement. By late 2000, the regime reunified around how to respond to Papua, and maintained a conservative militarized approach to the conflict. That the East Timor crisis caused serious fractures within the Indonesian political and military elite, which lead to the ultimately successful Timorese bid for independence, then itself contributes to the lack of internal dissent over the question of Papua. By 2001, the stakes were too high to disagree over the future status of Papua.

The second factor to explain divergent endings in these two cases is the quality and approach of senior leadership figures within the regime and the resistance, primarily, and the international community in part. The comparison across the two cases shows that even when the national military leadership promotes a militarized mode of settlement to civil war, and its associated atrocities, this did not necessarily triumph over all other options. When capable political leadership was demonstrated by a resistance organization, and that organization had a strong relationship with and across the civilian and military leadership in government, and members of the international community, alternative modes of ending were possible.

The third critical factor is the role of international diplomacy and civil society movements, at both the national and international levels. During the Cold War, the international diplomatic community actively supported mass atrocities within East Timor and Papua. But, following the fall of Suharto, this international dynamic changed towards East Timor. With this change, resulting partly from international and national civil society pressure, active international diplomacy pressured the Indonesian government toward a negotiated ending to the civil war. Papua received no such international support, and the national approach to ending civil war and atrocities in Papua was therefore very different.

The chapter proceeds as follows. In part one I discuss the main contentions surrounding the available data on mass atrocity in each of the two case studies. In part two, I outline the main phases of mass atrocity in each region during the high points of the Suharto regime, from the late 1960s to the mid-1980s. During this period, endings to mass atrocities took place in similar ways across both regions, usually via Indonesian military victory. Part three then discusses the main structural changes arising in the post-Suharto period, when all levels of political order came under contest within the Indonesian nation-state. I show how, when these processes of national and local change combined with new political challenges from external influences, multiple routes to ending mass atrocities opened up. I argue here how the three critical and interacting factors I have indentified help to explain the variation in how mass atrocities eventually ended in Papua and East Timor.

OVERVIEW OF THE DATA ON MASS ATROCITIES

In defining mass atrocities in Indonesia, I use the European Union/Institute for Security Studies definition, as the unlawful use of deadly violence against large numbers of civilians (Meyer et al. 2013, p. 31).[1] As the focus here is on explaining the *endings* to mass atrocities, counting the numbers of those directly killed is important. It is only by counting when the number of civilians killed has either dramatically declined, or indeed stopped, that we can know that a mass atrocity is over. But counting civilian deaths from mass atrocities is a notoriously difficult exercise. The case of Papua is no exception to the rule, due to the restricted access to the territory by independent observers since 1963. East Timor has much better data because, following Indonesian withdrawal and the establishment of international governance, a well-financed, independent, and methodologically rigorous truth commission and reconciliation process took place, known as the CAVR. The CAVR sponsored a thorough investigation into the entire period of conflict, from 1974 to 1999. For each of my two cases, I provide the best available estimates of mass killings, and the main controversies.

The data on mass atrocities in Papua

Although the data on Papua is sporadic, three broad phases of mass violence can be identified, two of which occurred under Suharto's regime. The first phase runs from 1963 (under Sukarno's presidency) to 1969 (under Suharto's rule). During this period, Indonesia took over governance of Papua from the UN in 1963, and Papua was then officially incorporated into Indonesia in 1969. The second phase runs from 1969 to 1998, corresponding to Suharto's New Order regime. Military and central government policy toward Papua did not shift significantly across these two phases: the second was in fact a more formal evolution of the strategies of the first. The third phase runs from 1998 to 2014, following the end of the New Order regime and the onset of democratization in Indonesia.

Due to the consistent restriction on independent observers since 1963, there is no systematic evidence for the total numbers of civilians killed for the entire period of Indonesian occupation and rule (1963–2014). There have been a few attempts to document mass atrocities in particular incidents, such as the Asian Human Rights Commission (2013) review of the 1978–1979 massacres in the Papuan highlands.

[1] Other definitions set a threshold of 1,000 civilian deaths per year (Ulfelder and Valentino 2008), or 5,000 civilian deaths per year (Bellamy 2011) as the minimum for a mass atrocity. Other definitions, instead, refer to acts that specifically fall within a class of international crimes, including crimes against humanity and war crimes (Evans 2008; Scheffer 2006). Both of the cases discussed here meet the first threshold. While the massacres in East Timor in 1999 do not meet the second higher threshold, they do meet the EU and international legal definition of a mass atrocity.

But no such parallel document exists covering the whole period. Despite joining the UN Commission on Human Rights in 2006 and becoming a non-permanent member of the UN Security Council in 2007, Indonesia continued to refuse permission to international observers to the region (Hedman 2007, p. 6). By 2014, no official UN documentation on human rights violations had taken place – marking a 50-year absence of formal reporting on human rights in Papua. National organizations have been frequently harassed and intimidated, thus further limiting the scope for data collection on victims of state violence (Hedman 2007, p. 6).

A wide range of informal estimates exists on total killings during the conflict, but these are rarely accompanied with detailed methodologies. Of the available estimates, the most commonly cited is the figure of 100,000 people directly killed since the commencement of Indonesian rule in 1963 (Wing and King 2005, p. 21). An estimated 30,000 were also killed during the period of de facto Indonesian rule between 1962 and 1969 (Robinson 2010, p. 176). Elmslie (2007) finds that 546,126 people were killed both directly and indirectly as a result of Indonesian occupation. Elmslie's research compared population growth in West Papua with Papua New Guinea – two otherwise similar contexts differentiated by exposure to conflict. The estimated death toll as a result of conflict is thus based on a population disparity estimate.[2] Direct killings and disappearances contribute to this figure, but no specific breakdown is provided. While the Elmslie estimation is useful to the wider study of poverty and conflict-related deaths in Papua, it is too inclusive of all possible conflict-related deaths to use as the best estimate of mass atrocity deaths.

One particular period stands out during the Suharto period – the extensive military operations of 1977–1978 in the Papuan highlands. These military operations appear to have resulted in the most intense period of killings and broader atrocities across the whole conflict. These operations were so extensive against the highland population that they are argued to amount to a "forgotten genocide" (AHRC 2013). The estimates on deaths and atrocities provided by the AHRC are based on direct testimony, field visits, and the use of historic documentation. The estimates produced range from 3,000 to 11,000 civilian deaths, across a one-year period, as a direct result of military operations. Based on interviews with survivors in fifteen districts, a minimum figure of 4,146 deaths is established with certainty, but this figure is conservative. It includes *only* those killed who could be specifically named by survivors. The estimated death toll in some individual villages alone was likely, therefore, to be above this figure (AHRC 2013, p. 8).

Wider research on the effects of the conflict on civilians indicates several other major episodes of violence where more than 100 people are estimated to have been

[2] The causes of this disparity are attributed to a combination of the following four factors: UN-funded contraception programs in highland areas; the disproportionate transmission of HIV-AIDS among the indigenous population; the dislocation of indigenous communities through conflict and logging, both of which have led to the decline of traditional agriculture; and direct killings, imprisonment, and disappearances. See Elmslie (2007, p. 5).

killed by bombing, strafing, and shelling for each known incident (Cann 2011).[3] Three events stand out – where between several hundred and several thousand people are estimated to have died in each attack. On March 12, 1967, at Manokwari, aerial and roadside strafings, bombings, and rocket attacks are estimated to have killed between 200 and 3,500 people (Cann 2011, p. 1). In late 1981, at Wissel Lakes, Paniai, the heavy bombing of villages, and the alleged use of napalm, is estimated to have killed between 2,500 and 13,000 people (Cann 2011, p. 7). In July 1984, at Cyclops Mountains, naval and aerial shelling is reported to have killed 200 (Cann 2011, p. 8). These three incidents illustrate the most typical forms of mass killing of indigenous during the New Order regime. These were very similar patterns to those taking place in East Timor, at the same time, with corresponding uncertainty surrounding the numbers killed.

The data on mass atrocities in East Timor

Significantly better data exists for East Timor, and this can be broken into three peaks of mass atrocity incidents. The first two peaks in mass killings took place during the Timorese civil war and the subsequent Indonesian invasion of 1975, followed by the counterinsurgency operations of 1978–1979. I locate these two peaks in killing within the first phase of mass atrocities. The third peak took place in the buildup to, but especially during the aftermath of, the independence vote in 1999, described here as the second phase.[4] The final report of the Commission for Reception, Truth and Reconciliation of Timor-Leste (CAVR), published in 2005, provides the most authoritative source of data on the killings resulting from Indonesian occupation of East Timor. The CAVR graphs in Figures 3.1 and 3.2 illustrate the total numbers of deaths and killings for the entire occupation period.[5]

The first peak of civilian killings – seen in both graphs – took place during the first phase of mass atrocities during the civil war and the initial period of the Indonesian invasion. The civil war between competing Timorese political

[3] This list is certainly not exhaustive: at least 40 other incidents linked to aerial bombardments were reported between 1965 and 1984 (Cann 2011). For most of those 40 incidents, there is no publicly reported estimate of victims, although reports of heavy bombardment-related casualties and refugee flight into Papua New Guinea were reported during this period as a result of the alleged incidents.

[4] For a more detailed analysis of phases in civilian killings and their endings between 1974 and 1999 in East Timor, including data by year and month for 1999, see Smith and Jarvis (2015)

[5] The CAVR estimates were gathered through the development of a human rights violation database (HRVD). This was based on narrative testimonies collected from witnesses and victim declarations made during the initial truth-telling exercise. Following this, the CAVR implemented a retrospective mortality survey (RMS) of 1,396 households – including data collection on residency and exposure to violence. Finally, the CAVR created a graveyard census database (GCD) of 319,000 unique graves in order to gauge the expected level of mortality that would have occurred without conflict, thus providing a baseline for the population-based mortality estimation (Silva and Ball 2006, p. 1).

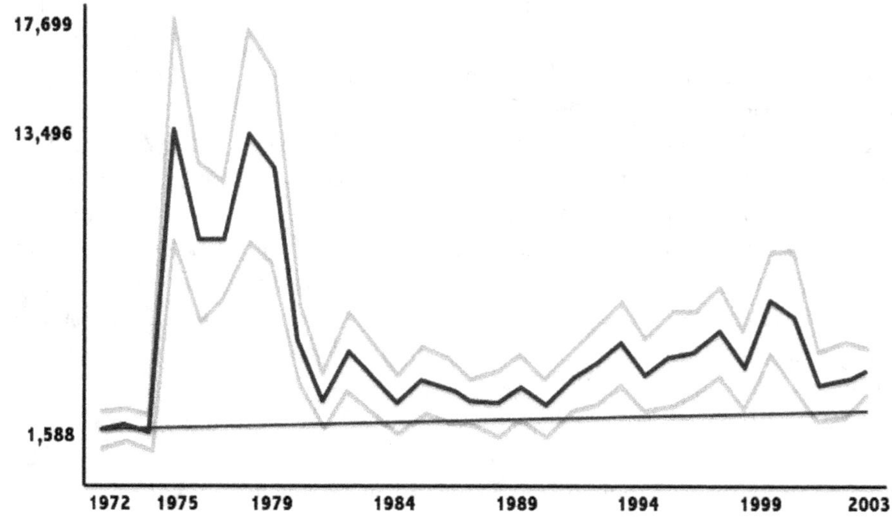

FIGURE 3.1: Estimated total deaths by hunger and illness in Timor-Leste.
Total estimated deaths by hunger/illness, 1972–2003: 161,098 (+/– 10,962)
Total estimated deaths by hunger/illness, 1975–1999: 135,017 (+/– 10,251)
Deaths in excess of estimated baseline, 1975–1999: 86,539 (+/– 10,251)
Data Source: Retrospective Mortality Survey by CAVR
Figure Source: T. Jarvis and C. Q. Smith

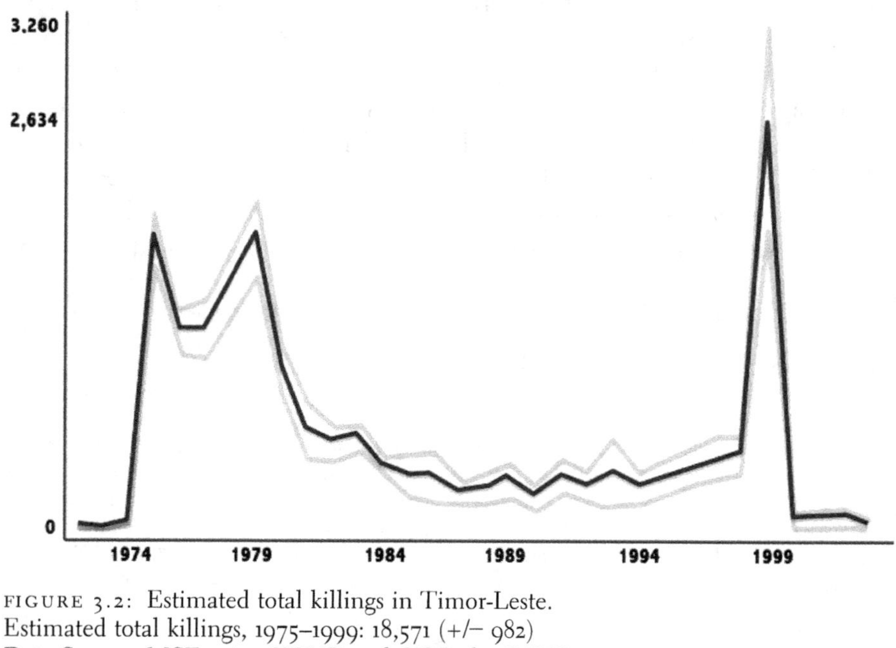

FIGURE 3.2: Estimated total killings in Timor-Leste.
Estimated total killings, 1975–1999: 18,571 (+/– 982)
Data Source: MSE using HRVD and GCD, by CAVR
Figure Source: T. Jarvis and C. Q. Smith

movements after the withdrawal of the Portuguese, namely, UDT, Fretelin, and Apodeti, caused intense violence against civilians of all allegiances (CAVR 2005, p. 42).[6] This period of violence ended when Fretelin established a de facto administration and declared Timorese independence (Braithwaite et al. 2010, p. 13). Almost half of all documented killings and disappearances in 1975 were attributed to Fretelin during this time.[7] The other direct contribution to civilian deaths during this peak of killings came from the Indonesian invasion, starting on December 7, 1975, with the targeted killing of Fretelin members and mass killing of civilians.[8] The intensity of violence during the invasion prompted the resistance, and many displaced civilians to move to inland mountainous areas (Simpson 2005, p. 297).

The second peak in killings seen in the graphs took place at the end of 1978 and in early 1979 during the Indonesian military's Operation Lotus (*Operasi Seroja*), with concentrated killings in the mountainous interior (Anderson 2001, pp. 233–235).[9] Civilians were transported by the military to enclosed camps where many subsequently died of starvation and illness (CAVR 2005). Following the fall of Fretelin's mountain strongholds, the final assault on Mount Matebian in the East, in November 1978, was one of the worst months of violence, remembered decades later as a period of particular brutality.[10] The military pursued a strategy named "Encirclement and Annihilation," which forced the resistance and civilians into small areas, where they were subsequently targeted by aerial and naval bombardment (Kiernan 2008, p. 163). Operation Lotus was disbanded on March 26, 1979, when the Indonesian military declared East Timor "pacified." Indonesian military victory thus brought the first phase of mass atrocities in East Timor to a close.

Thereafter, mass killings of civilians remained at much lower levels for the next twenty years, with two exceptions. In 1983 a wave of "overwhelming violence against the civilian population" was conducted by the Indonesian military in response to the death of a group of military support personnel in Viqueque (CAVR 2005, pp. 102–105). Later that year, Operation Unity *(Operasi Persatuan)*, also

6 The legacies of Fretelin's actions against rival Timorese political parties, as well as their own internal purges, continued to provoke political conflicts in 2014. Author interviews with former resistance members and former MPs, Dili, April–May 2014.

7 This percentage fell to 1.6% between 1976 and 1984, and 0.6% from 1985 to 1998. Of course, CAVR-interviewed Timorese may have underreported the violence committed by the resistance, but even accounting for underreporting, this cannot account for the magnitude decline observed in the data. By 1976, the resistance concentrated their fighting against the Indonesian security forces, inflicting an estimated 5,000 casualties by 1977 (Braithwaite et al. 2012, p. 50).

8 Among the civilian population of Dili, the ethnic Chinese were targeted with particular brutality during the invasion, with local accounts alleging that up to 500 ethnic Chinese residents of Dili were killed on December 8 alone (see Kiernan 2003, p. 210).

9 See also Saul (2001), text surrounding footnotes 32–47.

10 Author interviews with former resistance members in Baucau District, Timor-Leste, April–May 2013 and May 2014.

known as "Operation Clean Sweep" – in terms similar to those used in Papua – was then launched against the east of the territory. The 1991 Santa Cruz massacre was the second major reported incident for this period.

For the entire period of 1974–1999, the CAVR estimated a total of 102,800 (+/– 12,000) conflict-related deaths, including an estimated 18,600 direct killings (+/– 1,000) and a total of 84,200 (+/– 11,000) deaths due to illness, hunger, and other conflict-related causes.The highest concentration of deaths and killings took place in the immediate post-invasion stage between 1975 and 1980. It is important to note that the estimates provided by CAVR should be treated as a *minimum bound* for the total killings during the first civil war, the Indonesian invasion, and subsequent civil war (Cristalis 2009, p. 116).[11] This total estimate of killings stands out because it was produced via a relatively transparent, independent, and rigorous truth commission. As such, there is substantially less methodological contention for the East Timor data on mass atrocities than for the Papua case.[12]

The remainder of the chapter explains *how* these various peaks of mass violence in Papua and East Timor ended across the two regime periods: first, during Suharto's rule, and then following his resignation in the post-Suharto democratization period. During Suharto's rule, endings to mass atrocities and periods of massive violence were notably similar in form. However, the post-Suharto period, fundamental differences in the patterns of endings to mass atrocity appear. In the case of Papua, while incidents of mass atrocity waned after the fall of Suharto, sustained violence against the population continues. In the case of East Timor, mass atrocity halted completely following the withdrawal of Indonesian military and pro-Indonesian militia forces, and the establishment of a new independent government.

ENDINGS TO MASS ATROCITIES DURING SUHARTO'S RULE

During the Suharto regime, mass atrocities in Papua and East Timor, taking place between the Indonesian security forces and the civilian population, ended via military victories. When massive military operations against resistance forces and local civilian populations achieved military victory, the associated mass atrocities were no longer required by the regime. Other mass atrocity events, including the 1965–1966 anticommunist killings, and phases of killing during the civil war in

[11] Other estimates include 200,000 killed (Cristalis 2009, p. 116), but it is unclear how this estimate was reached. The pro-Indonesian UDT leader Lopez da Cruz claimed that at the height of the violence in 1976, 60,000 Timorese had been killed (Taylor 1991, p. 71).

[12] Contentions surround establishing responsibility for killings during the closing stages of violence in 1979. When the TNI encircled the remaining strongholds of the resistance, they forced parts of the civilian population to take part in the encirclement process (Taylor 1991, p. 92). The resistance forces also attempted to stop TNI's advancement by placing civilians within the crossfire (Cristalis 2009, p. 115). As a result of such strategies, particularly high numbers of civilian deaths took place during this phase of the conflict.

Aceh, ended in similar ways. At the central level, a relatively unified leadership supported a militarized approach to meeting the regime's security and political goals in both Papua and East Timor throughout the late 1960s and 1970s. By the 1980s, small but important variations started to emerge, which would set the stage for what would eventually become profound differences in how mass atrocities finally ended in the post-Suharto era.

Papua, 1963–1998

When Indonesia negotiated independence in the late 1940s from the Netherlands, the territory of West New Guinea, as Papua was then known, was deemed exceptional for several reasons.[13] Although West New Guinea had been part of the Netherlands East Indies, its territorial remoteness, strategic value as a gateway between the Pacific and Asia, its potential for resource extraction, and the opinion at the time that the territory was unprepared for self-determination, all combined to mean the Dutch government perceived Papua as distinctive. Papua was therefore excluded by the Dutch from the 1950 independence settlement, despite protests from the majority of the Indonesian Republican leadership.[14] From 1950, a growing local Papuan nationalist movement led to the 1961 establishment of the first Papuan National Council and a flowering of nationalist symbols and forums, which remained popular in 2014.

Under Indonesian pressure, however, the United States brokered an agreement between the Indonesians and the Dutch, placing the territory under UN Transitional Authority in 1962. In 1963 Indonesia took over the territory in preparation for the 1969 so-called Act of Free Choice, set to determine Papua's future status.

[13] Under Dutch rule, the territory was known as West New Guinea. Under formal Indonesian occupation by Suharto's New Order regime, from 1969, it was known as Irian Barat (West Irian). In 1973 it was renamed the province of Irian Jaya (Irian the Great). After the fall of Suharto, in 1999, and under the first elected and initially moderate President Wahid, it was renamed Papua. In 2003, under the more nationalist and conservative President Megawati, Papua was divided into two, into the provinces of West Papua and Papua. The two provinces are now widely known as either Papua or West Papua. I follow here the Asian Human Rights Commission definition, describing the two provinces collectively as the region of "Papua."

[14] Not all of the leading Republican independence leaders in the 1950s viewed Papua as an essential and necessary part of the republic, purely because it had been a part of the Dutch East Indies. Hatta, for example, was more concerned about maintaining control over Malaya, than Papua, deeming it more central to Indonesian interests and territorial land rights. Sukarno, in contrast, was consistent and vigilant on the point of Papuan inclusion in the republic. For a detailed anatomy of the process of Papua's initial exclusion from and later integration into the Indonesian republic, the most authoritative text is Drooglever (2009). This extensive historical analysis details the role of Indonesian, Dutch, and international negotiators in the decision-making process over Papua's international territorial status through the 1940s, 1950s, and 1960s, up to formal 1969 integration into Indonesia, following the General Assembly's supporting vote and subsequent Resolution 2504 (1969).

The ballot enabled 1,026 hand-picked Papuans to vote, from a population of 700,000, producing a unanimous choice for Indonesian rule. Indonesian sovereignty over Papua was then ratified by a majority vote at the UN General Assembly in November 1969.[15]

Between 1963 and 1969, violent clashes took place between the Indonesian military (TNI), and the Papuan Freedom Organisation (OPM), the main armed resistance group. Targeted violence against OPM sympathisers, arbitrary detention, and torture of suspected activists also took place. Throughout the 1950s and early 1960s, West New Guinea was viewed as a nationalist trophy for the Indonesian leadership, and particular significance for Sukarno (Chauvel and Bhakti 2004, p. vii; Drooglever 2009). The primary motivating factor for military-perpetrated violence against the population was therefore to ensure that the Act of Free Choice went in Indonesia's favor. The Indonesian Armed Forces largely controlled the election process, undermined the OPM, and subdued the rural population (Tebay 2005, p. 7). Many villages were reported to have been destroyed by aircraft attack and ground troop actions throughout this period (Cann 2011, pp. 1–2; Simons 2000, pp. 91–99).

The second phase of mass killings, from 1969 to 1998, followed the Act of Free Choice, and Papua's *de jure* incorporation into Indonesia. This period corresponds to the Suharto regime in Indonesia. Mass killings during this period peaked between 1977 and 1978, during the national elections of 1977 and related actions by both separatists and the military. There was another spike in violence between 1981 and 1985, related to a rise in military activities, and a final spike around 1996, toward the end of the New Order regime (Wing and King 2005, p. 2).[16] During the later periods, the TNI targeted remaining OPM, carrying out widespread operations in highland and border areas, where the OPM were believed to be based. International acceptance of the Act of Free Choice enabled Jakarta's hard-line security approach and the OPM provided little substantive resistance on the ground (Chauvel and Bhakti 2004, p. 22).

During the first and second phases of the conflict outlined earlier (1963–1998), the most violent acts against civilians took place in regions with suspected OPM supporters and following reported OPM attacks on military stations. For example, following the kidnap of seven high-ranking military and civilian officials by the OPM in May 1978, the army ran bombing sorties and burned villages along the Papua New Guinea border area (Brundige et al. 2004, p. 24). From 1978 to

[15] Agreement between the Republic of Indonesia and the Kingdom of the Netherlands concerning West New Guinea (West Irian), UNGA Resolution 2504, November 20, 1969.

[16] The text by Wing and King (2005) does not contain a systematic methodology and some of the data sources are unclear. The report by Brundige et al. (2004), published by Yale Law School, is more comprehensive, but large parts of the data are gleaned from media reports. Simons (2000) is also comprehensive, but again the data sources are unclear.

1979, military actions against highland communities were the most extensive of this time (Wing and King 2005, p. 2). When those who fled as refugees were forcibly returned, they were shot or disappeared on arrival (Asian Human Rights Commission 2013, p. 18).

By the late 1970s the Indonesian military began to shift from large-scale troop deployments toward a security agency approach.[17] By November 1978, the military launched the less hard-line "Smiling Operation" (*Operasi Senyum*). By this point, most of the resistance had been bombed, shot, disappeared, and displaced into submission. The strategy also shifted in East Timor around this time, following submission of that local population. However, as reports of anti-civilian violence continued into the 1980s in Papua, the shift may only have had a marginal effect on the ground, and may have been more of a propaganda operation.[18]

East Timor, 1974–1999

A former Portuguese colony, East Timor comprised the Eastern half of the island of Timor. After Indonesia invaded in 1975, the region became the 27th province of Indonesia, with the name of *Timor Timur* (East Timor). From 1975 through to 1999, various massacres of Timorese civilians by the Indonesian military took place, including the infamous 1991 massacre at Santa Cruz cemetery (Vickers 2005, p. 200; Wigglesworth 2013, p. 53).[19] The most accurate reporting estimates a total of 18,600 direct killings during this time period (CAVR 2005). Within the whole period, the first four years of invasion and occupation caused the greatest number of civilian deaths, followed by a second severe peak in 1999.

The first peak of mass killings immediately proceeded the Timorese civil war (1974–1975), following the withdrawal of the Portuguese from East Timor after the collapse of the Portuguese dictatorship, and the first brief interlude of Timorese

[17] In particular, the "Commands for the Restoration of Security and Order" (known as KOPKAMTIB) took over. On this shift, see Brundige et al. (2004, p. 20).

[18] During the same period, conflicts between communities and companies over control of natural resources and their revenues were ongoing. The central government took large tax revenues from mining and related industries in the region. The Indonesian military also profited at this time, by providing security to mining companies – most notably to the co-owned Indonesian-American company Freeport McMoRan Copper and Gold – as well as related legal and illegal business concessions, such as smaller scale mining operations and logging. For more details see the following: on the Freeport mine, see Mealey (1996) and IDMC (2010); on government revenues in Papua, see Smith (2009); and on logging in Papua, see Sebastian and Iisgindarsah (2013).

[19] Former members of both the civilian and student resistance reported that Santa Cruz formed a major turning point in the success of the resistance movement. The international publicity following Santa Cruz provided direct evidence of Indonesia's actions, and spurred global sympathy for the Timorese campaign. Author interviews in Dili, Timor-Leste, April–May 2014.

independence. The Indonesian government did not accept the leftist Fretelin movement's claim for independence and subsequently invaded in late 1975, with tacit international support from the United States and Australia. Between 1975 and 1979, the Indonesian military confined large sectors of the population to resettlement camps, and bombed and swept significant reaches of the highlands – in patterns very similar to those in Papua in the late 1960s and early 1970s. The displacement of the rural highland population forced a majority of the population to the arid lowlands. This further restricted communication and recruitment to the resistance forces, as tens of thousands of people were rounded up into military-run camps. Mass killings waned by 1979 as the Indonesian military secured an almost-complete total victory over the Timorese resistance, with the remaining fighters – numbering a few hundred – confined to the remote eastern mountains (Niner 2009).

The second highest peak in mass killings took place in 1999, around the UN-sponsored Popular Consultation on East Timor's future status. Under intense international pressure, with the mistaken, but widely held, belief in the Indonesian political elite that the Timorese population would prefer to remain within Indonesia, and intending to mark a political break from the past, the newly appointed President Habibie agreed to the UN-supervised ballot in mid-1999. Despite months of violent intimidation by the Indonesian security forces and their militia, the East Timorese voted overwhelmingly for independence at the August 1999 ballot, with over 78% supporting independence. Violence escalated immediately after the results were announced on September 4, leading to the final wave of mass killings of the civil war. This final phase of mass killings, displacements and related atrocities lasted until the Indonesian military imposed martial law in mid-September, just prior to the arrival of the UN-lead international force.[20]

Throughout the whole civil war, the intensity of killings perpetrated by the Indonesian security forces against the Timorese population was most severe during the first four years of invasion and occupation. Indeed, the initial invasion has been described as one of the most brutal operations in modern twentieth-century warfare against a civilian population (Kiernan 2003, p. 210). The early phases of occupation saw the military violently forcing separation of the population from the resistance by directly killing or arresting suspected members, sympathisers, and bystanders (Kiernan 2003, p. 212). The extent of resistance from Fretilin's armed wing Falintil (the Timorese resistance army), which caused the deaths of thousands of Indonesian troops, in turn motivated further revenge attacks by the Indonesian armed forces against Timorese civilians (Braithwaite et al. 2012, p. 48). Between September 1977 and February 1979, the Falintil's central command was almost entirely destroyed, with only a small branch under Xanana Gusmão's command

[20] For a detailed breakdown of the timeline of Indonesian military withdrawal and the UN's military intervention in late August and early September 1999, see Smith and Jarvis (2015).

surviving the extensive and sustained Indonesian military campaign (Kiernan 2003, p. 219; Niner 2009). The level of killing peaked with the assault on Mount Matebian in the East, the last stronghold of Falintil (Robinson 2008, p. 97). Indonesian military strategies during this time, which have been well documented, included daily bombing and strafing, public executions in villages with forced participation from other villagers, mass drownings, mass cliff pushings, sea droppings of victims from helicopters, mass public rapes, mass public torture, and indiscriminate killings of large numbers, including children, in confined and public spaces (CAVR 2005, p. 7).

The effect of these multiple strategies of violence led to a declared victory against Falintil by the Indonesian military in March 1979, with the widespread destruction of Falintil's remaining forces (Cristalis 2009, p. 115). The success of the Indonesian military's campaigns at this time explains the significant reduction in mass atrocities after 1979: it was no longer strategically necessary to conduct mass atrocities to meet the miltary's political or security goals.The data shows this, for example, after the sustained military attack on Mount Matebian, when a large reduction in civilian deaths followed the surrender of remaining resistance forces in that area (Cristalis 2009, p. 115). International relief agencies were finally granted access to East Timor in September 1979, following four years of closure to international organizations. This move signaled an important shift in government policy. Following the military victory, a small degree of (controlled) international observation was deemed permissible as the Indonesian government faced little risk of further public resistance to their presence.

Global factors had of course affected the scale of killings committed by the Indonesian military between 1975 and 1979, but they did not determine – in this instance – its ending. The Cold War political environment, which had aided the rapid rise of Suharto to the Presidency, and sustained his elimination of the entire leftist movement in Indonesia between 1965 and 1966, then continued to enable his ambition to eliminate any remaining leftist elements in the archipeleago via the invasion of East Timor. The Indonesian government successfully depicted Fretilin to the international community as "communist dominated"; the United States and its allies avoided criticism of the invasion; and the invasion received little international attention (Simpson 2005, p. 291). The sale of A4E Skyhawk bombers to the Indonesian Air Force in 1978 by the United States, and their subsequent deployment in the attacks on Mount Matebian, along with other airforce operations, directly enabled the huge scale of civilian killings during this period (Cristalis and Scott 2005, p. 32). Due to the lack of scrutiny from Indonesia's allies, and the closure of the territory to international organizations, the international public had limited awareness of the mass atrocities taking place. As such, the first phase of mass killings and associated atrocities in East Timor came to an end when the Indonesian regime had eliminated sustained armed resistance, thus achieving its national security and political goals.

Political shifts in the 1980s and 1990s

Several important shifts took place in the final decade of the Suharto era in relation to Indonesian government and international policy on East Timor, but not in relation to Papua. Whereas the Papuan resistance was shattered and isolated by the last decade of Suharto's government, the Timorese had managed to communicate internationally with their supporters both inside and outside government channels. The sustained support of the Catholic Church internationally, the widespread support of international civil society organizations, and Xanana's strategic political leadership at the head of the Timorese armed resistance movement together combined to enable the survival of the Timorese resistance against Indonesia's sustained military and political campaign.

The internal reorganization of the Timorese resistance in 1981, lead by Xanana, and the relaunch of Indonesian military operations at the same time, demonstrated that the civil war was not yet over for either party. The Timorese armed resistance was, however, quickly undermined by renewed military operations, and Xanana finally sought a cease-fire in 1983. Whilst low-level conflict continued, the early 1980s saw a major transition in the relationship between the Indonesian armed forces and Falintil on the ground in East Timor, with unofficial agreements to hold cease-fires at the local level operating in several areas (Cristalis 2009; Niner 2009). During the post-1983 period, particular incidents of brutality appeared to directly follow killings or attacks on Indonesian soldiers by Falintil (Taylor 1991, p. 69). It is therefore possible that as the number of reported attacks on the Indonesian military by Falintil declined after 1983, so too did the Indonesian killing of Timorese civilians in retaliation.[21] These micro-peace deals appear to have prevented the need for the Indonesian military to launch further *large-scale* killings against the civilian population. The leadership and policies of Falintil during this particular phase played a crucial role in minimizing further mass killings against civilians – by restricting their own attacks on the military forces present.

Two other factors reduced further violence in the 1980s. First, Xanana focused on hiding the remaining resistance fighters, thus avoiding direct armed resistance to the Indonesian military. Second, the Indonesian military saw that another large-scale attempt to wipe out the few hundred remaining insurgents was too costly for the effort involved, especially with thousands of potential pro-Timorese recruits remaining in the civilian population. Local decisions to restrict violence, within both Falintil and the Indonesian military, therefore minimized mass civilian killings during this relatively quieter phase of Indonesian occupation.

Despite a decline in mass killings, throughout the 1980s, civilian supporters in both East Timor and Indonesia, members of the clandestine Timorese network, Timorese community leaders, and the Catholic clergy nonetheless remained

[21] Further research with Indonesian military sources would be necessary to substantiate this claim.

targets for the Indonesian security forces and their allied militia groups. Their victims were not solely targeted for their Timorese ethnicity: members of the local police, military, and militia carrying out atrocities in East Timor were frequently East Timorese themselves.[22] Instead, the violence through this period was largely political in nature (Vickers 2005, pp. 193, 229).[23] The clergy were targeted due to their political views (Robinson 2010, p. 229; Saul 2001, pp. 209–211), as the Catholic Church provided refuge to resistance members and civilian sympathizers (Anderson 2001, p. 238). The Indonesian military also targeted their efforts on the resistance leadership and remaining cadre, using the anti-guerrilla techniques of assassination and terror (Vickers 2005, p. 167). Forced resettlement, forced control of crop cultivation, political infiltration, arrests, torture, and disappearances of suspected resistance supporters were all used against the population throughout this phase of the civil war (Taylor 1999, p. 158). Meanwhile, the Timorese resistance switched to a wider form of political resistance, with the widescale destruction of its armed wing. The persistence of the small group of armed resistance fighters was essential to maintaining wider morale in the resistance movement, but by the mid 1980s it was a symbolic rather than genuinely capable armed force (Niner 2009, p. 122).[24]

Through the early to late 1980s, a national Indonesia-wide campaign for East Timorese human rights and national independence, led by an underground student network bridging both Timorese and Indonesian students, became a critical wing of the resistance movement. In Papua, in contrast, no equivalently effective national network of student and supportive activists existed at this time on such a scale. Pro-Timorese demonstrations in Jakarta; smuggled information; and the Timorese national solidarity networks were all run by Timorese student organizations, the most prominent and organized of which was Renetil.[25] This political student network kept the Timorese resistance organization alive nationally, once the armed resistance in East Timor was largely defeated by 1983. International support also began to grow as a global civil society campaign in support of East Timor's independence gained gradual traction in Europe, Australia, and the United States. The leadership of several civil society figures in the Timorese resistance movement was essential.

East Timor's overseas independence activists' in-exile rallied international civil society support throughout the 1980s.[26] Jose Ramos-Horta (Fretelin's overseas representative) played a major role in maintaining pressure at the UN and on

22 See also Saul 2001 (text surrounding footnotes 130–150).

23 See also Saul 2001 (text surrounding footnotes 223–243 and 252–253).

24 Reported in interviews by the author with former armed and civilian resistance members, in Dili, Timor-Leste, April–May 2014.

25 Author interviews with former Renetil members and members of other pro-Timorese student resistance networks, in Dili, Timor-Leste, April–May 2014.

26 Author interviews with former national and international independence activists, in Dili, Timor-Leste, April–May 2014.

European governments, especially in Portugal and at the UN in Geneva. This international campaign followed an internal Fretelin decision to prioritize the global civil society campaign toward independence *over* a military strategy, given the widespread destruction of Falintil by 1983 (Niner 2009). International outreach by the Catholic Church also assisted the civil campaign, and the UN finally gave recognition to East Timor's right to independence in 1983. Huge international media publicity then followed the 1991 Santa Cruz massacre: an Indonesian military massacre of Timorese civilians at the Santa Cruz cemetery, caught for the first time on camera by the documentary filmmaker Max Stahl. This footage was released internationally, further fueling the international civil campaign for East Timorese human rights and national independence. The awarding of the 1996 Nobel Peace Prize to Bishop Carlos Belo and Jose Ramos-Horta also contributed to raising awareness of the campaign for East Timor's independence (Niner 2009; Sword Gusmão 2003).

East Timor's growing presence in the global human rights movement came – for the large part – from the efforts by a small group of Timorese civil society leaders and international supporters, who were able to lobby effectively at the international level. This lobbying formed an essential component in the eventual success of Timor's secessionist campaign, and was without parallel in the Papua case through the Suharto years, and at the end of the regime. While it took two decades, the gradual change in the international attitude to Indonesia's occupation of East Timor slowly chipped away at Western support for the Indonesian government's stance, coming to a head in the late 1990s as the Cold War era waned and the Suharto government fell (PERI 2002; Robinson 2010).

The resistance leadership of Xanana throughout the 24-year occupation was also critical – both to maintaining morale within the resistance locally and nationally, and providing a public figure to the global campaign. His continuous presence first as the head of armed resistance in Falintil and later of the unified political body, the National Council of the Maubere Resistance (CNRM), provided leadership to both the political resistance and the Timorese civilian population (Niner 2009; Sword Gusmão 2003).[27] When Xanana was captured and arrested by the Indonesian military in East Timor in November 1992, and removed to Cipanang Prison in Jakarta, it was at first seen as a devastating blow to the resistance movement. But this relocation meant Xanana was actually more easily able to coordinate with the resistance in exile, as well as to communicate with supportive foreign governments and human rights organizations (Niner 2009, p. 161). Xanana's imprisonment eventually benefited the movement for Timorese independence.

Xanana's international although informal recognition as the Timorese national leader was confirmed by his official 1997 meeting with Nelson Mandela, in Jakarta,

[27] This point was also emphasized in interviews conducted by the author with former armed and political resistance members, in Dili, Timor-Leste, April–May 2014.

in the company of President Suharto. At this meeting both the political options of greater regional autonomy for East Timor, and a longer term peace plan to end the civil war, were discussed. This meeting was critical in raising Xanana's international profile and garnering further international support for East Timorese independence, as well as securing East Timor's place as an issue of national importance for Indonesia. The organizational and personal leadership capacity of Xanana within of the East Timorese independence movement was vital when the geopolitical and national political shifts affecting Indonesia in the late 1990s. The combined impact of international geopolitical and national political shifts forged a unique moment for change in the Indonesian government's approach to the civil war.

In summary, then, the first and largest wave of mass atrocities in East Timor – lasting between 1975 and 1979 – came to an end when the perpetrating Indonesian regime achieved its military and political goals of occupation and has almost entirely eliminated the Timorese armed resistance. This outcome was very similar to that in the Papua case at that time. In the context of Cold War global politics, and by ensuring little information leaked out, the Indonesian regime could pursue its military goals in both East Timor and Papua without any significant political risk. The only real cost to the regime during this period was the loss of military personnel killed in action. These losses were initially significant during the first phases of invasion of East Timor, in the face of an unexpectedly strong armed response from the Timorese. But this factor alone was insufficient to prevent ongoing military operations and their related mass atrocities. From 1979, following Indonesian military success, the overall campaign switched to a lower level strategy of violence-including civilian confinement, suppression, intimidation, arrests, disappearances, and torture, as in the Papua case. This policy only shifted during the 1980s and 1990s in East Timor, when the scope for political negotiations rose in the face of a changing national and international climate towards East Timor, while not in the case of Papua.

Within the context of the Cold War, a strong, militarized Indonesian state pursued militarized endings to mass atrocities with overpowering military force, retaining their key Western international allies of the United States and Australia while doing so. Activists from Papua were effectively silenced and were unable to build a national or transnational network of civil society support to match that of the East Timorese. In contrast, the East Timorese independence activists, via strength of leadership and relying on a range of civilian activist networks and resources, used this time in exile and in prison to cement international interests in the global justness and importance of their cause.

POST-SUHARTO ENDINGS TO MASS ATROCITIES

Following Suharto's resignation, his Vice President J.B. Habibie stepped into the presidency. Given his long history as a key Suharto ally, Habibie was keen to distance himself from Suharto's government and establish himself as a genuine political reformer, both nationally and internationally. However, in 1998, he was not yet able to consolidate political or military power, and the future direction of his government was unclear. This limitation on his power meant that during the immediate transition period after Suharto's resignation, with the political uncertainty created by Habibie's appointment, unique openings for political change opened, which the Timorese resistance immediately grasped. These political openings were highly contingent and constrained by internal dissension, both within the Indonesian military, and across the military and civilian branches of government, over Timorese policy. They were also highly contingent on the shifting international legitimation of – and support for – both the Indonesian government, and the Timorese resistance and supportive civil society organizations acting against the goverment. Only such a unique set of highly contingent conditions enabled East Timor's successful bid for independence from Indonesia, and a political end to the civil war.

By late 1999, following the East Timor debacle (as the Indonesian government saw it), the first Indonesian national elections brought a new president to power, the Islamic moderate Wahid. Habibie had lost the confidence of the military after the loss of East Timor, and was not selected again by the ruling party Golkar to run in the first national post-Suharto elections. His Presidential (though not party) successor Wahid was known nationally as a reformer – and he had the mass support of civil society as the leader of one of the largest moderate Islamic movements in Indonesia, which numbered in the tens of millions. However, while Wahid at first extended an open and conciliatory hand to the Papuans, and encouraged open public dialogue on the Papuan situation, very quickly, Wahid found he could not control the military or wider political forces, and coerce them into supporting this open stance. Wahid eventually did not command sufficient political power over either the military or political branches of government to stave a renewed militarized response to the Papuan conflict, especially following what (to the Indonesian government) was the disaster of Timorese secession in late 1999.

Shifts in policy and violence in Papua, 1998–2014

The final phase of mass atrocities in Papua was very different both in character and impact from the first two phases of mass atrocity ending in the region. The final phase ran from the 1998 change in national government, through to 2014. The beginning of this final phase coincided with the monumental changes in East Timor, both taking place within the same evolving international context. Even as Jakarta made major concessions to East Timor in 1999, for example, by allowing the international consultation on East Timor's status, the central government firmly renewed their stated position against any such political activities or changes in Papua. While the new post-Suharto government allowed a brief flowering of local Papuan political and social aspirations to develop in 1999 and early 2000, this openness was rapidly squashed. When community and political leaders in Papua publicly rallied, following positive statements from Wahid on the scope for reforms in Papua, and in the face of the widespread belief at the grassroots level, that Papua, too, was about to get its independence, the military and police rapidly responded by brutally squashing this rising Papuan public activism.

The post-Suharto period in Papua started with the "Papuan Spring," as President Habibie then President Wahid opened limited dialogue with Papuan community and political leaders following public calls for political and military reform in Papua. In December 1999 President Wahid even announced a radical new position, deeming that pro-independence political views, including raising the Morning Star Papuan flag, were protected by free-speech laws. This statement represented a dramatic political shift from Jakarta towards Papua. While Wahid stated that there was no scope for actual independence, this important new political freedom inspired the Papuan leadership. Wahid further allowed the region to be renamed "Papua." Most significantly, Wahid also permitted Papuan leaders to hold the Second Papuan Peoples' Congress, which was attended by over 500 representatives and led to the creation of the Papuan Presidium of 18 Papuan elders (Human Rights Watch 2001).[28] The Congress announced a unanimous call for independence and unanimously rejected the Act of Free Choice that had subsumed Papua within the Indonesian nation state. Some Papuan communities indeed believed at this time that independence was imminent, which itself fuelled further local political activity and pro-independence support.

By October 2000, this rising Papuan public activism triggered military dissent in the government in Jakarta, and Wahid was forced to reverse his open position. As with East Timor, the military leadership reacted forcibly against a political shift in policy towards Papua and demonstrated that there would be no more toleration of the Papuan independence movement. But unlike Habibie's stance on Timor, President Wahid did not hold to his stance on Papua in the face of military opposition. He did not have any mass civil society groups backing greater openness to Papua, nor international civil or government supporters for opening the dialogue between Jakarta and Papua.

The reversal in Wahid's policy on Papuan dialogue was marked by serious security incidents against Papuan protestors in Wamena in October 2000 and Abepura in December 2000, where mass arrests, beatings, and shootings of civilians took place (Human Rights Watch 2001, pp. 10–11). These two incidents signaled the end to the Papuan Spring, the death knell for which came when the leading

[28] The key role of then Indonesian President Wahid in enabling this new dialogue process was stressed by Benny Wenda, exiled Papuan political activist, and Leader of the Free West Papua Campaign, author interview, November 10, 2014, Oxford, UK.

pro-negotiation Papuan independence elder Theys Eluay was assassinated by Indonesian Special Forces in 2001. The central government retrenched to a hard-line and unified anti-independence and anti-dialogue position on Papua from late 2000 onward, and no return to dialogue or negotiations had been signaled even by 2014.

President Wahid (like President Habibie before him) did not have the confidence of the military throughout his Presidency. He was eventually impeached by parliament, meaning many of his political reforms were shortlived (Mietzner 2006). Following the militarized end to the Papuan Spring, the military reasserted control across the Papuan territory. The military carried out a number of sweeping operations, and the police arrested a number of Papuan leaders on various charges, as well as conducting the shooting of civilians (Human Rights Watch 2001). After an armed group of suspected Papuans killed 5 members of the mobile police, the Indonesian security forces then launched operations that displaced an estimated 5,000 people (Chauvel 2007, p. 44). Between 2000 and 2014, state agents reportedly arrested and tortured suspected separatists, killed several leading Papuan independence leaders, and intimidated ethnic Papuans in multiple locations, alongside continuing militarized sweeping operations (Human Rights Watch 2001).[29] In June 2000, a leaked Indonesian military document detailed, "the formation of militias, targeting human rights defenders and black operations against independence leaders" (Wing and King 2005, p. 2). Sweeping operations in rural and urban areas were reported well into the 2010s (ICP 2013, p. 21).[30] These ongoing militarized activities and leaked military documents indicate that it was not only Wahid's government, but successive post-Suharto democratic governments that retain a similar overall perspective on and policy towards the Papuan resistance, Papuan civil society organizations, and the wider civilian Papuan population to that of Suharto's former military regime.[31] The only obvious major change has been that

[29] These operations were also reported in interviews with Benny Wenda, and various international human rights organizations working on the Papuan human rights situation, who requested anonymity. Author interviews, November 2014.

[30] As well as anti-political and sweeping operations, state killings of civilians around resource extraction sites were also ongoing at this time, peaking around 2009, when the TNI were deployed to protect the gold and copper mine operated by PT Freeport. Between then and January 2010, 28 separate violent incidents were reported by observers to have taken place between security forces and locals (as reported by *West Papua Netzwerk Imparsial* 2009: 43). These incidents helped create a context for ongoing anti-civilian violence from the security forces, and made it difficult for observers to map human rights violations in more remote areas (ICP 2013: 21).

[31] Leaked documents of the Indonesian military, from around 2008, suggested that the remaining Papuan armed resistance forces contained approximately 1,129 people, with an addition 16,867 people associated with the pro-independence *Bintang Kejora* (Morning Star) political grouping "with capabilities in propaganda and political diplomacy" (as cited in Elmslie et al. 2011, pp. 8–15).

mass bombings were no longer being reported after the transition to democratic government.

Despite formal changes to the structure of the Indonesian government, and concessions toward greater regional autonomy, political groups with Papuan nationalist viewpoints were met with harsh repression and targeted violence from late 2000 onward. Wider military operations (if not bombing campaigns) against civilians continued. The Baptist Church reported that an estimated 6,300 people were displaced in a military operation in 2005, leading to widespread malnutrition following the burning of villages, and that villagers took refuge far from their sources of food (ICTJ 2012). While these wider military activities did not always lead to direct mass killings, they indicated a continued climate of aggression and intimidation toward the Papuan population, as an apparent strategy to eliminate opposition to the Indonesian government.

The military presence in Papua remained pronounced after 1998, with as many as 100 army posts and 10,000 troops estimated present in 2009 (Conoras 2009, p. 4). The central highland areas of the newly created Papua province were reportedly undergoing military operations through 2003 and 2005 (Hedman 2007, p. 9). The Wamena incident in 2000 was the most violent post-Suharto incident reported, with nearly 30 people estimated killed and 65 wounded (Chauvel 2007, p. 44; Human Rights Watch 2001; Giay 2005, p. 212).[32] The Abepura incident in late 2000, where an alleged separatist killed members of the police, led to the mass arrests, beatings, and torture of highland students. This incident demonstrated how severely the security forces would respond to civilians following antigovernment actions (Human Rights Watch 2001). Between 2011 and 2013, further cases of extrajudicial killings and torture incidents were also reported, demonstrating a sustained and ongoing level of violence lasting well over a decade into the new democratic government (ICP 2013, p. 1).

The only significant changes in government policy toward Papua to that of the former Suharto regime came via the post-2001 local governance reforms, rather than changes to overall security policy. A new province was created in 2001, and local government was reorganized into new regions following that, with direct elections also introduced in 2005. Given the ongoing security approach to the territory, in many areas, these governance policies formed a "divide and rule" approach – part of an illiberal peace-building strategic approach to ending the civil war. The reforms were an attempt by the central government to attract and nurture pro-Indonesian Papuan leaders toward the financial, social, and political benefits and rent-seeking opportunities of a role in either local or regional government (Smith 2014). The ongoing killing of Papuan leaders by

[32] Author interviews with Benny Wenda and members of other international human rights organizations working on Papua, October to November 2014, confirmed that this was the most violent post-Suharto incident from the end of the Suharto government in 1998 up to 2014.

security forces, including the high-profile extra-judicial state killing of the leading pro-independence Papuan political figure, Theys Eluay, in 2001, highlighted the danger of being in vocal and public opposition to the Indonesian government. The security risks of maintaining public opposition to Indonesian government policy caused many senior Papuan activists to seek exile from 2001 onward.[33]

Thus, while the *scale* of anti-civilian violence by the Indonesian security forces shifted between the Suharto and post-Suharto regimes, the nature and purpose of anti-civilian attacks did not. To the extent that information is available, aerial bombardments and mass killings by shooting, drowning, and disappearances had waned by the 1980s. But mass arrests, torture, disappearances, targeted killings of suspected activists, village burnings, forced displacement, and smaller scale killings continued right through to 2014: sixteen years after the official transition to democratic rule. The increased securitization in Papua since the government's reversal on political dialogue policy in late 2000 has been enabled by the continued impunity of the security forces and the great difficulties posed to any external or independent human rights monitoring.[34] In 2014, public lawyers in Indonesia remained reluctant to defend accused political separatists, and investigations into human rights violations continued to be incomplete and inadequate (TAPOL 2013).

The "ending" to mass atrocities in Papua therefore took place via a gradual military victory, rather than a negotiated settlement. This type of ending was reflected in a downward shift from mass killings and mass displacements to lower levels of direct violence and other human rights violations. This shift in policy was enabled via the destruction of sustained military and political resistance from the Papuan military resistance organization, the OPM, by the Indonesian military in the late 1970s. Ongoing violence against the Papuan population in 2014 reflected a lack of complete political victory for the government, but large military operations were no longer feasible, or indeed necessary, after the democratic transition in 1998.

Three critical variables therefore explain the transition from mass atrocities to lower levels of anti-civilian state violence as part of an overall government strategy toward Papua by the Indonesian government.

The main issue defining policy toward all conflict-affected regions of Indonesia since 1998 has been the balance of power between the president and his civilian and military adversaries in Jakarta.[35] While this power balance shifted nationally

33 Reported in an interview with Benny Wenda by the author, November 10, 2014.

34 The murder of Theys Eluay by the Indonesian Special Forces in 2001 lead to the trial of several low-ranking officers, but the trial process was deemed highly partial and inadequate by observers (Araf et al. 2011, p. 153).

35 Human Rights Watch (2001, p.22) argue that this is the primary reason for limited reforms in Papua, as no Indonesian president since 1998 has had the interestor strength over the military to force wider reforms in this region.

after 1998, internal dissent over Papua was very brief and was not sustained against significant military protest. President Wahid did not command sufficient power over either the military or the parliament in late 2000 to sustain his policy of political openness toward Papuan leaders – and there was no other important national political faction who was behind such efforts at the time. The balance of power in government from late 2000 led to policy reversal – a step back to a renewed hard-line security-based policy to Papua. This hardline policy toward Papua was then greatly exacerbated by the loss of East Timor from the Indonesian nation state in late 1999, following Indonesian military withdrawal and the establishment of a transitional international government in East Timor. The perceived risks of political negotiations with Papua increased greatly after East Timor seceded, the national parliament retreated to a hard-line approach to perceived national security matters, and the military remained outspoken against further negotiations with all separatist movements within the nation-state.[36]

The second crucial factor was the limited coordinated local resistance in Papua. By the late 1990s, armed resistance in Papua was already severely limited, following three decades of sustained military action. However, despite the destruction of the armed wing, effectively over by the late 1970s, during the Papuan Spring of 2000 it was clear that – given the political space to air their views and attempt negotiations – the majority of Papuan leaders were soundly pro-independence. When the nascent political spring was crushed by mass arrests of students, activists, and Papuan leaders, shootings of Papuan civilians, the murder of key Papuan leaders, and renewed intimidation against the indigenous highland population, the independence movement was forced again underground and their leadership dispersed into exile.[37] The scope for security forces to act with impunity was only briefly halted by then President Wahid's invocation of the right to free speech in 2000. But with no significant national support, and limited international support from either governments or civil society, the independence movement could not sustain widespread political resistance beyond the brief Papuan Spring.

The third critical factor missing for Papua, in contrast to East Timor, was that both international civil society movements and international governments had limited interest in the Papuan situation. During the critical period of national

36 The prospect of national negotiations with separatists only shifted later, with a shift in policy towards the Acehcivil war , in 2005. When the newly elected President Yudhoyono showed a sustained interest in ending the Aceh conflict, he commanded sufficient power within relevant branches of the military to force them to accept his policy of political negotiation in Aceh. He also had the backing of a popular majority in parliament, and faced significant international pressure to find a negotiated ending to the war following the 2004 *tsunami*. Only under these conditions, was a negotiated ending to that particular civil war possible. Without the unique national balance of internal power and international interest, no national shift in policy towards Papua was possible, even under President Yudhoyono's government.

37 Author interviews with Benny Wenda and other members of international human rights organizations working in Papua, October to November 2014.

political transition between 1998 and 1999, when the window for national political change briefly opened, there was no serious international support for Papuan negotiations in place. Although several active human rights networks within Indonesia lobbied against ongoing violence in Papua – with some support from international human rights organizations – the movement was very small in contrast to the campaign for East Timorese rights and freedoms. Small networks of civil society groups and some global parliamentary networks had supported Papuan human rights at the UN since 2000. For example, the International Parliamentarians for West Papua and the Free West Papua Campaign groups pushed Papua to the forefront of foreign policy for several small Melanesian countries. Vanuatu, for example, started to lead international support for West Papuan independence at the UN in the early 2010s.[38] But without more widespread civil international support for Papuan self-determination, and with a greatly constrained local civil society movement, there was no significant movement towards or growing international pressure for a negotiated solution to the Papuan situation by late 2014.

Western government interest in the Papuan situation was also very limited between 1998 and 2014. Some argue that this minimal concern for the human rights situation and ongoing violence against civiliants in Papua is due to Western commercial interests in the territory, with the Indonesian government viewed as a better partner to protect large commercial interests in Papua than a small and relatively unknown independence movement.[39] However, while this factor may have constrained Western government support for Papuan rights to self-determination, large Western commercial interests were *also* at stake in the cases of East Timor and Aceh, yet the international community supported a political settlement to those conflicts. The post-September 11 international security context may provide a more convincing explanation for continued Western governmental support to Indonesia, and limited interest in Papua.

Indonesia has been a key security ally to Western governments since September 2001, and the United States, the United Kingdom, and Australia regard the secular Indonesian government as a strategically crucial ally among majority-Muslim countries.[40] International government support for East Timor's campaign for independence was crucial to the change in Indonesian policy toward the territory, but – critically – this support took place *prior* to the events of September 11, 2001 in the United States. The lifting of the U.S. embargo of weapons sales to Indonesia

[38] The importance of the international role of Vanuatu in lobbying for Papuan indigenous rights was reported in interviews with Benny Wenda, November 10, 2014; Lord Harries (member of the British House of Lords and the International Parliamentarians for West Papua campaign group), November 24, 2014; and members of international human rights organizations working in Papua, October to November 2014.

[39] Reported to the author in interviews with members of human rights organizations working in Papua, October to November 2014.

[40] Reported in author interview with Lord Harries, November 24, 2014.

in 2010 and Australia's ratification of the ASEAN Charter – a founding principle of which is noninterference in the internal affairs of member states – have added to a conservative international policy toward Papua in the 2010s (Trajano 2010, p. 30). The combined effect of these various international factors meant there was little interest for the major Western states to push the Indonesian government to change its policy on Papua by 2014.

Overall then, by 1998, with the onset of democratization and a long-established military victory over the armed resistance movement, the need and scope for ongoing mass atrocities by the security forces in Papua, in order to meet their security goals, had been substantially reduced. Informal political scrutiny of the Indonesian government by the surviving Papuan resistance groups had increased – via the availability of new communication technologies – and several undercover studies by international human rights organizations had provoked some concerns for the Indonesian government regarding continuing their securitized policy towards Papua. But this scrutiny was insufficient for the government to end all violence against Papuan civilians in the 2000s and 2010s.

Further, the creation of new Papuan political bodies in 2000, the adoption (if not practice) of Special Autonomy measures in 2001, partial decentralization in 2001, and the introduction of direct elections in 2005 had a cumulative effect on Papuan politics. This package of governance reforms meant some Papuan elites were more mobile economically and politically, and had access to much wider rent-seeking opportunities at the local and provincial government levels. In the context of ongoing security operations, these government reforms served to "divide and rule" the Papuan political elite.[41] The post 9/11 international security context also played a crucial role in maintaining international support for Indonesia, despite known ongoing human rights violations in Papua. By 2014, the combined effect of an Indonesian leadership united behind maintaining a securitized policy toward Papua, an effective divide-and-rule governance strategy at the local evel, limited global civil society interest in the territory's human rights problems, weak local resistance organizations, and firm international government support for the Indonesian government, all undermined the scope for a political negotiated settlement to end anti-civilian violence in Papua.

The ending to mass atrocities in East Timor in 1999

The third and final wave of mass violence in East Timor broke out in the months leading up to and rapidly ended after the September 4, 1999 UN-sponsored ballot on autonomy or independence, known as the UN Popular Consultation. The

41 For a more detailed analysis of the post-Suharto government's illiberal peacebuilding strategy in Papua, covering a package of governance reforms, dispersal of additional revenues, and continued securitization, see Smith (2014).

process leading up to the ballot has been discussed in detail in other sources. I focus here on outlining the scale and changes in patterns of state violence, and the key factors that brought it to a final close.[42] September 1999 was the most critical month of political change for East Timor since the 1974 civil war and Indonesia's subsequent invasion in 1975. This single month included mass destruction and killings following the September 4th announcement of the ballot's result; the intense diplomatic negotiations between the 5th and 12th to force Indonesia to impose martial law and to accept an international force; and to the eventual arrival of UN forces on the 20th September.

The violence of September 1999 was one of the worst since the Indonesian invasion in 1975.[43] Commencing immediately after the announcement of the result on September 4, widespread killings of civilians were conducted by pro-Indonesian Timorese militias, and supported by the Indonesian military.[44] Four factors were critical in the decision for the Indonesian military to end the violence and withdraw – rapidly changing national level dynamics with sustained leadership dissent over the policy on East Timor; sustained and coherent local political resistance; sustained and high-pressure international diplomatic efforts; and an active and well-organized international civil society movement.

National level political dissent in Indonesia – both across and within civilian and military leadership – provoked a crisis over East Timor, leading to the political space for a drastic policy change. On the civilian side, the referendum on Timor's future is highly unlikely to have taken place without President Habibie's desire to mark himself out both nationally and internationally from the Suharto era and to demonstrate his credibility as a reformer and moderate (Lloyd 2000, p. 84).[45] But Habibie *did not* seek East Timor's independence. He feared, as with the entire political elite, that the Indonesian nation state could break apart if that happened. Instead, Habibie and his advisors were so disconnected from the

[42] On this, in particular, see Robinson 2001, Martin 2001, Sword Gusmão 2002, and Greenlees and Garran 2002. For a more detailed analysis of the factors ending military-sponsored violence in 1999, see Smith and Jarvis (2015).

[43] For a detailed breakdown of killings in East Timor, with monthly and daily averages across 1999, see Smith and Jarvis (2015).

[44] See Robinson (2005) and Moore (2001) for detailed discussion of the role of militia. The CAVR found that "... militia groups were formed, trained, armed, funded, directed and controlled by the Indonesian security forces" (CAVR 2005, p. 8). The CAVR also found that the violations in 1999 "were facilitated through both the direct participation and the inaction of members of the Indonesian police force" (CAVR 2005, p.8). Throughout the occupation, pro-Indonesian militias of East Timorese origin were recruited as agents of the Indonesian state (Robinson 2012, p. 230). The more organized militias grew in the 1990s via "a network of army-sponsored thugs, known as Ninja, whose role was to provoke violence, and terrorize or kill alleged supporters of independence" (Robinson 2012, p. 232).

[45] Sources close to the Indonesian and UN negotiations at the time reported to the author in interviews that under a different Indonesian president, the referendum would never have been permitted.

political reality in East Timor that they believed Indonesia would win the vote. Indeed, his spontaneous bravado in announcing the referendum – without prior consultation with either his foreign or defense ministers – demonstrates his confidence that the result would be in Indonesia's favor (Greenlees and Garran 2002).

Despite his bravado, Habibie's position in Indonesian politics was fragile throughout 1999, and even more so around the time of the referendum result in September, with the lead-up to national elections in October. Habibie wanted to be "the reformer" to his national and international audiences, but he also needed to maintain his links with the military, who held a significant number of seats in parliament and without whose support he could not govern (Mietzner 2006, p. 15). His initial decision to hold the referendum, but his subsequent reluctance to allow international intervention during the crisis, reflected this political tension.

Dissent within the military – and its eventual resolution under Armed Forces Chief Wiranto's final decision to withdraw – was also a critical factor in determining the end to mass violence. Leadership chains of command within the military were highly contested throughout 1999 and internal dissent within the military affected the response to the East Timor referendum. For some in the military, the crisis was an opportunity for different factions to seize power. Wiranto had struggled to maintain power over the military through 1999. Like Habibie, he was attempting to appease both reformist and hard-line wings within the Indonesian Armed Forces (Mietzner 2006, p. 13).

General Wiranto faced particular pressure from Prabowo, a hard-line nationalist who had served extensively in Timor as head of the Special Forces. While Prabowo had been removed from military office in 1998, over a separate military scandal, he still commanded influence over certain branches of the military, especially those connected to the Timorese militia. One theory purports that Prabowo influenced the Timorese militia towards great violence as a means to destabilize Wiranto's position (Schulze 2001, p. 80). But it is also conceivable that Wiranto himself orchestrated the violence as a means to damage Habibie's reputation, and secure his own, and that he only brought it to an end when he had achieved this objective (Schulze 2001, p. 80). A definitive view on internal military politics and motivations through this period has not yet been reached, despite a prevalence of leaked military documentation (Robinson 2005, p. 72).[46] But significant internal dissent within the military between forces loyal to Wiranto and Prabowo – as well as civilian dissent between Habibie and Wiranto (Virgoe 2008, p. 99) – certainly appears to have exacerbated the national political crisis over East Timor's future. Only the (temporary) united front between Habibie and Wiranto, against widespread national political and military opinion, for a few brief days in

46 Further discussion on the role of the military in controlling the militia in the September 1999 violence is provided in Smith and Jarvis (2015). For detailed analysis of the role of the militia in East Timor, see Wandelt (2007), Robinson (2001), Sebastian (2006), CAVR (2005), Van Klinken and Bourchier (2006), and Gledhill (2012).

mid-September 1999, eventually resolved the crisis and enabled a political settlement to be reached on East Timor's future.

It is evident that there was a degree of Indonesian military planning for the September violence in East Timor, largely carried out by the military's proxy militia groups.[47] But senior UN staff, with access to senior Indonesian military and government personnel at the time, also report there was significant command-level chaos within the Indonesian military during September 1999. Organic troops and militia were not directly responsive to regional or national command in the immediate weeks following the election result.[48] While Wiranto's claim that the military were not responsible for the militia's actions is untenable, a degree of disorganization within senior levels of the Indonesian military through late August and early September 1999 appears to have aided the crisis. It took weeks for regional command officers to take control of the militia, via the reorganization of military leadership and troops, as well as the imposition of martial law, which took some days to take effect.[49]

Violence eventually declined following the imposition of martial law on September 6. This decision placed Kiki Syahnakri in charge of military operations across East Timor from around September 9 (CAVR 2005, p. 2). Kiki offered an alternative power base to Prabowo and brought in new battalions to replace those troops deeply connected to the militia (Moore 2001, p. 43).[50] But martial law did not enable Kiki to gain full control of the security situation (Lowry 2013, p. 90). The UN Security Council's visit on September 11th and the debate on the 12th at the Security Council spurred on the momentum for decisive international intervention. Heightened international pressure on the Indonesian military then forced Wiranto – and thereby Kiki – to assert control of the situation in East Timor just

47 Greenlees and Garran (2002) uncovered evidence that central military planning for the 1999 violence had taken place, and argue that the violent aftermath was part of a routine Indonesian military strategy upon forced departure from a site of military defeat. Robinson (2005) makes a strong case for military leaders' direct complicity in the killings. Documentary footage filmed during the September violence in and around Dili, on the sites of recently abandoned military-occupied buildings, and in displacement camps, contains interviews with victims of military and militia violence, footage of paperwork from military records, and both of these confirm that the military ordered anti-civilian violence following a vote for independence. This original film footage, dated September 15–19, 1999, was viewed by the author on 3 and 4 May, 2014, at the *Centre Audio-Visual Max Stahl* (CAMS), Dili, Timor-Leste.

48 Author interviews with a former UNAMET official involved in the case, July 2 and 3 2014.

49 See Smith and Jarvis (2015) for graphic representations of the daily and monthly rise and decline in civilian killings through August and September 1999, in response to policy decisions in the Indonesian government, Indonesian military, the UN and international governments.

50 The replacement of organic with non-organic troops was cited by the former UN chief of mission at the time, Ian Martin, as a key factor in bringing the militia violence to an end. The new troops had no relationship with the militia, and were drafted in under Wiranto's authority during martial law, reflecting a new and clear chain of command. Interview with author, London, July 2 2014.

one week prior to the arrival of international troops. On September 11th, Wiranto indicated that he would accept an international force. By the 12th, President Habibie formally accepted UN peacekeeping assistance. This incredibly rapid shift in a deeply rooted and long-standing Indonesian policy towards East Timor – taking place between September 5 and 12, 1999 – reflected Habibie's vulnerability to international diplomatic pressure, as well as the military's temporary loss of direct control over the security situation in the province. UN military troops did not actually arrive until the 20th, but once it was confirmed that Australian forces would lead the intervention, Wiranto finally gave into international pressure, with no stomach for Indonesian troops facing Australian forces on the ground without a prior agreement to cease hostilities in place. The Indonesian Army chief directly ordered the pro-Indonesian militia to leave the province, under the military escort of all remaining battalions, prior to a full military withdrawal over the following few months.[51]

Adding to the national political crisis in Indonesia, international diplomacy played a major role in pressuring the Indonesian government to withdraw from East Timor. Pressure came first on the economic front. In September 1999 Indonesia was still recovering from the 1997 economic crisis: the IMF was in the process of delivering a $12.3 billion bailout, three quarters of which had yet to be transferred (Lane et al. 1999, p. 4). The IMF and World Bank took an unprecedented political step at this time, and linked continuation of international loans to the government to the ending of the violence in East Timor. Indeed, on September 8, 1999, World Bank President Wolfensohn wrote to President Habibie stressing that the restoration of security in East Timor was essential for continued financial support (Connery 2000, p. 78). The U.S. State Department made a similar demand to the President (Greenlees and Garran 2002, p. 52). However, while Habibie was sensitive to the dangers of further economic crisis to his presidency, this pressure on its own was still insufficient to force a change in his national policy. On September 9th, Habibie reiterated his resistance to international intervention and repeated that *only* when Indonesia had relinquished sovereignty could UN forces go into East Timor – a position backed by both Armed Forces Chief Wiranto and Foreign Minister Alatas (Greenlees and Garran 2002, p. 252). According to the UN Mission Chief in East Timor at the time, the deeply held issue of Indonesian national pride, in both the civilian and military leadership, was still at stake. International economic pressure alone was insufficient to change their policy (Martin 2001, p. 157).

It was only when two further factors were added to international diplomatic efforts that Habibie – and eventually General Wiranto – accepted UN military intervention. The first was the intense media scrutiny and public reporting by the UN Mission in East Timor (UNAMET) staff on the violence in Dili, which in turn

[51] This timeline is drawn from Greenlees and Garran (2002) and Martin (2001).

pressured the UN Security Council to debate the issue (Wheeler and Dunne 2001, p. 821). Senior UN figures feared that their continued failure to protect the East Timorese following a UN-mandated referendum would seriously damage the UN's reputation (Martin 2001, p. 110).[52] The UN Security Council was, however, united on the policy that Indonesian government consent was an essential precondition to intervention (Martin 2001, p. 157). The highest levels of individual international government lobbying conducted by UN Secretary General Kofi Annan, U.S. President Clinton, and Australian Prime Minister Howard to President Habibie were all essential in persuading the Indonesian leadership to eventually accept international intervention.

Australian Prime Minister Howard also faced considerable domestic pressure to force intervention (Soderlund and Briggs 2008, p. 251). President Clinton too faced increasing pressure from the US Congress (Jago 2010, p. 385). When Clinton assured Howard the United States would support the military intervention, it finally began to look like a realistic option for Australia (Braithwaite et al. 2012, p. 101). The final straw appears to have been U.S. Admiral Blair's meeting with General Wiranto in Jakarta, where he warned him of the consequences of continued violence: U.S. suspension of $100 million in military cooperation (Berrigan 2001). The combined effect of UN and international bilateral diplomatic pressure, the suspension of international loans and direct U.S. military support, and the increasingly genuine threat of international intervention by an Australian-led, U.S.-supported, UN armed force eventually convinced both Habibie and Wiranto to accept international military intervention. As the UN mission chief at the time reported, Wiranto could not risk the Indonesian Armed Forces facing Australian troops on the ground in East Timor: he had too much to lose from such a scenario. Faced by this imminent threat, even the Indonesian military's senior rank conceded to the withdrawal.[53] But without a national level Indonesian acceptance of the international force, the UN intervention would not have taken place. National level dynamics and decisions within the Indonesian government, therefore, played the central role in the final decision for Indonesia to withdraw.

The third factor enabling an ending to the East Timor crisis was the combined pressure of national and international civil society on Western governments. From 1997, and the start of protests against the Suharto government, Timorese student groups, including Renetil, joined with human rights organizations and ramped up protests on international embassies, attracting significant

[52] Senior UN negotiators were not unanimous on the preferred outcome for East Timor, with some committed to persuading Indonesia to accept autonomy, and others more committed to independence, having observed the UN's failure to provide a fair referendum on self determination in Papua in the 1960s. See Marker (2003) and Martin (2001) for further details of this internal UN debate on East Timor's future. This point was also discussed in an interview with a former senior UN negotiator, London, July 3, 2014.

[53] Interview with Ian Martin, former UN Secretary-General's Special Representative in East Timor, and head of UNAMET, London, July 2, 2014.

global media attention. The Catholic Church also played a role in maintaining international pressure. Bishop Belo's residence – host to hundreds of displaced Timorese – was attacked by militia on September 6th. In response, Pope John Paul II urged international action (Robinson 2009, p. 285), which affected U.S. politics, by adding to U.S. public opinion that the United States should intervene. Ramos Horta's role as special representative of the Timorese resistance abroad was also important. During 1999, the Timorese resistance organization "went into overdrive" (Martin 2001, p. 107). The international network supporting East Timor lobbied the U.S. Congress, Australian nongovernmental organizations, EU member states, and the international media (Simpson 2004, p. 471). These international civilian networks contributed to pushing the East Timor crisis onto national political agendas. This active role of civil society on the status of East Timor directly contrasts with the lack of international interest in the comparable situation in Papua.

The international and national context had changed enough for Indonesia by the late 1990s to create a national political crisis, leading to the removal of Suharto and the rise of Habibie. But this political change itself is not enough to explain East Timor's particular ending. By September 1999, three further critical dynamics had changed: internal dissent within the regime had reached a fracturing point, there was rising international support for the independence movement in East Timor, and, finally, international diplomatic efforts succeeded in making the risk of continuing violence too great for the military to sustain its policy in East Timor. In relation to the principal argument of this chapter, then, the final wave of mass atrocities in East Timor ended due to the Indonesian regime's incapacity to sustain mass violence against the population and to achieve a decisive victory over the resistance via such methods. The East Timor case illustrates how national-level political decisions determined military withdrawal, when the risks of retaining the territory via violent means became too great for the government. While the nationalist motivation to retain East Timor remained consistent at the highest levels of leadership, and ran across most of the political elite, it was a *strategic* decision to withdraw that eventually formed the national policy towards East Timor, and only then under great and sustained international pressure. No such strategic decision was ever necessary for the Indonesian government towards civil war and its associated state violence against civilians in Papua.

CONCLUSION

I have outlined here the different endings to two episodes of mass atrocity, taking place during the civil wars in two regions of Eastern Indonesia, and how they varied across two regime periods: the Suharto era, and the post-Suharto era of democratization. The contrast between the Indonesian government's response to the two conflicts and associated mass atrocities demonstrates how a complex interplay of national and international factors created an environment for a negotiated ending to mass atrocity in one region, and undermined the scope for such a political change in the other.

The political space that opened with *reformasi* in Indonesia was seized by independence movements in both Papua and East Timor. Democratization presented the possibility for conflict within the internal leadership. This meant a hard-line security approach to Indonesia's civil war-affected regions was no longer the only viable option toward dealing with those conflicts. The reform process opened up the civilian leadership to other sources of pressure, from both international and national civil society movements, and pressure from those international governments that had previously supported the regime. However, national democratization and post–Cold War international geopolitical changes *alone* were insufficient to dispel the efficacy of military force in maintaining territorial control over the two regions. This was demonstrated in 1999 in East Timor, in the final wave of mass atrocities following the independence ballot, and with the constant, low-level violence continuing in Papua into 2014. The endings to mass atrocity in both regions ultimately varied because of the combined effect of three key factors: internal regime dissent; the quality and character of resistance leaders; and pressure generated by international civilian society, diplomacy, and threatened economic and military consequences.

A combination of these three factors produced a particular level of risk to the Indonesian regime in terms of continuing civil war and associated mass atrocities in East Timor. When the combined risks produced by these three factors outweighed the benefits to the regime of maintaining those mass atrocities, a negotiated response finally became preferable. This led to the Indonesian regime changing tack, with eventual military withdrawal. In Papua, *none* of these three factors were present by 1999, and the regime could assert political control of Papua via a different pattern of violence against the population, once mass atrocities were no longer required. A combination of less intense killings, widespread incarceration on political grounds, and the displacement and intimidation of particular groups has been sufficient to maintain Indonesia's political authority over Papua. This policy continues without significant international, national or local resistance.

Had these three other factors been in place for Papua, it is possible that a political settlement could also have been reached: if not for independence, for more genuine regional government autonomy and civil freedoms. But the balance of power between the civilian and military leadership in Indonesia never shifted in Papua's favor. Thus, while mass atrocities ended in Papua, this was not due to national dissent, a sustained local resistance, or strong international pressure. Rather, it was because they were no longer necessary to subdue the civilian population. However, as East Timor shows, if any of these factors change in the future, then the opportunity for a genuine political dialogue to end the civil war in Papua may once again open up.

WORKS CITED

Anderson, Benedict. 2001. "Imagining East Timor." *Lusotopie*, 233–239.

Araf, A., A. Aliabbas, A. Manto, B.I. Reza, C. Satriya, G. Mabruri, J. Nurhasya, J. Simun, M.A. Safa'at, and P. Indarti. 2011. "Securitisation in Papua: The Implication of Security Approach towards Human Rights Condition in Papua." Jakarta: Imparsial, The Indonesian Human Rights Monitor.

Asian Human Rights Commission (AHRC). 2013. *The Neglected Genocide: Human Rights Abuses Against Papuans in the Central Highlands, 1977–78*. Hong Kong: Asian Human Rights Commission and Wuppertal: Human Rights and Peace for Papua.

Bellamy, Alex J. 2011. *Global Politics and the Responsibility to Protect: From Words to Deeds*. New York: Routledge.

Berrigan, Frida. 2001. *Indonesia at the Crossroads: U.S. Weapons Sales and Military Training*. New York: World Policy Institute Arms Trade Resource Centre Special Report.

Braithwaite, J., V. Braithwaite, M. Cookson, and L. Dunn. 2010. *Anomie and Violence – Non-Truth and Reconciliation in Indonesian Peacebuilding*. Canberra: The Australian National University E Press.

Brundige, E., W. King, P. Vahali, S. Vladeck, and X. Yuan. 2004. *Indonesian Human Rights Abuses in West Papua: Application of the Law of Genocide to the History of Indonesian Control*. New Haven: Allard K. Lowenstein International Human Rights Clinic, Yale Law School.

Cann, Esther. 2011. *The Indiscriminate Use of Explosive Weapons against Papuan Civilians*. London: Background report, TAPOL.

Chauvel, Richard. 2007. Refuge, "Displacement and Dispossession: Responses to Indonesian Rule and Conflict in Papua." In *Dynamics of Conflict and Displacement in Papua, Indonesia*, edited by E. Hedman. Oxford: Refugee Studies Centre Working Paper No. 42.

Chauvel, R. and I. N. Bhakti. 2004. *The Papua Conflict: Jakarta's Perceptions and Policies*. Washington: East-West Center.

Commission for Reception, Truth and Reconciliation Timor-Leste (CAVR). 2005. *Chega! The Report of the Commission for Reception, Truth and Reconciliation Timor-Leste: Executive Summary*. Dili: Commission for Reception, Truth and Reconciliation Timor-Leste (CAVR).

Connery, David. 2000. *Crisis Policymaking: Australia and the East Timor Crisis of 1999*. Canberra: ANU E Press.

Conoras, Yusman. 2009. "Analysis of the Human Rights Situation in Papua, April–July 2009: Papua in a Cycle of Conflict: Violence Is Still Occurring." *TAPOL*. Accessed October 23, 2013. www.tapol.org/sites/default/files/sites/default/files/pdfs/Papua%20cycle%20of%20violence%20report%202009.pdf.

Cristalis, Irena. 2009. *East Timor: A Nation's Bitter Dawn*. London: Zed Books Ltd.

Cristalis, I. and C. Scott. 2005. *Independent Women: The Story of Women's Activism in East Timor*. London: Catholic Institute for International Relations.

Drooglever, Pieter. 2009. *An Act of Free Choice: Decolonisation and the Right to Self-Determination in West Papua*. United Kingdom: Oneworld Publications.

Elmslie, Jim. 2007. *West Papua: Paths to Justice and Prosperity*. Sydney: Sydney University.

Evans, Gareth. 2008. *The Responsibility to Protect: Ending Mass Atrocity Crimes Once and for All*. London: International Crisis Group.

Giay, Benny. 2005. "The Role of the Church in West Papua." In *Bridge or Barrier: Religion, Violence and Visions for Peace*, edited by G. Harr and J.J. Busuttil, pp. 203–224. Leiden: Brill.

Greenlees, D. and R. Garran. 2002. *Deliverance: The Inside Story of East Timor's Fight for Freedom*. Crows Nest, NSW: Allen and Unwin.

Hedman, Eva-Lotta E. 2007. "Papua: The Last Frontier for Democratisation, Demilitarisation and Decentralisation in Indonesia." In *Dynamics of Conflict and Displacement in Papua, Indonesia*, edited by E.E. Hedman. Oxford: Refugee Studies Centre Working Paper No. 42.

Human Rights Watch. 2001. *Violence and Political Impasse in Papua*. New York: Human Rights Watch.

Internal Displacement Monitoring Centre (IDMC). 2010. *Papua: Papuans Displaced by Military Operations in the Central Highlands Remain Unassisted*. Geneva: IDMC.

International Centre for Transnational Justice (ICTJ). 2012. *The Past That Has Not Passed: Human Rights Violations in Papua Before and After Reformasi*. New York: ICTJ.

International Coalition for Papua (ICP). 2013. *Human Rights in West Papua 2013: The Third Report of Human Rights and Peace for Papua – The International Coalition for Papua (ICP) Covering Events from October 2011 until March 2013*. Wuppertal: Human Rights and Peace for Papua.

Jago, Marianne. 2010. "INTERFET: An Account of Intervention with Consent in East Timor." *International Peacekeeping* 17: 3, 377–394.

Kiernan, Ben. 2008. *Genocide and Resistance in Southeast Asia: Documentation, Denial and Justice in Cambodia and East Timor*. New Brunswick: Transaction Publishers.

2003. "War, Genocide and Resistance in East Timor 1975–1999: Comparative Reflection on Cambodia." In *War and State Terror: The United States, Japan and the Asia-Pacific in the Long Twentieth Century*, edited by M. Selden and Y. Alvin. Lanham: Routledge.

Lane, T., A. Ghosh, J. Hamann, S. Phillips, M. Schulze-Ghattas, and T. Tsikata. 1999. *IMF-Supported Programs in Indonesia, Korea and Thailand*. Washington DC: International Monetary Fund Occasional Paper 178.

Lloyd, Grayson J. 2000. "The Diplomacy on East Timor: Indonesia, the United Nations and International Community." In *Out of the Ashes: Destruction and Reconstruction of East Timor*, edited by J.J. Fox and B. Soares, pp. 74–98. Canberra: The Australian National University.

Lowry, Bob. 2013. "Timor Timur: The Untold Story by Lieutenant General Kiki Syahnakri (retd.), Indonesian Armed Forces." *Australian Army Journal Summer Edition*, X, 4, 84–94.

Martin, Ian. 2001. *Self-Determination in East Timor: The United Nations, the Ballot and International Intervention*. London: Lynne Rienner Publishers.

Mealey, George. 1996. *Grasberg: Mining the Richest and Most Remote Deposit of Copper and Gold in the World in the Mountains of Irian Jaya, Indonesia*. United States: Freeport-McMoran Copper & Gold.

Meyer, Christopher O., Karen E. Smith, C. De Franco, L. Peral, and E. Strauss. 2013. *The EU and the Prevention of Mass Atrocities: An Assessment of Strengths and Weaknesses*. Budapest: Budapest Centre.

Mietzner, Marcus. 2006. *Military Politics, Islam and the State in Indonesia: From Turbulent Transition to Democratic Consolidation*. Singapore: ISEAS.

Moore, Samuel. 2001. "The Indonesian Military's Last Years in East Timor: An Analysis of Its Secret Documents." *Indonesia* 72, 9–44.

Niner, Sara. 2009. *Xanana: Leader of the Struggle for Independent Timor-Leste*. Melbourne: Australian Scholarly Publishing.

Political Economy Research Institute (PERI). 2002. "Modern Conflicts. Conflict Profile: East Time–Indonesia (1975–1999)."University of Massachusetts. Accessed January 4, 2014. www.peri.umass.edu/fileadmin/pdf/Easttimor.pdf.
Robinson, Geoffrey. 2009. *If You Leave Us Here, We Will Die: How Genocide Was Stopped in East Timor.*Woodstock: Princeton University Press.
2008. "People Power: A Comparative History of Forced Displacement in East Timor." In *Conflict, Violence and Displacement in Indonesia*, edited by Eva-Lotta E. Hedman. Ithaca: Cornell Southeast Asia Program Publications.
2005. "East Timor 1999: Crimes against Humanity." In *Chega! The Report of the Commission for Reception, Truth and Reconciliation Timor-Leste: Executive Summary*. Dili: Commission for Reception, Truth and Reconciliation Timor-Leste (CAVR).
Robinson, Jennifer. 2010. "Self-Determination and the Limits of Justice: West Papua and East Timor, Future Justice." *Future Justice.* Accessed October 20, 2013. www.futureleaders.com.au/book_chapters/pdf/Future_Justice/Jennifer_Robinson.pdf.
Saul, Ben. 2001. "Was the Conflict in East Timor 'Genocide' and Why Does It Matter?" *Journal of International Law* **2**: 2, 477–522.
Scheffer, David. 2006. "Genocide and Atrocity Crimes." *Genocide Studies and Prevention: An International Journal*, 1; 3, Article 3.
Schulze, Kirsten E. 2001. "The East Timor Referendum Crisis and Its Impact on Indonesian Politics." *Studies in Conflict and Terrorism*, **24**: 1, 77–82.
Sebastian, L. C. and Iisgindarsah. 2013. "Taking Stock of Military Reform in Indonesia." In *The Politics of Military Reform*, edited by J. Rutland, pp. 29–56. Berlin: Springer-Verlag.
Silva, Romesh and Patrick Ball. 2006. "The Profile of Human Rights Violations in Timor-Leste, 1974–1999." A Report by the Benetech Human Rights Data Analysis Group to the Committion on Reception, Truth and Reconciliation. February 9, 2006.
Simons, Geoff. 2000. *Indonesia: The Long Oppression*. London: Palgrave Macmillan.
Simpson, Brad. 2005. "Illegally and Beautifully: The United States, the Indonesian Invasion of East Timor and the International Community, 1974–1976." *Cold War History* **5**: 3, 281–315.
2004. "Solidarity in an Age of Globalisation: The Transnational Movement for East Timor and US Foreign Police." *Peace and Change* **29**: 3 and 4, 453–482.
Smith, Claire Q. and Tom Jarvis. 2015. "Contested politics, democratization and intervention: The ending to mass atrocities in East Timor." Conference paper, "States of Peace in Asia Workshop." University of Yangon, June 29–30, 2015.
Smith, Claire Q. 2014. "Illiberal peacebuilding in hybrid political orders: managing violence during Indonesia's political transition." *Third World Quarterly* **35**, 8.
2008. "Indigenous Welfare and HIV-AIDS Risks: The Impacts of Government Reform in the Papua Region, Indonesia." *AIDS, Conflict and Security Initiative (ASCI) Report No. 12*, New York/Hague: Social Science Research Council and Netherlands Institute of International Relations.
Soderlund, W.C. and E.D. Briggs. 2008. "East Timor (Timor-Leste), 1999." In *Humanitarian Crises and Intervention: Reassessing the Impact of Mass Media*, edited by W.C. Soderlund, D.E. Briggs, K. Hildebrandt, and A.S. Sidahmed, pp. 231–258. Sterling, VA: Kumarian Press.
Sword Gusmão, Kirsty. 2003. *A Woman of Independence*. Macmillan: Sydney.
TAPOL. 2013. "No Political Prisoners? The Suppression of Political Protest in West Papua." *TAPOL*. Accessed December 19, 2013. http://tapol.org/sites/default/files/sites/default/files/pdfs/Suppression%20of%20political%20protest%20in%20West%20Papua.pdf.
Taylor, John G. 1999. *East Timor: The Price of Freedom*. London: Zed Books.

1991. *Indonesia's Forgotten War: The Hidden History of East Timor*. London: Zed Books Ltd.

Tebay, Neles. 2005. *West Papua: The Struggle for Peace with Justice*. London: Catholic Institute for International Relations.

Trajano, Julius Cesar I. 2010. "Ethnic Nationalism and Separatism in West Papua, Indonesia." *Journal of Peace, Conflict and Development* 16, 12–35.

Ulfelder, Jay and B. Valentino. 2008. "Assessing Risks of State-Sponsored Mass Killing." Working Paper. SSRN: http://ssrn.com/abstract=17033426. Last accessed: July 13, 2015

Vickers, Adrian. 2005. *A History of Modern Indonesia*, 1st edn. Cambridge: Cambridge University Press.

Virgoe, John. 2008. "Impunity Resurgent: The Politics of Military Accountability in Indonesia, 1998–2001." *Asia Affairs* **39**: 1, 95–108.

West Papua Netzwerk Imparsial. 2009. "Human Rights in Papua 2009." *West Papua NetzwerkImparsial*. Accessed December 19, 2013. www.humanrightspapua.org/images/docs/HumanRightsPapua2009-FBN.pdf.

Wheeler, N. J. and T. Dunne. 2001. "East Timor and the New Humanitarian Interventionism." *International Affairs* **77**: 4, 805–27.

Wigglesworth, Ann. 2013. "The Growth of Civil Society in Timor-Leste – Three Moments of Activism." *Journal of Contemporary Asia* **43**: 1, 51–74.

Wing, J. and P. King 2005. *Genocide in West Papua? The Role of the Indonesian State Apparatus and a Current Needs Assessment of the Papuan People*. Sydney: West Papua Project at the Centre for Peace and Conflict Studies, The University of Sydney.

Sudan

Patterns of violence and imperfect endings

Alex de Waal

INTRODUCTION

Mass atrocities in Sudan have no clear endings. The country's protracted civil wars have been punctuated by major military campaigns that involve large-scale killings and war crimes perpetrated by regular and irregular forces. Four times over the last thirty years, operations of this kind have killed tens of thousands of civilians, and caused hundreds of thousands to die from displacement, hunger, and disease. Each episode of mass atrocity occurs for different reasons, including fear-driven counter-insurgency, ideological ambition, and clearing areas to seize their resources, but they resemble one another in their pattern of ethnically targeted destruction of civilian communities. These episodes do not end clearly or decisively. Rather, killings diminish as the pattern of violence changes from a bipolar confrontation to fragmented or anarchic conflict. This is related to the way in which Sudan's wars end neither in outright victories nor durable peace settlements, but rather in political realignments that reconfigure and may reduce violence. Sudanese live under the constant threat that war and mass atrocity may flare up again. Even the separation of South Sudan was not a decisive break: a new episode of mass atrocities is unfolding in South Sudan during the writing of this chapter.

This chapter examines the pattern of mass atrocity in Sudan between the outbreak of the second civil war in 1983 and the independence of South Sudan in 2011 with a focus on how the episodes ended. The background section examines some patterns that emerge from the data on atrocities in Sudan, in particular its recurrent nature and the link between violent killing and death through hunger and disease. I digress briefly into identity politics as a framework for narrating Sudan's conflicts. Then I turn to four episodes or patterns of mass atrocity, and to their endings, sequelae, and comparative null cases. The first case is the militia war of the north-south borderlands during the late 1980s. This established the pattern of irregular counter-population warfare that has been the framework for the conduct of wars ever since. This way of conducting hostilities has a particular logic, which determines escalation and de-escalation. The second case is the jihad in the Nuba Mountains in 1992: an important, under-documented case, which illustrates a related set of political dynamics that influence how mass atrocities end. Third is the case of Darfur: a richly documented episode that reprises themes from both the prior cases. Last, I examine the different pattern of atrocities committed by southern Sudanese armed groups against the southern Sudanese population.

Members of Sudan's political-military leadership have organized or authorized mass atrocities for diverse reasons: extending or consolidating power, with ideological, political, or economic rationales, or responding to threats. All occur in the context of war.

The principal hypothesis for the ending of atrocities perpetrated by the Government of Sudan and its proxies is that large-scale killings come to an end when the Sudanese Armed Forces (SAF) have achieved immediate military goals, but do not sustain the effort to decisive victory. The reasons for that inability include (a) internal dissension among the ruling elite; (b) resistance from local rebels; and (c) resource and organizational constraints on sustaining a campaign. The immediate outcome is not a definitive "ending," but a different pattern of violence, less polarized and more "anarchic," less intense but perhaps more widely spread. Irrespective of the rationale for initiating the violence, the patterns of (incomplete) endings are similar.

Within southern Sudan, the violence perpetrated by the Sudan People's Liberation Army (SPLA) – both as a rebel army (1983–2005) and as the army of a semi-autonomous government following the Comprehensive Peace Agreement (CPA) (2005–11) – has a variant pattern, without a clear distinction between intense polarized violence and more anarchic violence. The bureaucratic element of power in southern Sudan is vanishingly small, and the patrimonial element is pervasive.

Throughout this chapter, an important recurring theme is that the key elements in episodes of large-scale, one-sided violence require an understanding of two levels of violent contestation. One is political struggle within and between the centers of power: the seat of government in Khartoum and the leadership of the SPLA and its subordinate political movement, the Sudan People's Liberation Movement (SPLM). Drawing on Stathis Kalyvas (2006) and Sydney Tarrow (2007, pp. 587–699), I describe these contests as "Schmittian" in the twin senses that they are within entities that exercise forms of sovereign authority beyond the rule of law (entitled to dictate the exception) and their politics is a contest between "friends" and "enemies."

The second level of violent contestation is that of the intermediate elites – the individuals who have political constituencies and who control military instruments at a subnational level, usually in the provinces. These are struggles for position, including place in a patrimonial hierarchy and control over constituencies, territory, and resources. Given the weak and contested nature of sovereign authority in provincial Sudan and in all parts of South Sudan – the absence of a Leviathan – I describe these as "Hobbesian" contests. Thomas Hobbes's famous description of "warre" compared it to the English weather, which does not always rain but has a general disposition to rain at any time (1651, p. 62). Similarly, "anarchy" is not ever-present violence but the continual risk of such unregulated violence. Sudanese understand this well (Fadul and Tanner 2007). The peripheries of Sudan, especially the South, are without institutionalized political authority and are characterized by multiple forms of violent contention. They are situations in which law and procedure is subordinate to contingent political calculation. Thus, "anarchy" is given order by certain accepted modes of political bargaining, but those forms of bargaining involve violence and continually run the risk of breaking down and generating more widespread armed contestation.

Mass atrocities typically occur when the organizers of violence at the two levels coordinate with one another, and decline when that coordination is broken. When the organizers at a higher level decide not to pursue group-targeted violence, lower level leaders may commit sporadic atrocities but these do not escalate into mass atrocity.

PATTERNS IN THE DATA

There are few reliable data for the human costs of Sudan's wars, and methods used to estimate war-related deaths are opaque and inconsistent. The data are also controversial: there have been acrimonious exchanges between the proponents of higher figures and those who are more cautious (General Accountability Office 2006; Reeves 2007; de Waal 2007). Rather than dive into the methodological issues, in this section I provide indicative figures and patterns without claiming to be definitive.

Figure 4.1 is an indicative graph of war-related deaths in southern and northern Sudan – a category that includes direct killing and also a considerably larger subcategory of people who perished from war-related famine. The graph shows that the second civil war witnessed three main episodes of large-scale loss of life, alongside chronic heightened mortality numbering in tens of thousands each year. The Darfur war constituted a fourth peak in killing and dying, and the war that broke out in December 2013 in South Sudan may be a fifth peak.

The figure tells three major stories, two reliable and one less so. First, reliably, the long war was punctuated by episodes of more intense killing and dying, and other periods of lower levels of violence and suffering. More than two-thirds of the estimated fatalities occurred in 1986–88, 1991–94, and 1998, just seven of the twenty years of the war. Second, there are no definitive endings, rather reductions, pauses, and reconfigurations. Any horizontal line drawn across the graph, below which the level of fatalities is no longer counted as "mass," will be arbitrary.

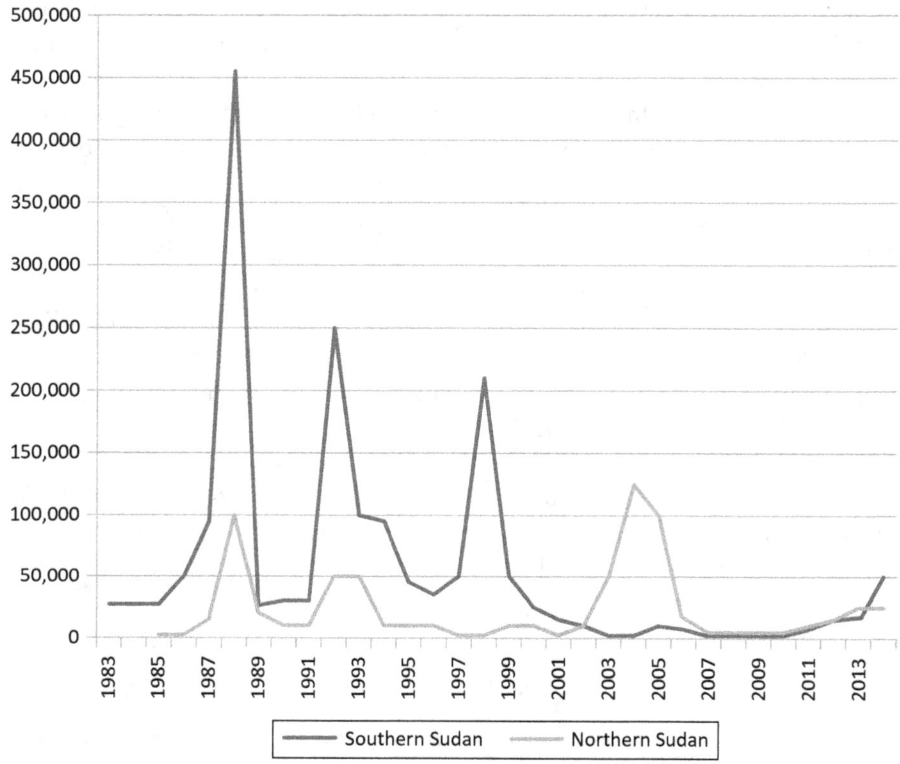

FIGURE 4.1: War-related deaths in Sudan 1983–2014.
Sources: Estimates for southern Sudan 1983–98 from Burr (1998); for Darfur from CRED (2005).

Third, and less reliably, each peak is less high than the one before. This may be an artifact of estimation, because better information commonly leads to lower numbers (de Waal 1987), and there are better data for more recent incidents. Additionally, because most deaths are due to hunger and disease, improved humanitarian response would reduce fatality numbers over time.

The graph is not an indication of absolute numbers of dead. There are many biases in the estimations. For example, humanitarian agencies tend to use upper-limit figures, giving reason to suspect inflated estimates. On the other hand, there have been no systematic efforts to compare general population mortality levels with a prewar baseline, and thereby generate overall estimates of excess mortality, comparable to the International Rescue Committee surveys in the Democratic Republic of Congo (Coghlan et al. 2006).

Additionally, the relationship between deaths caused by direct violence and overall excess mortality is complicated. The case of Darfur, for which the data are better than elsewhere, is a good illustration of this. The pattern of violent killing was documented by the International Criminal Court.[1] The most reliable, and not coincidentally, the lowest estimates for overall mortality is the review of surveys generated by the Centre for Research on the Epidemiology of Disasters or CRED[2] (Guha-Sapir and Degomme 2005a; Guha-Sapir and Degomme 2005b). These indicate that approximately 40,000 civilians were violently killed in 2003-05 and about a further 120,000 people died as a result of displacement, disease, and malnutrition in this period. Subsequent studies show that excess mortality continued thereafter, though at a diminished level. The ratio of direct as opposed to indirect deaths changed over the different periods of the conflict. Figure 4.2 represents this.

For southern Sudan, the standard compendium of war-related deaths is the work of Millard Burr (1998),[3] whose estimates amount to approximately 1.55 million up to 1998.[4] A simple tabulation of known incidents of large-scale killing, set alongside Burr's gross numbers, suggests that the proportion of deaths attributable to direct violence is in the range of 10–15%. There are too many unknowns to make any inference from this. However, the relationship between the two kinds of fatalities is likely to be similar to that documented for Darfur: a spiky line with early peaks for violent deaths, and a smoother epidemic curve, peaking slightly later and continuing much longer, for other causes of death.

IDENTITY POLITICS

The dominant framework for predicting and preventing genocide and mass atrocity, both in Sudan and globally, focuses on inter-group hostility and hatred. This chapter emphasizes other factors. This is in line with the dominant approaches to the study of ethnic conflict that treat ethnic and religious mobilization and contestation as instruments used by political and societal leaders

1 The ICC figures tabulate approximately 13,000 deaths from violence from July 2003 to January 2005. For the purposes of this analysis, I take this to be one-third of the real figure. The prosecutor of the ICC did not use the evidence and analysis provided by his staff in his request for an arrest warrant against President Omar al Bashir.

2 The CRED estimates begin in September 2003 and estimate twenty-six percent of deaths due to violence between then and January 2005. If the CRED team had consistently followed the method of medium estimates, its overall figures would in fact have been lower, but such was the poisonous atmosphere surrounding the debate on numbers that their estimates, even though lower than others', still have upward biases built in. The CRED estimates begin only in September 2003, and the ICC data indicate that one-third of the violent deaths were between May and August 2003, which is a reason to increase the overall figure. However, on the basis that this is an indicative rather than a definitive graph, I have not further adjusted the numbers.

3 Burr's figures have several upward biases built into them. For example, he gives excess death figures of 100,000 per year for the Nuba Mountains for the mid-1990s, which is certainly a huge overestimate.

4 Including the war-affected areas of northern Sudan, his estimate was 1.9 million, the basis for the oft-cited figure of two million dead overall.

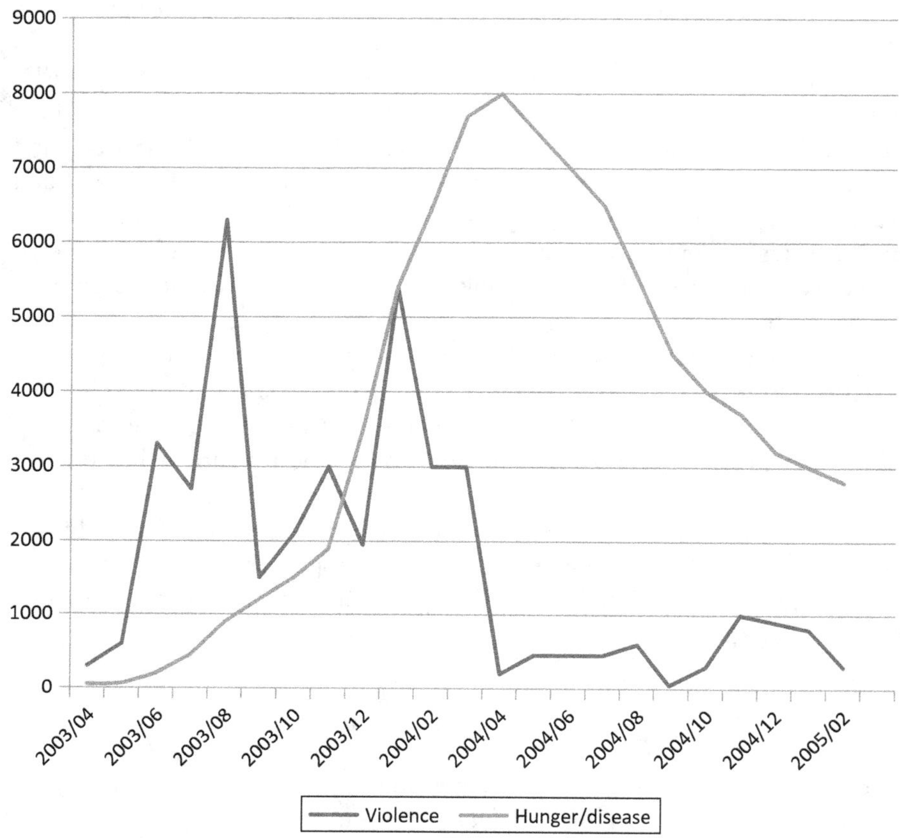

FIGURE 4.2: Causes of death in Darfur 2003–05.
Sources: Violent deaths: ICC, scaled by a factor of three to be commensurate with the CRED estimate; hunger/disease: CRED, smoothed.

(Fearon and Laitin 2000). There is a rich literature on the role of identity in conflict and mass atrocity in Sudan, which both confirms and elaborates these instrumentalist explanations (Deng 1995, 2015; Beswick 2004; Jok 2004; de Waal 2005; Komey 2012). It is a fundamentally pessimistic corpus of writings. Violence has long played an important role in the construction and maintenance of identities in Sudan. Ethnic and religious scripts are used by political actors to organize and justify violence, and one of the reasons for the effectiveness of identity politics as political instrument is that ordinary people often subscribe to primordial accounts of ethnic identity and difference. Writers concur that inter-communal hostility and hatred is a product rather than a cause of conflict and atrocity, but also that violence creates its own self-reinforcing cycle.

The literature on identity conflict in Sudan has little to say about war endings and nothing that directly addresses the question of how mass atrocities end.

The logic of identity-based conflict narratives leads to purported solutions based either on separation or on reconciliation.

The rationale for establishing ethnically based governance entities, either new sovereign states or units within a federal system, is that dividing people into administrative units according to identity markers will resolve conflict, by meeting the aspirations of hitherto-repressed minorities for self-government. *In extremis* this led to the secession of South Sudan. Insofar as administrative or sovereign partition is relevant to ending atrocities, the implied logic is that atrocities are an inter-communal affair, and that separating the two groups – if necessary by reciprocal ethnic cleansing – will serve as a kind of permanent ceasefire. The experience of Sudan and South Sudan is that these measures reconfigure conflict rather than resolve it, and often generate deeper conflicts and more atrocities.

The rationale for reconciliation is that forgiveness will heal rifts, and that conflicts can be transformed by new paradigms of common future. Close study of inter-communal reconciliation processes suggests that there is a self-reinforcing cycle at work here also, in which the conflict resolution mechanisms serve to reinforce ethnic identity, notably insofar as they strengthen the authority of tribal leaders (Abdul-Jalil 1984; Schomerus and Allen 2010). The logic of reconciliation subsumes atrocities and war crimes within the overall losses of war, and submits them to measures ranging from amnesia, through amnesty, to mutual apology and forgiveness. This also implies new narratives of inclusion and tolerance. These are all, however, normative recommendations based on deduction, rather than empirical or historical evidence.

THE MILITIA WARS AGAINST SOUTHERN SUDAN

From the beginning of the war, the Government of Sudan mounted counter-insurgency "on the cheap" through tribal militia (de Waal 1994). The unstated rationale for this was the parlous condition of government finances throughout the 1980s (de Waal 2015). The earliest militia included southern Sudanese "friendly forces," which carried out widespread killings, mainly of ethnic Dinka civilians and SPLA recruits (Anonymous 1987; Africa Watch 1990). The most notorious militia were drawn from the Arab groups who lived on the northern side of the internal north-south boundary, which practiced a scorched earth policy, destroying communities suspected to support the SPLA, and rewarding themselves by stealing cattle and looting whatever else they could find. Commonly known as *murahaliin* ("nomads"), these militia killed, plundered, burned, and raped their way through a huge swathe of southern Sudan from 1985 to 1989 (Amnesty International 1989). They also abducted thousands of women and children into servitude and created a famine of exceptional severity among the displaced (Keen 1994). In 1987, when the militia unexpectedly encountered a large SPLA unit and suffered many fatalities, they took reprisals on displaced civilians in the southeastern Darfur town of ed Da'ien, killing more than 1,000, many by burning alive inside railway wagons (Mahmoud and Baldo 1987).

Large-scale killing and displacement reached a peak in 1988. This episode of mass atrocities began to subside when the areas accessible to the militia had been thoroughly ravaged, and because SPLA units penetrated the area and could now challenge the army. The dry season of 1989 witnessed reduced raids (Mawson 1991). Political factors also contributed to this incomplete ending. One element was local. The tribal leadership of the Baggara Arabs prevailed upon their kinsmen who were commanding the militia that they should reduce the violence, on the grounds that they would need at some point to live together with the Dinka as neighbors. During 1990–94 there were a number of local truces that included setting up seven cross-border "peace markets" and some cooperation in finding and returning abducted children.[5] At a national level, the army's General Headquarters was opposed to the war in general and the militia strategy in particular, and pressed the government to rein in the militia and to engage in peace talks. As a compromise, the government formalized the militia into the Popular Defence Forces (PDF), putting them on salaries and within the command and control structure of the army. The more consolidated control mechanisms limited the license for atrocities that served no military purpose, and the level of raiding by the murahaliin never again reached the same levels as 1985–89.

Finally, there was an international dimension. While the war did not spark international outrage, and the first reports by human rights organizations were published in 1989 (Amnesty International 1989) and 1990 (Africa Watch 1990), the humanitarian disaster did belatedly generate a response. Journalists visited the displaced camps in the summer of 1988, alongside aid workers. Meanwhile, aid workers reported on death rates in the camps that were higher, by an order of magnitude, than those recorded in other famines of the 1980s. The fact that internationally donated aid had stood untouched in railway wagons for over a year, just yards from a camp where children were starving to death, caused outrage. This generated pressure on the government to allow relief to reach the famine victims, and in time led to the launch of Operation Lifeline Sudan (OLS) in January 1989. The presence of aid workers made it impossible for the slaughter to continue in secret.

A Sequel: The Clearance of the Oilfields

The center of gravity of the war shifted southward in 1991 when the SPLA split and SAF fought the SPLA near the Ugandan border. For some years, the areas close to

[5] The issue of slavery later became highly emotive, with inflated numbers cited by slave redemption groups, which ran highly lucrative, and largely fraudulent, exercises in raising money for "buying back" slaves to return to their homes. See de Waal (1998).

the north-south boundary were in a situation of low-intensity conflict, with local truces and various forms of *modus vivendi* between belligerents.

This changed in 1997, as the government made a major effort to control the oil-producing areas (Patey 2014). Its main tool was renting the allegiance of local leaders so that military activities were undertaken under the command of local men (Christian Aid 2000; European Coalition on Oil in Sudan 2001; Human Rights Watch 2003). Hundreds of fighters were killed in battles and hundreds more civilians killed in massacres, and by 2001 more than 200,000 people were displaced (Human Rights Watch 2003, pp. 313–19). It was an anarchic conflict, organized around loyalty payments to militia. After the majority of the local militia commanders defected and made alliances with the SPLA in 1999–2000, the government strategy changed to one of dispatching its own forces and northern militia to clear the oil-producing areas, leading to the deaths of many thousands and the displacement of a further 130,000 (de Guzman 2002). This phase of the conflict was polarized, targeted, and systematic, which distinguishes it from most other large military offensives in Sudan. However, estimates for total fatalities do not match those of other major episodes of mass atrocity. It is notable that the peak in war-related deaths in 1998, as reported by Burr, refers almost entirely to the famine that resulted from the rampages of the Dinka forces of Kerubino Kuanyin, a renegade SPLA commander who was terrorizing Bahr al Ghazal at the time, rather than the oilfields fighting and the heightened mortality associated with forced displacement. The atrocities in Upper Nile subsided when the government had achieved its immediate military objectives, which were securing the area for oil production. However, the SPLA's military threats to the oil-producing areas ended only with the peace negotiations that brought an end to the civil war itself, and it was only during the period of the Comprehensive Peace Agreement that displaced people were able to return home in relative security.

THE *JIHAD* IN THE NUBA MOUNTAINS, 1992

The campaign mounted by the Sudanese government in the Nuba Mountains in 1992 was only thinly documented at the time (Africa Watch 1992; African Rights 1995; BBC 1995). It was not the bloodiest campaign in the Sudanese civil war, but it was an unparalleled effort at total social transformation by force, including the complete relocation of the Nuba population residing in the hills where the SPLA had its strongest support, which were also the communities most resistant to the Islamist "Civilization Project" (de Waal and Abdelsalam 2004). The campaign was heralded as a *jihad*, and in intent if not in outcome, it most closely resembled the paradigmatic genocides theorized by Raphael Lemkin, who saw genocide as consisting not only in the destruction of the identity of the targeted population but also the imposition of the pattern of the oppressor (1944). The campaign failed, for four reasons: dissension among the perpetrators of the attack; resistance from the targeted group; the exhaustion of the efforts of the army and associated militia, as they ran out of money, logistics, stamina, and passion; and (a lesser factor) opprobrium in wider society (de Waal 2006).

The war in the Nuba Mountains began in 1985 and escalated over the following six years. It was marked by mass killings of educated people and community leaders, and government plans for mass relocation of the population to "peace camps." The campaign reached a climax in 1992–93 with the declaration of *jihad* and the adoption of a plan for systematic forced resettlement of the people out of the mountains. It was a fusion of coercive social planning and counterinsurgency.

A group of militant Islamists and security officers led the *jihad*. They mobilized comparatively vast resources, including aircraft and foreign military advisers. However, while they were fighting their *jihad*, they were also engaged in an internal power struggle with others within the government and army who wished to pursue a less radical approach, including some who (even at that date) sought a ceasefire and a negotiated settlement.

The Kordofan *jihad* is most closely associated with the governor of Kordofan, the newly promoted Lt. Gen. Sayed Abdel Karim el Husseini, and his notably zealous commissioner for South Kordofan, Abdel Wahab Abdel Rahman Ali. They were assisted by many others, such as the head of Military Intelligence in Kadugli, Major Ahmed Khamis. Their motivations were mixed. El Husseini was a career military officer who seized the openings offered by the Islamist government, and who opportunistically tried to prove both his loyalty and his new-found Islamist credentials during the campaign. Abdel Wahab Abdel Rahman was a middle-ranking civilian Islamist cadre trained in social mobilization. The most ideological of the three, he ranked low in the Islamist hierarchy: he too was trying to prove his credentials. Major Ahmed Khamis was a military officer who had acquired a reputation for cruelty. His career illustrates how those with a penchant for unflinching violence can thrive in such situations.

The military campaign was the largest offensive of the war to date, but it suffered weaknesses in planning. The most serious of these was an underestimation of the tenacity and skill of the SPLA forces. Ideologues are often let down by their neglect of practicalities, and especially tend to overlook contingency planning for when things go awry. There was a vast gap between the moral purity of the ideal *jihad* and the tawdry realities of counterinsurgency. The Nuba *jihad* contains many examples of the triumph of faith over caution, for example, the propensity of the *mujahidiin* commanders to alert the SPLA troops of imminent attacks by ordering their troops to cry "Allahu akbar!" as they leapt out of their trenches.

Without a quick victory, the spirit of *jihad* was soon exhausted. The *jihadist* language was reduced to mere formula, cited by officers in their reports for the benefit of superiors. There was neither heroism nor combat in the service of God, just a dirty little war, involving dejected and frightened soldiers killing poor and frightened villagers.

The government was united in support of the 1992 military offensive, but there was bitter dispute over the policy of relocation. At the height of the campaign, internal dissension erupted into a series of dismissals, reinstatements and re-dismissals of officials, and abrupt reversals of policy. Professional army officers were dismayed at the discontent among the army's noncommissioned officers over the atrocities, and were unhappy at the diversion of manpower and resources to the Nuba front when there were urgent demands elsewhere on the warfront. The civilian Islamists were divided too. Notably, the Islamists' leader Dr. Hassan al Turabi remained studiously quiet on the question of the *jihad*, waiting on the sidelines to see how the power struggles would play out and whether the campaign would succeed or not.

The failure of the campaign was expedited by the SPLA's defensive capability. By 1992, the SPLA troops in the Nuba Mountains were battle hardened and knew their strength. When they confronted the *mujahidiin* columns, they were confident, knowing the inexperience of the latter. Nonetheless, the fighting was sustained and ferocious, with day-and-night bombardment of the SPLA stronghold at Tullishi Mountain, and repeated infantry attacks. A small but determined SPLA force held them off (NAFIR 1997). After four months of failed assaults, the government finally declared it had captured Tullishi Mountain and withdrew. But the SPLA forces were still in control.

Throughout the early 1990s, the Nuba SPLA was cut off from the world. There was no resupply: they had no vehicles, had no heavy weapons, and sometimes had just a handful of bullets each. There was no humanitarian presence in the SPLA-held areas at all. There was no news coverage. Facing collective annihilation and with nothing but themselves to rely on, the Nuba people found the necessary determination and reserves of energy.

The SPLA governor Yousif Kuwa Mekki was pivotal to sustaining resistance during the hardest years. A former schoolteacher and cultural activist, Kuwa was close to his people, full of enthusiasm for their culture, and ready to share their hardship and suffering (Mekki 2001). The BBC film *Sudan's Secret War* captures an unscripted (and untranslated) moment in which he remarks to a villager, "I also ate *mukheit*," referring to a bitter berry that is used as a famine food. He continued his community mobilization during the war, convening an "advisory council" to debate whether to continue the war or surrender, and organizing a conference to promote religious tolerance between different faiths.

The Nuba SPLA steadily lost territory during the 1990s, but a mountainous base area remained impregnable. Their resistance lasted long enough to put the Nuba issue on the international human rights agenda in 1995, and then on the agenda for peace talks. Kuwa died of cancer in 2000, fearful that the future of his people still hung in the balance.

A final supplementary reason for the reduction in mass atrocity was wider opposition in Sudanese society. The leaders of the *jihad* tried to keep the real nature of their activities secret. But, by relocating destitute and starving Nuba civilians to the outskirts of towns outside the region, they inadvertently advertised what they were up to. The townspeople were shocked by what they saw and began to bring food and clothing to the Nuba people dumped on their doorstep. They were still more shocked when the security forces stopped their charitable activities. The groundswell of popular disgust, expressed through social networks rather than publicly, contributed to the retreat of the militants.

Sequelae

After the jihad ended, the war continued, as a dirty and fragmented counter-insurgency, with multiple militia on the government side, and several fragments of the SPLA breaking off and allying themselves with the government. Most of the fighting in the last years of the war was between units composed of Nuba.

The use of local people as government proxies changed the pattern of violations. In the earliest years of the war, Military Intelligence officers who were from elsewhere in Sudan rounded up educated Nuba and community leaders in an indiscriminate fashion and executed hundreds of them, on the flimsiest of evidence or allegation. The 1992 *jihad* similarly mobilized army and militia from outside the Nuba Mountains, and targeted entire communities. Thereafter, Nuba chiefs who collaborated with the government ran security operations. They had much better intelligence and their agents – also local people – could easily slip across the frontline and enter villages without being noticed, and assassinate individuals such as SPLA officers, chiefs, or administrators. Atrocities therefore continued, but were mostly targeted killing.

BLUE NILE: A NULL CASE

It is interesting to compare the Nuba assault with the conflict in Blue Nile. This took place at the same time and was intermittently just as fierce, with battles between conventional forces of SAF and the SPLA and Ethiopians. The Blue Nile occupies a strategic position as it is home to the Roseires Dam that provides electricity to Khartoum and irrigation water to the Gezira Scheme, the country's biggest agricultural project. In the 1990s, the region was also the centerpiece of the government's Islamization program. Three times, the SPLA, backed by the Ethiopian army, mounted major military operations that occupied much of Blue Nile and threatened the dam in 1987, 1989, and 1996–97. These attacks caused panic in the government far greater than anything occasioned by the war in the Nuba Mountains, including calling on Arab countries for assistance and bringing in commandos from the Eritrean People's Liberation Front (EPLF) to spearhead a counterattack (de Waal 2004). There were many violations in Blue Nile, but it never saw the same level of systematic abuses as the Nuba Mountains.

There are three likely reasons for this. The first is that the population was smaller and could flee across a nearby international border and take refuge in Ethiopia. The second is that the main military threat in Blue Nile was a conventional assault by mechanized and infantry brigades, and the component of guerrilla war was smaller. Once the conventional military threat had been seen off, the counterinsurgency was minor. The third was that in each case, the SPLA attack was directed by Ethiopia, and the Ethiopian leadership sent a message about what the Sudan government needed to do in order for the Ethiopians to stop. In 1989, this was to stop support to the EPLF – which was in turn the reason why the Eritreans led the counterattack. In 1996–97, the message was to dismantle bases used by the Ethiopian opposition, and the Sudanese complied. By remaining in direct communication with the Sudanese leadership about their intentions, the Ethiopians allowed the Sudanese to calibrate their actions in response.

DARFUR

Significant conflicts occurred in Darfur over the fifteen years prior to the recognized insurrection that erupted in February 2003 (Flint and de Waal 2008). Darfur's conflicts included different configurations of the following factors: local ethnic disputes, spillover of the Chadian civil war, SPLA incursion from southern Sudan, and government overreaction to local rebellion, especially by mobilizing proxy militia forces.

The 2003 rebellion was more significant than its predecessors because of the large-scale involvement of Chadian army officers in supporting the rebels, the extensive military supplies provided by the SPLA (which was at the time negotiating a peace agreement with Khartoum) to the Sudan Liberation Army (SLA), the emergence of the Justice and Equality Movement (JEM) drawn from former Darfurian Islamists suspected of having ties to would-be putschists in Khartoum, and the extent to which local state officials were backing and arming Arab militia. After the rebels overran Darfur's main airbase in April 2003, the government decided on a military response at scale. True to form, it used proxy militia in the frontline of its offensives, in this case drawn principally from camel-herding Arab tribes, and popularly known as *janjawiid*.

From June 2003 to January 2005, SAF, militia, and airforce mounted three vast scorched earth offensives in Darfur. The main method of the forces was targeting civilian communities, especially Fur, Masalit, and Zaghawa, the groups that formed the mainstay of the SLA and JEM. Estimates for the numbers of civilians killed are in the scores of thousands. The scorched earth tactics combined with obstruction of relief created a humanitarian disaster that caused a further 150,000 deaths. More than two million people were forcibly displaced.

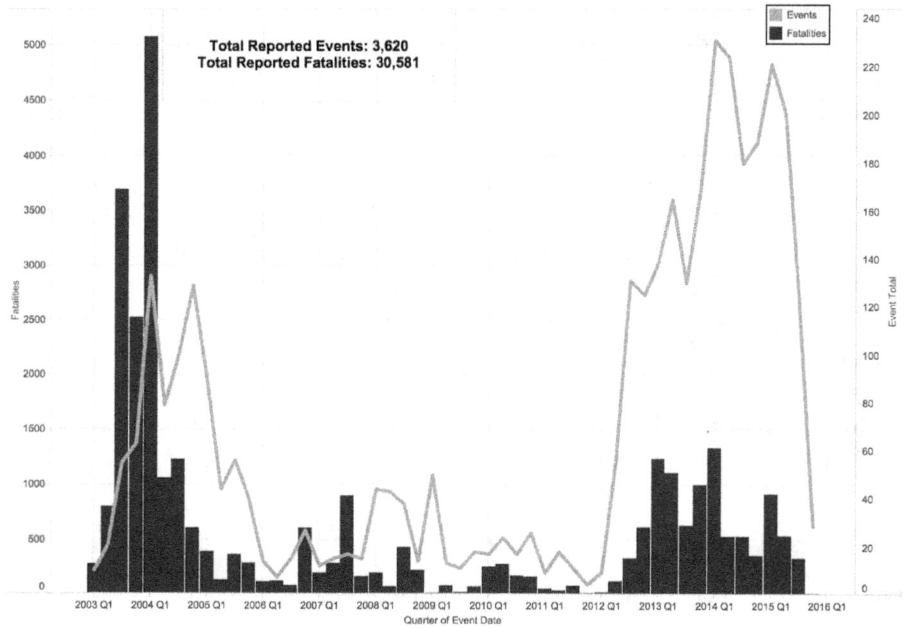

FIGURE 4.3: Violent incidents and fatalities in Darfur 2003–14.
Source: ACLED. Note that the figures are certainly an underestimation for 2003 and early 2004.

ENDING

The first and most dramatic drop in the number of killings in Darfur coincided with the end of the government's second major offensive and the signing of the N'djamena Humanitarian Ceasefire Agreement in early April 2004. The government had achieved its principal military objectives, and the army had reached the limits of its immediate operational capacity, having exhausted its supplies.

International pressure was also a factor. The U.S. administration had been alerted early to the Darfur war and its humanitarian implications, and a major USAID response was underway in the second half of 2003. A political response from the United States was slower, but by March 2004, the United States was actively backing Chadian and African Union (AU) initiatives for a ceasefire and peace talks, held in the Chadian capital N'djamena. These efforts climaxed, coincidentally, in early April 2004, just as the AU held a day of commemoration for the 10th anniversary of the Rwanda genocide. The AU Chairperson Alpha Oumar Konaré met President Bashir and urged him to sign a ceasefire at once. Bashir passed his instruction to his negotiator in N'djamena, Major General Ismat al Zain. Ismat responded that another few days' talks were required to resolve a key issue over where the rebels would be located during the ceasefire and adopt a map.[6] Ismat was overruled, but his reservation was prescient: the absence of an agreed map made the ceasefire impossible to enforce, and the SLA groups headed by Minni Minawi decided to expand the war to eastern and southern Darfur shortly thereafter, sparking a third large-scale government counteroffensive.

The ceasefire, albeit only partially respected, allowed for a rapid scale-up in humanitarian operations. This was possible only because of the initiative taken by senior officials at USAID (Andrew Natsios and Roger Winter) eight months earlier. The data for general mortality in Darfur, overwhelmingly caused by hunger and disease, indicate that it fell more rapidly than in other comparable crises, reaching levels approximately equal to normal by the end of 2005. The credit for this success belongs to the early USAID response and the ceasefire.

The third government campaign, between June 2004 and January 2005, was just as large as the previous ones, but both less bloody and less militarily successful. There is anecdotal evidence to suggest that one reason for the reduced level of killing of civilians was the presence of military observers, mostly Africans but also some Europeans and Americans, as part of the African Union Mission in Sudan (AMIS) set up by the N'djamena agreement. The AMIS force commander was also proactive, both in deploying his troops, often stretching his mandate, and in his public pronouncements. Although AMIS later came in for serious criticisms for its inadequacies, its first deployment coincided with a substantial reduction in both fighting and one-sided violence, and the third army campaign killed many fewer civilians. At the same time, an enormous international humanitarian effort was gearing up, with a much-increased presence of aid workers. This had been set in motion by USAID in mid-2003. The aid that began to arrive six months later undoubtedly saved many lives, and there is also anecdotal evidence that the presence of aid workers served as a deterrent to mass killing.

The second drop in levels of killing occurred in January 2005, when that campaign ended. This also followed the signing of the Comprehensive Peace Agreement between the Government of Sudan and the SPLM/A, and John Garang's subsequent commitment to assist in resolving the Darfur conflict. Displacement continued for considerably longer, though the reasons for people leaving their villages became more complex, less to do with mass attack and more to do with generalized insecurity and collapse of the rural economy.

Aftermath

The situation thereafter was one of a low-intensity conflict, with the rebel groups fragmenting and occasionally fighting one another, and the government's erstwhile proxies losing their enthusiasm for the war and either becoming freelance, turning on one another, or turning their guns on the government. The conflict after

[6] Ismat al Zain, personal communication with the author, March 2006.

2005 consisted of a mixture of banditry, interethnic conflict, harassment of civilians including displaced persons, and occasional offensives and counteroffensives by the government and rebels. The pattern was a familiar one from the protracted wars in the south and elsewhere, of a background level of killing (in this case, perhaps 100 people per month) with occasional sharp spikes with several hundred being killed. From December 2005 to December 2009 (until the governments of Sudan and Chad reached a rapprochement), Darfur's war was intermingled with the conflict in Chad, with many of the belligerent forces fighting on both sides of the border.

During this period, international engagement may have complicated and prolonged the war. The U.S. policy priority of bringing United Nations peacekeepers to Darfur certainly distorted and possibly derailed the AU-led efforts to find a negotiated settlement to the conflict in 2006. Sudanese peace agreements double as security pacts: they are a means whereby the government makes a deal with one rebel group in order to fight other rebels. The May 2006 Darfur Peace Agreement turned out this way, when the only rebel leader to sign was Minni Minawi. This shifted the pattern of fighting instead of ending it, and did not promote reconciliation. Even had all the rebel groups signed, the exclusion of the Darfurian Arabs from the peace agreement would have generated another round of violence. Nonetheless, the distortion and mishandling of a peace process, due to a "security-first" U.S. agenda, contributed to ongoing conflict.

Data for violent incidents for the period 2008–09 allow us to investigate more rigorously the pattern of conflict at this stage (de Waal et al. 2014). What these show is a shift from a two-sided conflict including asymmetric violence against civilians to a diverse set of interlinked conflicts, including fighting between government forces and rebels, violence by both the government and rebels against civilians, intertribal conflicts, banditry, and – most interestingly – conflicts among the different pro-government forces.

It is striking that there is a significant amount of violence perpetrated among members of government forces, both regular (uniformed) and irregular. This arose from the government strategy of establishing new paramilitary units in parallel to existing ones, often by incorporating irregular militia into the command structure and putting them on the payroll. Thus, some Arab militia (*janjawiid*) were given uniforms and ranks and reconstituted as the Border Intelligence. Others joined the Central Reserve Police. There were cases in which these units fought against the army, police, or National Intelligence and Security Service.

Another striking feature of this period was that most of those killed were Arabs. This reflects a particular feature of the conflict during this stage, which was the prevalence of "rent-seeking rebellions" by Arab militia that had been armed and used by the government to fight the rebels. Arguing that they had been unfairly treated, militia leaders rebelled against their sponsors, demanding back pay, compensation, promotion, and benefits for their communities, and used fiery rhetoric against the government (Channel 4 News 2008). They bargained well and won most of their demands (Flint 2008). The following year, it was the turn of Zaghawa groups that had joined the government in 2006 to mutiny, with comparable demands. Some were bought back in to the government, and others joined the growing new rebellion sponsored by South Sudan and Uganda (Gramizzi and Tubiana 2012). In addition, throughout this entire period there were numerous conflicts between Arab groups, particularly over control over land and local administrative units (Gramizzi and Tubiana 2012).

After 2011, there was another uptick in violence, as the opposition reorganized and obtained renewed support from the newly independent South Sudan. However, this was not a return to straightforward two-sided violence, but also a complicated picture.

ANALYSIS

This account points to a pattern whereby a polarized conflict along political-ethnic lines became disaggregated into a multisided conflict with diverse actors and diverse kinds of violent contestation: a shift from "Schmittian" to "Hobbesian" violence. As the government withdrew from coordinating the violence in Darfur, but failed to assume the role of Leviathan, it abandoned the region to anarchic violence. Many Darfurians regarded this as just as reprehensible as the tyranny on display of the height of the war (Fadul and Tanner 2007, p. 295).

As the levels of central financial patronage and instruction declined, local political factors became more salient and national ones became less so, and the level at which violence was organized accordingly shifted to the local level. However, opportunistic violence was routinely at risk of escalating into coordinated destruction. And indeed, this is precisely happened with the JEM attack on Khartoum in 2008 and the escalation of the war in 2012–13. These represent not just an increase in the overall levels of violence, but also a higher level of coordination and a different and more "Schmittian" logic. Interestingly, as explored later, the 2008 JEM attack, while it led to a high level of military combat, did not result in a commensurate level of violence against civilians.

Darfur provides a number of important null cases. The first is the SPLA incursion of 1991, intended to foment a civil war. This was a serious military and political threat, but it was rapidly defeated and, most interestingly for our purposes, the campaign did not involve large-scale violence against civilians. There were violations, including the burning of a dozen villages and the rounding up and incarceration of SPLA sympathizers. The major difference between 1991 and 2003, according to persuasive analysis by Philip Roessler (2014), was that in 1991, the Islamist government possessed an extensive political apparatus in Darfur, which provided it with good intelligence at the level of individuals. The intelligence was also aided by the capture of the rebel leader, Daud Bolad, whose notebooks contained every detail of the SPLA network (Flint and de Waal 2008, pp. 24–25). Therefore, it was possible to organize a precisely targeted repression campaign.

In 2003, by contrast, the government had lost the Islamist movement in Darfur, which had either gone over to the rebels or was uncooperative. Without the granular intelligence it could have deployed earlier, it was blundering around in the dark. This was illustrated in July 2003, when the officer commanding the western region, Major General Ismat al Zain, distributed arms to a wide range of communities, Arab and non-Arab, to fight the rebels. Very large numbers of the recruits immediately defected, especially from the non-Arabs. Consequently, the government resorted to using community or ethnic labels as the basis for targeting its violence (Roessler 2014).

A second and complementary explanation for the difference between 1991 and 2003 was the military tactics used by the rebels. The Bolad incursion was an irregular infantry attack of the kind that the SPLA conducted in southern Sudan and the Nuba Mountains. The SAF commanders were used to this. However, the attacks of 2003 were conducted using desert warfare tactics of high mobility, using land cruisers. These tactics had been widely used in Chad but never on this scale in Sudan, and SAF was unprepared. Throughout 2003, the SLA and JEM fighters were running rings round SAF, winning almost every encounter (Flint and de Waal 2008, p. 119). Not only was SAF operating in the dark, but it was being stung every time it moved.

In light of the Sudanese government's normal *modus operandi*, which consists in paying off sufficient members of the provincial elite to maintain sufficient control over its peripheries, the question arises, why did national security and party officials not just pay off the rebel leaders? At this time – 2003 – it had been enjoying oil revenues for three years and the national budget was rising fast. One reason is that government business managers miscalculated the price, or were not prepared to pay it. Khalil Ibrahim reports that, when Vice President Ali Osman Taha was warned of imminent revolt in Darfur, he contemptuously dismissed the possibility on the grounds that Darfurians were "too hungry to stage an armed revolution" (el-Tom 2011, p. 211). Khalil puts the miscalculation down to racism. Another reason is that they did not anticipate the degree of escalation: after the rebels' humiliating attack on al Fashir airbase, the logic of reprisal set in, and this led to reciprocal escalation on a runaway path.

The violence in the far west of Darfur (Dar Masalit) in 1995–97 and 1999 originated over land disputes and especially the control of the provincial administration, between the Masalit (who had customary jurisdiction) and Arabs (who were growing in number and political influence). Clashes escalated into massacre and flight, with hundreds killed, disproportionately on the Masalit side. Government officials were complicit: the more powerful ones favored the Arabs. But the higher levels of the government were not actively involved. Indeed, the government analysis was that the violence stemmed from lack of authority, and when the president sent a retired general, Mohamed al Dabi, as his envoy, al Dabi insisted on putting on his uniform and organizing a show of force by military helicopters in order to quell the violence (Flint and de Waal 2008, pp. 62–63). This illustrates a distinction between the central authorities permitting local violence and actually instigating it. In 1997 and 1999, the government could (in a cynical exercise of double standards) stop violence at a certain point.

The 2008 null case is another interesting variant. The background to this is the way in which relations between Sudan and Chad degenerated into an intense proxy war in 2006. In February 2008, a column of Chadian rebels, armed and supported by Sudan, reached as far as the Chadian capital N'djamena and were at the point of victory when their leaders disagreed over who should become the next Chadian president and on what terms, which allowed the incumbent, Idriss Déby, to reorganize and counterattack. A few months later, an almost identical reciprocal attack by JEM forces, assisted and armed by Chad and Libya, reached the Sudanese capital and was blocked only at the bridges across the River Nile. This attack shook the Sudanese political and security establishment to the core.

In the immediate aftermath of the attack, there were fears of ethnic pogroms, targeted especially at members of the Zaghawa, who constituted the bulk of the JEM fighters. There were arrests and some killings, but the feared mass reprisals did not occur. Indeed, the UNAMID incident database does not register any increase in killings at that time. (The fatalities in the fighting in Khartoum are excluded from the dataset as they occurred outside Darfur, but as most Zaghawa live in Darfur, and JEM was based in Darfur, any retaliation would be expected there.)

We can surmise two reasons for this lack of violent response. The first is that by 2008, the Sudanese intelligence service had rebuilt its information network, and could therefore reliably identify who was involved and who was not, and could target its actions on an individual basis. In this respect, the 2008 response was similar to the 1991 counterinsurgency.

The second is that the core of the threat emanated from the governments of Chad and Libya, and Sudan was in direct communication with both. What followed was that, over the remainder of 2008, both Chad and Sudan engaged in an arms race, taking the form of sponsoring and equipping one another's rebels, until both realized the futility of this exercise (Tubiana 2011). In 2009, Sudan's President Omar al Bashir and Chadian President Idriss Déby – who knew each other well from their days as close allies from 1990 to 2004 – met and decided on a truce. Throughout this period of conflict and rapprochement, each understood the other's constraints and likely courses of action. This mutual confidence – common understanding rather than unconditional trust – was then enough to make a workable agreement. The third party in this drama, Libya's brother leader Muammar Gaddafi was trusted by neither, and both had a strategy of managing his erratic ambitions. In 2011, Sudan took the opportunity of actively supporting Gaddafi's military overthrow.

The endings and, even more so, the null cases, illustrate the importance of a central authority in determining the level of violence against civilians. The government is never fully in control – it cannot instigate a high level of violence without enlisting others, and neither can it wholly suppress violence – but it is, nonetheless, a key actor. The government's ability to obtain, process, and act upon intelligence is important in determining whether to use violence to target selected individuals, or whether to target entire groups.

INTERNECINE KILLINGS IN SOUTHERN SUDAN

Since its very earliest days in 1983, the SPLA perpetrated atrocities against southern Sudanese. Violence against recruits and resisters, internal dissenters, external challengers and their constituencies, and any civilian populations that its troops encountered was its consistent modus operandi. In comparison to the Khartoum government, the SPLA had less capacity to dial the level of violence up or down, and the distinctions between politically organized "Schmittian" killing and "Hobbesian" violence are less clear-cut.

Atrocities 1983–91

The SPLA was never a guerrilla force in the strict sense. It began as a coalition of mutinous units from SAF, organized in a conventional manner, supplemented by ethnic units. The SPLA grew extraordinarily fast, and within two years it was "in full-scale conventional warfare" (Madut-Arop 2006, p. 112). From the outset, the people of southern Sudan identified the SPLA as a *hukuma* ("government"), differing from Khartoum chiefly in that, for many, it was their government. Cherry Leonardi describes how young people in southern Sudan sought to escape the clutches of each of the two "governments," or joined one (preferably the SPLA) in order to mediate between its power and their own communities (Leonardi 2007). Killing with impunity was the hallmark of its governmental authority, and as the SPLA sought to establish that authority, it tried to destroy all intermediate structures (Hutchinson 1998). Its determination to "smash" the existing order verged on nihilism, as exemplified in the slogan taught to SPLA recruits, "You must live through the barrels of your guns. Food, wife and property wherever you find them are to be acquired through your might" (African Rights 1997, p. 84).

The most infamous internecine brutalities in southern Sudan occurred in 1991, but the previous eight years consisted of a litany of atrocities by SPLA forces and rival southern militia (Nyaba 1997; African Rights 1997). The government and the SPLA were jointly responsible for inflicting famine on southern Sudan and impeding humanitarian relief (African Rights 1997). While the government army and militia ravaged the countryside, the SPLA laid siege to the towns. Garang made no secret of this, saying in a radio interview that, "garrison towns in the South are famine-stricken and are real disaster areas, and this is good; our military strategy is working" (Garang 1987, p. 71). The largest and widest-ranging SPLA force was the Locust Division, which swept through the countryside devouring everything like its totem (Madut-Arop 2006, pp. 111–12).

The political function of the SPLA's violence was an attempt to create a new, state-like power center, by instrumentalizing opposition to a common enemy (Khartoum) to justify the elimination of internal challengers and the imposition of centralized dictatorial machinery. But for most southern Sudanese, the experience of the war was lawlessness. In the light of this, the subsequent internecine massacres and man-made famines of the early 1990s, when the SPLA turned on itself, appear less as an aberration and more as the inevitable outcome when this hyper-militarized political authority ran into crisis.

The 1991–94 Internecine Killings

Centralized militarism was sustainable only for as long as the SPLA could call upon the state power of Ethiopia. When that failed in May 1991, the SPLA collapsed. That ushered in the most conspicuous mass atrocities of the internal conflicts within southern Sudan.

The collapse began in August 1991 when three senior SPLA commanders, Riek Machar, Lam Akol, and Gordon Kong, based in the town of Nasir, declared that they had overthrown Garang. Their platform was that the SPLA had been run in a dictatorial and incompetent manner. They did not intend an ethnic coup, but they did not succeed in obtaining the timely support of key Dinka commanders who sympathized their position, and within days the split degenerated into a confrontation between the rebellious "Nasir Faction," mainly ethnic Nuer and Shilluk, and the mainstream "Torit Faction" led by Garang, retaining the loyalty of the Dinka, and named for his headquarters. An attempt by Riek Machar to march on Torit turned into an exercise in mobilizing a Nuer tribal force, popularly known as the White Army, which got as far as Garang's home town of Bor, in Jonglei, where they massacred 2,000 civilians on November 15, 1991. This was the signature atrocity of a period of internecine killings that continued throughout the decade. But, as indicated previously, it was different mainly in visibility rather than scale to what had gone before.

The SPLA largely disintegrated at that time. From a strength of over 100,000, it was reduced to an estimated fighting force of less than 10,000. What emerged was a constellation of ethnic militia, whose commanders were ready to rent their allegiance to the highest bidder, or to whoever would license them to pursue their local agenda, alongside a core of veteran SPLA commanders who retained a political vision, but lacked the organizational means to pursue that vision. In part this was an organizational capitulation to the model of the militia war adopted by the Sudanese security chiefs who ran a tribally based counterinsurgency, and were ready to supply arms to any southern leader ready to cooperate. In part it was because Garang ensured that there was no organizational capability within the SPLA that might challenge his power. He made sure that he monopolized the SPLA's intelligence gathering and mobilized large units only for specific operations, disbanding them into dispersed reserves afterward, to prevent them developing *esprit de corps* and loyalty to their commanders.

The period of the most intense reciprocal ethnic killings came to an end in 1994. The mechanism for ending this was a political process of internal reconciliation. It began with junior commanders in a place called Lafon, who saw no rationale to killing one another. Under pressure from commanders, chiefs, religious leaders, and a wide array of southern Sudanese, in the country and abroad, the SPLA leaders were pushed to reconcile. Garang was also pressed to turn the SPLM from an empty shell into a substantial entity with consultative mechanisms. This culminated in early 1994 in the SPLM's first convention, at which delegates welcomed back dissenters and adopted a program of institution building and democratization (Rolandsen 2005). Garang subsequently circumvented or subverted most of the decisions of the convention, but it nonetheless served a purpose of creating a forum in which southern Sudanese could meet, legitimizing discussions outside the tight control of the commander in chief, and reducing internal violence. It took some years for the key mutinous commanders to return to the fold, and other discontented commanders mutinied in the meantime – leading to a particularly vicious round of killing and starvation in 1998 – but the worst of the atrocities were over.

Wars of Peace: Jonglei 2005–13

Throughout the civil war, Jonglei was the cockpit of southern Sudan, strategically adjacent to the SPLA's bases in Ethiopia, where the fiercest fighting and most atrocities occurred. The legacy of this militarization lives on. Fighting in Jonglei continued throughout the CPA Interim Period (2005–11) and into the independence of South Sudan. This violence lacks clear pattern, constantly reconfiguring itself with a week-to-week unpredictability, as new armed actors emerge or disappear, merge or divide, or reconfigure themselves (Thomas 2015).

Peace in southern Sudan in 2005 meant war. The initial fear was that the SPLA, at that time a relatively small force in comparison to the numerous other armed groups in southern Sudan, would create new alliances to exclude those groups from power, using force. The prospect of large-scale civil war was averted after John Garang died in July 2005, and his deputy Salva Kiir became president of the Government of Southern Sudan. Kiir immediately began a process of reconciling with non-SPLA southern militia, bringing them into the SPLA and onto its payroll. His strategy was to outbid the northern security chiefs by renting the allegiance of the militia, simply by paying them more money. The largest number of these militia were ethnic Nuer, organized as the South Sudan Defence Force, including large numbers from Jonglei. This culminated in the Juba Agreement of January 2006.

This is southern Sudan's null case for comparative purposes: the large-scale internal war that was feared following the CPA. The conflict was avoided by negotiating an agreement.

Although the wars of peace that followed were much smaller scale than might otherwise have occurred, they nonetheless involved large-scale killing. The White Army was not included in the Juba Agreement, and as a result the SPLA began a campaign to dismantle it later that year, under the rubric of civilian disarmament. An estimated 1,200 White Army and 400 SPLA soldiers were killed along with hundreds of civilians (Small Arms Survey 2006–2007, p. 4). The SPLA burned, looted, and lived off the land. The exercise ended with the White Army temporarily disbanded.

Two rebellions by disaffected provincial politicians followed in 2011. The first was a mutiny by a defeated gubernatorial candidate, General George Athor. The second was a rebellion by David Yauyau, and raids by his ethnic Murle forces. In response, a coalition of SPLA troops and ethnic militia destroyed Murle communities. Humanitarian crisis followed, exacerbated by SPLA attacks upon health centers (Médecins Sans Frontières 2012).

Each episode of violence ended in its own way. The disarmament campaign ended when the SPLA forces were exhausted and decided that the White Army was sufficiently weakened. George Athor's rebellion ended when Athor was killed. The Yauyau rebellion ended when the civil war broke out in December 2013, and President Kiir and Yauyau found it opportune to combine forces against ethnic Nuer rebels. But the overall pattern of violence shows no sign of ending.

PATTERNS TO MASS ATROCITY

Internal factors have dominated how mass atrocities end in northern Sudan. The international role has been secondary. If we compare Darfur 2003–05 (with a high level of international engagement) to the Nuba Mountains 1992 (with none), the overall pattern is similar. International presence and pressure appear to have helped bring down the level of killings, especially in the third offensive in Darfur in 2004–05, and international assistance undoubtedly reduced the death toll from the humanitarian crisis.

In Sudan, mass atrocities occur when a high-level political conflict is articulated with capabilities for inflicting violence at a lower level in the political or administrative hierarchy. On their own, low-level social and political formations lack the capacity for large-scale sustained violence. Higher-level political leaders must make exceptional efforts if they are to organize violence at scale. It is when the two levels function together that large-scale killing is most likely.

In most cases, this coordination comes about when the government feels threatened and unable to muster a sufficient response using its conventional army or its political machinery. A combination of fear and lack of good information about the threat causes the political leadership to target violence at entire communities, defined by ethnicity or location. These campaigns ended when the immediate threat had passed, although the underlying political conflict had not been resolved. The endings involved a shift in the coordination of the violence and the salience of short-term destruction. While the central command may have stepped back from directing large-scale operations, local actors continued to inflict violence, in diverse ways.

Occasionally, the government acted not through fear but strategically in order to gain political advantage. Examples are the Nuba Mountains jihad, which failed, and the clearances of the oilfields in the late 1990s, in order to pave the way for extracting and exporting oil, which succeeded.

The pattern of sequelae to large-scale killing is consistent: a lower level, more widespread, and more fractured form of violence takes over. This pattern occurs regardless of the original motive or goal of the perpetrator. However, the pattern of endings indicates that an instrumental calculus triumphs over other logics.

In southern Sudan, the SPLM/A and the government it has headed have less organizational capacity, and a less sophisticated management of the patronage system. Whereas Khartoum has institutions and an associated capacity for a large-scale mobilization, Juba is run entirely as a militarized patronage system. Consequently, in the south, the distinction between high-level, political violence and lower level violence is less clear-cut. This can be seen in the continuities between the patterns of violent turbulence in Jonglei before the CPA, during the CPA Interim Period, and subsequently.

The atrocities committed internally within the SPLA after the failed coup against Garang in 1991 and again on the outbreak of civil war in 2013 represented ethnically brokered reciprocal escalation. These were inherently unsustainable because of the organizational weaknesses of southern Sudanese political and military institutions.

The internal-external dichotomy is blurred in southern Sudan. Since the early 1990s, the SPLM/A has become deeply enmeshed in regional and international politics including resource flows, military cooperation, and advocacy narratives and networks. In the 1990s, the violations were reduced by the southern Sudanese activating a web of cross-cutting networks including the churches, community leaders, and SPLA commanders themselves, supported by international partners. Since 1997, successive U.S. administrations have stood in solidarity with the SPLA, and have put little pressure on the southern Sudanese authorities to reform a governance system that has persistently reproduced patterns of violence that represent a chronic mass atrocity against their own people.

Peace Agreements

Sudanese and their foreign sympathizers have hoped that peace agreements would spell a decisive end to armed conflict and mass atrocity. This was the hope of the 2005 CPA and the 2006 Darfur Peace Agreement. Those hopes were not fulfilled. Just as SAF was never able to achieve a decisive military victory, so too do formal peace agreements not represent the decisive triumph of peacemakers. The CPA was the victory of one political coalition in Sudan – the National Congress Party and the SPLM – over others, and those others needed to be contained or suppressed, by force if need be. The prospect of large-scale internal violence in southern Sudan after the CPA was forestalled only by the 2006 Juba Declaration between President Salva Kiir and his main domestic challenger, Gen. Paulino Matiep. That agreement sowed the seeds of future conflict. In Darfur, the 2006 agreement in Abuja turned out not to be the end of that region's armed conflict, but rather a reconfiguration of that conflict. The hope that the independence of South Sudan would herald a resolution of the country's problems, replacing two neighboring states at peace with one another, to replace a single quarrelsome state, also proved transient. Peace agreements have been more akin to contingent bargains struck in a turbulent market, good for only as long as market conditions remain favorable, rather than durable proto-constitutional political settlements.

International Roles

The role played by international actors has been secondary throughout but is gradually increasing. This is associated with the growing visibility of atrocities in Sudan and (belatedly) South Sudan.

The reduction in the militia campaigns in 1989 was associated with a shift in the U.S. position on Sudan. Formerly an accommodating patron of Khartoum, Washington lost its fear that Sudan might switch to the Communist bloc, and lost patience with its government's shambolic political and economic performance. In January 1989, the incoming George H.W. Bush administration tied economic assistance to relief programs, including Operation Lifeline Sudan, and steps to end the war. Prefiguring wider patterns across the Greater Middle East, however, hopes of democracy and peace were snuffed out by a military-Islamist takeover.

There is recurrent circumstantial evidence to suggest that international scrutiny does reduce violations. Instances include the humanitarian concerns over the internal conflict within the SPLA in 1991, the impact of the BBC and African rights investigation in 1995, and the presence of AMIS monitors in Darfur in late 2004. International pressure on the South Sudanese parties in 2013–14 probably dampened the escalation of the war.

Darfur is a test case for international measures to reduce atrocities. Early international engagement by USAID and the African Union contributed to the N'djamena ceasefire of April 8, 2004, which coincided with the scaling up of the humanitarian operation and the most significant drop in lethal violence. The high-profile international campaign to "save" Darfur began after this date and cannot, therefore, be credited with these successes. The small number of AU ceasefire monitors in 2004–05 was associated with a major reduction in atrocities, and the large Chapter VII peace enforcement mission from 2008 onward was associated with no reduction in violence.

Concluding Reflections

One substantive conclusion is that all endings are relative, and are embedded within the political and governance framework available at the time. Sudanese and southern Sudanese peace agreements are primarily political bargains that, while they create new alliances, also create new exclusions, and thereby generate new violence. The CPA and Darfur Peace Agreement do not represent a "success" and a "failure" but different points on a spectrum of outcomes.

The main policy conclusion is that most instances of mass atrocity occur in the context of war, especially where there is heightened political polarization, develop an escalatory logic, and then follow a different logic as they de-escalate. However, it is also important to recognize that "peace" can also mean war, in the form of the enforcement of the new governing coalition, through, for example, forced disarmament. We sorely need policy tools to deal with the aftermath of these peaks in violence, which are typically marked by poorly coordinated but destructive and protracted levels of violence, where governance has broken down. While the resolution of "Schmittian" violent contention demands mediation, perhaps backed by an enforcement capacity, the subsequent "Hobbesian" violent contention that typically occurs in the aftermath demands the (re-)construction of government authority.

WORKS CITED

Abdul-Jalil, Musa. 1984. "The Dynamics of Ethnic Identification in Northern Darfur, Sudan: A Situational Approach," in Bayreuth African Studies Series, *The Sudan: Ethnicity and National Cohesion*, Bayreuth.

African Rights. 1995. *Facing Genocide: The Nuba of Sudan*. London: African Rights.

1997. *Food and Power in Sudan: A critique of humanitarianism*. London: African Rights.

Africa Watch. 1990. *Denying "the Honor of Living," Sudan: A human rights disaster*. London: Africa Watch.

1992. *Sudan: Eradicating the Nuba: Africa Watch Calls for the United Nations to Investigate Killings, Destruction of Villages and Forced Removals*. London: Africa Watch, September 9.

Amnesty International. 1989. *Sudan: Human Rights Violations in the Context of Civil War*. London: Amnesty International.

Anonymous. 1987. "Sudan's Secret Slaughter," mimeo.

BBC. 1995. *Sudan's Secret War*, television program, July.

Beswick, Stephanie. 2004. *Sudan's Blood Memory: The Legacy of War, Ethnicity, and Slavery in South Sudan*. Rochester, NY: University of Rochester Press.

Burr, Millard. 1998. *Quantifying Genocide in Southern Sudan and the Nuba Mountains*. Washington, DC: Committee of Refugees.

Channel 4 News. 2008. *Meet the Janjaweed*, television program, March 13.

Christian Aid. 2000. *The Scorched Earth: Oil and war in Sudan*. London: Christian Aid, October.

Coghlan, Benjamin, Richard J Brennan, Pascal Ngoy, David Dofara, Brad Otto, Mark Clements, and Tony Stewart. 2006. "Mortality in the Democratic Republic of Congo: A nationwide survey." *Lancet* 367, 44–51.

Deng, Francis. 1995. *War of Visions: Conflict of identities in the Sudan*. Washington, DC: Brookings Institution Press.

2015. "Foreword." In *Genocidal Nightmares: Narratives of insecurity and the logic of mass atrocities*, edited by Abdelwahab El Affendi, pp. xi–xix. London: Bloomsbury.

de Guzman, Diane. 2002. *Depopulating Sudan's Oil Regions*, edited by Egbert G. Ch. Utretch: ECOS, May 14.

de Waal, Alex. 1987. "The Perception of Poverty and Famines." *International Journal of Moral and Social Studies* 2: 3, 251–262.

1994. "Some Comments on Militias in Contemporary Sudan." In *Civil War in the Sudan*, edited by Martin Daly and Ahmed al Sikainga, pp. 142–156, London: British Academic Press.

2004. "The Politics of Destabilization in the Horn, 1989–2001." In *Islamism and Its Enemies in the Horn of Africa*, edited by Alex de Waal, pp. 182–230. London: Hurst.

2005. "Who are the Darfurians? Arab and African Identities, Violence and External Engagement." *African Affairs* 104/415: 181–205.

2006. "Averting Genocide in the Nuba Mountains of Sudan." *How Genocides End*, Social Science Research Council Web Forum. http://howgenocidesend.ssrc.org/de_Waal2/ Accessed 29 June 2015.

2007. "Deaths in Darfur: Keeping Ourselves Honest." *Making Sense of Sudan* blog, August 16.

1998. "Exploiting Slavery: Human Rights and Political Agendas in Sudan." *New Left Review*, February 1998, 135–46.

2015. *The Real Politics of the Horn of Africa: Money, War and the Business of Power*. London: Polity.

de Waal, Alex and A. H. Abdelsalam. 2004. "Islam, State Power and Jihad in Sudan." In *Islamism and Its Enemies in the Horn of Africa*, edited by Alex de Waal, pp. 71–113. London: Hurst.

de Waal, Alex and Chad Hazlett, Christian Davenport, and Joshua Kennedy. 2014. "The Epidemiology of Lethal Violence in Darfur: Using Micro-data to Explore Complex Patterns of Ongoing Armed Conflict." *Social Science and Medicine* 120: 368–377.

el-Tom, Abdullahi Osman. 2011. *Darfur, JEM, and the Khalil Ibrahim Story*. Trenton, NJ: Red Sea Press.

European Coalition on Oil in Sudan (ECOS). 2001. *Documentation on the Impact of Oil in Sudan*. Utrecht: ECOS, May 29.

Fadul, Abdul-Jabbar and Victor Tanner. 2007. "Darfur After Abuja: A View from the Ground." In *War in Darfur and the Search for Peace*, edited by Alex de Waal, pp. 284–313. Cambridge: Harvard University Press.

Fearon, James D. and David D. Laitin. 2000. "Violence and the Social Construction of Ethnic Identity." *International Organization*, 54: 4, 845–877.

Flint, Julie. 2008. "Beyond 'Janjaweed': Understanding the militias of Darfur, Small Arms Survey." Sudan Working Paper 17.

Flint, Julie and Alex de Waal. 2008. *Darfur: A New History of a Long War*. London: Zed.

Hobbes, Thomas. 1996. *Leviathan, Part 1*. Student Edition, edited by Richard Tuck. Cambridge: Cambridge University Press (Originally published 1651).

Garang, John. 1987. *John Garang Speaks*. Edited and introduced by Mansour Khalid. London: Kegan Paul.

General Accountability Office. 2006. *Darfur Crisis: Death Estimates Demonstrate Severity of Crisis, but Their Accuracy and Credibility Could Be Enhanced*. Washington, DC: Report GAO-07-24, GAO, November.

Gramizzi, Claudio and Jérôme Tubiana. 2012. *Forgotten Darfur: Old Tactics and New Players*. Small Arms Survey, HSBA Working Paper 28.

Guha-Sapir, Debarati and Olivier Degomme. 2005a. *Darfur: Counting the Deaths: Mortality Estimates from Multiple Survey Data*. Brussels: CRED, May.

2005b. *Darfur: Counting the Deaths (2): What Are the Trends?* Brussels: CRED, December.

Human Rights Watch. 2003. *Sudan, Oil and Human Rights*. New York: Human Rights Watch.

Hutchinson, Sharon. 1998. "Death, Memory and the Politics of Legitimation: Nuer Experiences of the Continuing Second Sudanese Civil War." *In Memory and the Postcolony, African Anthropology and the Critique of Power*, edited by Richard Werbner, pp. 58–70. London: Zed Books.

Jok, Jok Madut. 2004. "The Legacy of Race." In *Race and Identity in the Nile Valley: Ancient and Modern Perspectives*, edited by Carolyn Fluehr-Lobban and Kharyssa Rhodes. Trenton, NJ: Red Sea Press.

Kalyvas, Stathis. 2006. *The Logic of Violence in Civil War*. Cambridge: Cambridge University Press.

Keen, David. 1994. *The Benefits of Famine: A political Economy of Famine and Relief in Southwestern Sudan*, 1983–1989. New Haven: Yale University Press.

Komey, Guma Kunda, 2012. *Land, Governance, Conflict and the Nuba of Sudan*. Oxford: James Currey.

Lemkin, Raphael. 1944. *Axis Rule in Occupied Europe: Laws of Occupation, Analysis of Government, Proposals for Redress*. Washington, DC: Carnegie Endowment for International Peace.

Leonardi, Cherry. 2007. "Liberation or Capture: Youth between Hakuma and Home during Civil War in Southern Sudan and Its Aftermath." *African Affairs* 106/424: 391–412.

Madut-Arop, Arop. 2006. *Sudan's Painful Road to Peace: A Full Story of the Founding and Development of the SPLM/SPLA*. North Charleston, SC: Booksurge, LLC.

Mahmoud, Ushari and Suleiman Baldo. 1987. *El Diein Massacre and Slavery in the Sudan*. Khartoum: Mimeo.

Mawson, Andrew. 1991. "Murahaleen Raids on the Dinka 1985–89." *Disasters* 15:2, 137–149.

Médecins Sans Frontières. 2012. *South Sudan's Hidden Crisis: How Violence Against Civilians is Devastating Communities and Preventing Access to Life-Saving Healthcare in*

Jonglei. Paris: 27 November. Available at: www.doctorswithoutborders.org/sites/usa/files/Jonglei%20Report%20Single%20Page.pdf Accessed December 8, 2015.
Mekki, Yousif Kuwa. 2001. "Things Would No Longer Be the Same." In *The Right to Be Nuba: The Story of a Sudanese People's Struggle for Survival*, edited by Suleiman Rahhal, pp. 25–35. Trenton, NJ: Red Sea Press.
NAFIR. 1997. *The History of the Battle of Tullishi Mountain*. NAFIR: The Newsletter of the Nuba Mountains, Sudan, Nuba Mountains Solidarity Abroad, 3.3, October.
Nyaba, Peter Adwok. 1997. *The Politics of Liberation in South Sudan: An Insider's View*. Kampala: Fountain Press.
Patey, Luke. 2014. *The New Kings of Crude: China, India, and the Global Struggle for Oil in Sudan and South Sudan*. London: Hurst.
Reeves, Eric. 2007. "How Many Dead in Darfur?" *The Guardian: Comment is Free*, November 20.
Roessler, Philip. 2014. *In the Shadow of the Coup d'Etat: The Strategic Logic of War and Peace in Africa*. College of William and Mary, book manuscript.
Rolandsen, Oystein H. 2005. *Guerrilla Government: Political Changes in the Southern Sudan during the 1990s*. Uppsala: Nordiska Afrikainstitutet.
Schomerus, Mareike and Tim Allen, 2010. *Southern Sudan at Odds with Itself: Dynamics of Conflict and Predicaments of Peace*. London, England: London School of Economics and Political Science, 2010.
Small Arms Survey. 2006–2007. *Anatomy of Civilian Disarmament in Jonglei State*. Small Arms Survey, Sudan Issue Brief No. 3.
Tarrow, Sidney. 2007. "Inside Insurgencies: Politics and Violence in an Age of Civil War." *Perspectives on Politics* 5: 3, 587–699.
Thomas, Edward. 2015. South Sudan: A Slow Liberation. London: Zed.
Tubiana, Jérôme. 2011. *Renouncing the Rebels: Local and Regional Dimensions of Chad-Sudan Rapprochement*. Small Arms Survey, HSBA Working Paper 25.

Bosnia-Herzegovina

Endings real and imagined

Bridget Conley-Zilkic

INTRODUCTION

On November 26, 2005, a flashy-golden statue of Bruce Lee striking a defensive posture was installed in the Bosnian city of Mostar.[1] Vesilin Gatalo of the Mostar Urban Movement, who spearheaded the effort, explained why a man known for his fictional exploits was an appropriate subject for tribute in post-war Bosnia. The monument, Gatalo stated, was dedicated to the idea "that justice, knowledge, honesty, good intentions can fight against corruption, evil, ignorance. . . ." He continued:

> He is a hero from childhood of every one of us. Nobody will ask what kind of activities his people made during Second World War, First World War, in Turkish times [. . .] it makes him an ideal hero.
>
> (Siegle 2005)

Reflecting disillusionment with the real-life leaders that the post-war environment offered, the Mostar Urban Movement wisely invested in a fictional embodiment of the ideals that inspired them. They understood a simple fact of the post-war landscape: if you want a story of archetypal heroes, stick to fiction. It is an insight overlooked in the extraction of atrocity prevention and response lessons from Bosnia.

In her influential book that helped inform the atrocities prevention and response agenda, Samantha Power described the two-week NATO bombing campaign in August–September 1995 thus: "backed by a newly credible threat of military force, the United States was easily able to convince the Serbs to stop shelling civilians" (Power 2001, p. 440). All that was needed, so the story went, was a show of international force to push petty Balkan war criminals to stop killing civilians and

[1] The statue was crafted by Croatian sculptor Ivan Fijolić. Vandalized in 2005, it was taken down shortly after its unveiling. It was remounted in the city park in 2013.

make concessions at the peace table. Closer analysis of endings in Bosnia, however, reveals that despite important variations in the patterns of atrocities, the first year of the war, 1992, witnessed the overwhelming concentration of killing and ethnic cleansing of civilians (UNHCR 1992). A second spike of lethal violence occurred when Srebrenica fell to the Bosnian Serbs in 1995. Neither of these spikes of violence concluded because of international military action. Further, while the NATO bombing was significant, its impact on the perpetration of atrocities and armed conflict can only be assessed in relation to a broader array of factors: shifts in regional alliances; the ground war; the abandonment of both the maximalist ethno-national and an integrated, multiethnic visions of the state; and – the most important international contribution – a change in approach to diplomacy.

This chapter explores four primary questions with regard to ending mass atrocities during the 1992–1995 war in Bosnia-Herzegovina: first, *how did atrocities end?* The first wave of violence began to decline in summer 1992, when the Bosnian Serbs nearly completed their plan of creating a contiguous, ethnically homogenized Serb Republic (Republika Srpska). I also point to some areas of variation from this pattern: the fate of camp detainees, human rights abuses against Bosnian Serbs, the outbreak of conflict between the Bosnian government and Bosnian Croat forces, the siege of Sarajevo, and systematic killing following the fall of the UN "safe haven" of Srebrenica in 1995, which I contrast with the aftermath of the Bosnian Serb takeover of a second "safe haven," Žepa. As part of demonstrating *how* atrocities end, I also discuss a second question: *why* they ended. Third, I address the closely related but separate question of *how the war ended.*

The fourth question concerns *why the complexity of endings was diminished in anti-atrocities stocktaking from the 1990s Yugoslav experience.* We will address this question at the beginning and the end of this chapter, drawing out how the story of endings in Bosnia has been transformed into a simple narrative of using international military power for a humanitarian good. As such, it is less a tale of Bosnia and more concerned with self-imagination of the international community, led by the United States

PART ONE: CONTEXTUALIZING SOUTH SLAV ENDINGS

Bosnia has a special place in the development of an anti-atrocities imagination, which can only be understood in relation to the expectations and then disappointments of the post–Cold War dispensation. It is difficult now, more than two decades deep in the quandaries that have emerged since, to recall the hubris of the time. Francis Fukuymama's influential thesis of the "end of history" perhaps captures it best:

> The century that began full of self-confidence in the ultimate triumph of Western liberal democracy seems at its close to be returning full circle to where it started:

> not to an "end of ideology" or a convergence between capitalism and socialism, as earlier predicted, but to an unabashed victory of economic and political liberalism.
>
> (Fukuyama 1989, p. 3)

This victory was accompanied by the "dawn of Europe" as new political and economic unity seemed to unite the continent and the "new world order" to describe the ascendancy of the United States internationally. It included principles of human rights, rule of law, democratic governance, and economic liberalism – each assumed to be mutually reinforcing. And yet, when met with the resurgence of violent European nationalism, these hopes were devastated. In Bosnia, tens of thousands were killed *despite* a peacekeeping force, the United Nations Protection Force (UNPROFOR); 24-hour media coverage; a massive aid operation run by the UN High Commissioner for Refugees (UNHCR) involving a host of international humanitarian aid organizations; human rights investigations; and high-level mediation efforts. The Bosnian war burst on the scene in all its brutality and the failures of the new international system were exposed; they further collapsed in face of the 1994 Rwandan genocide. However, in Bosnia – unlike Rwanda, where there was no redemption for the international community – international conscience seemed to awaken in 1995 with the deployment of NATO airpower and a shift in diplomatic strategy. The change in policy toward Bosnia, spearheaded by the United States and epitomized in memory by the use of coercive force, seemed to confirm not only the moral value of the liberal state triumph but its efficacy and potency as well. Thereafter, wholesale disappointment could be replaced with newly energized initiative to convert ideals into policies.[2] Bosnia's place was to serve as the signature lesson in the virtues of confrontation, especially through international coercive military action.

However, if we look across twentieth-century South Slav (encompassing the area of the former Yugoslavia) periods of atrocities, the 1990s does not seem to herald an abrupt break with history, rather a life-saving, but more modest alteration to historical patterns. One clear, important difference is the scale of atrocities against civilians, which is undeniably reduced in 1990s from the hundreds of thousands killed during the two earlier periods: the Balkan Wars through the end of World War I (1912–1919) and World War II through 1948. The South Slav wars of the 1990s were not caught up in wider international conflicts as previously periods were. An international environment of peace, coupled with monitoring and condemnation of violence against civilians, no doubt contributed to the overall reduction in the number of civilians killed.

2 See, for instance, the International Commission on State Sovereignty and Intervention that noted, Somalia, Bosnia, Rwanda, and Kosovo occurred at a time "when there were heightened expectations for effective collective action following the end of the Cold War. All four of them [. . .] have had a profound effect on how the problem of intervention is viewed, analyzed and characterized" (ICISS 2001, p. 1).

TABLE 5.1: *South Slav periods of twentieth-century atrocities*

Period of atrocities	Description	Fatalities	Ending
1912–1919	Balkan Wars 1912, 1913 World War I (WWI) 1914–1919	Balkan Wars: est. Montenegro, 3076 (135) (military); Serbia 82,000–91,000 (Hall 2000, p. 135); "uncounted numbers of civilians perished or fled" (Hall 2000, p. 138). "From first to last, in both wars, the fighting was desperate as though extermination were the end sought"(Carnegie Commission to Inquire into the Causes and Conduct of the Balkan Wars 1993, p. 265). Entire period (1912–1918): 1 million total; 300,000 (Biondich 2011, p. 87)–500,000 (Wachtel 2008, p. 84) civilians in Serbia. Estimate of 1 million civilians with Serbia and Montenegro bearing the brunt (Pawlowtich 1999, p257).	Balkan Wars: Ottoman Empire retreats from Balkans; Serbia and Greece defeat Bulgaria. WWI: Austro-Hungarian Empire defeated; coalition of local actors forms Yugoslav Kingdom of Serbs, Slovenes, and Croats; international recognition at the 1919 Paris Peace Conference.
1941–1948	World War II 1941–1945	Est. total of 1,027,000 killed, of which an estimated 501,000 were "victims." (Žerjavić 1992).	Germany, Italy, Croatian Ustashe regime, and associated local groups fought against Chetnik (Serb royalist forces), and Communist partisans. Partisans resist international forces, which are defeated elsewhere in Europe and retreat, and defeat local forces.
	Post-war violence 1945–1948	100,000–140,000 fatalities within populations associated with Croatian and Slovene fascist forces (Mozjes 2011, pp. 126–127), and from the ethnic German (Mozjes 2011, p. 114). and Hungarian communities (Levene 2013, p. 374).	Communists consolidate their government, and, following the split with Stalin in 1948, their position between the Soviet bloc and West.

(*continued*)

Table 5.1: (*continued*)

Period of atrocities	Description	Fatalities	Ending
1991–2001	Dissolution of former Yugoslavia	Slovenia, 1991: 12 civilians (Government of the Republic of Slovenia, Public Relations and Media Office. 2001).	Slovenia defeats Yugoslav National Army.
		Croatia, 1991, 1995: total of 10,000–15,000 killed (Mozjes 2011, p. 162) including both civilians and combatants.	Croatian army defeats Croatian Serb separatists.
		Bosnia 1992–1995: 39,684 civilians killed (Research and Documentation Center Sarajevo, 2008).	Ethnic partition. Internationally negotiated peace agreement.
		Kosovo and Serbia, 1998–1999: est. 13,000 (Brunborg 2002). civilians, mostly ethnic Albanian, including 500 Serbian civilians (Human Rights Watch 2000).	NATO military defeat of Serbia, internationally imposed peace terms.
		Macedonia, 2001: est. 106–117 (Schneider 2013, p. 639). civilians.	Internationally mediated agreement between Macedonian populations.

However, some of the overall patterns are more resilient. Across periods, the nature of the violence follows a hauntingly similar logic. The following description from a 1913 report of the Carnegie Balkan Commission could apply to any period of South Slav atrocities from the twentieth century:

> Houses and whole villages reduced to ashes, unarmed and innocent populations massacred en masse, incredible acts of violence, pillage and brutality of every kind ... Since the population of the countries about to be occupied knew, by tradition, instinct and experience, what they had to expect from the armies of the enemy and from neighboring countries to which these armies belonged, they did not await their arrival, but fled ... .
>
> (Carnegie Endowment for International Peace 1993, p. 151)

While not labeled "ethnic cleansing" until the 1990s, the pattern of South Slav violence has long adhered to the contemporary understanding of the term:

> the enactment of an explicit policy of elimination or removal by one group against another that is defined in religious, ethnic, national, or racial terms and is

> organized in relation to an identified geographic area by military or socio-political means ranging from discrimination to extermination.
>
> (Hagan and Haugh 2011, p. 201)

Similarities in the patterns of ethnic cleansing over South Slav history serve as grist for the view that bone-chilling violence against neighbors of different ethnic backgrounds is inherent in ethnic difference,[3] particularly its "Balkan" manifestation. This view was influentially propagated by Robert Kaplan (1993), as well as some international leaders, and logically led to the argument that endings could only be produced through partition (Kaufman 1998). It is a gross simplification. Among the contradictions of the South Slav region is that its periods of violence intermingle with peaceful coexistence and solidarity across communities. There has been enough South Slav unity, *Yugoslavism*, that it has twice in the past century contributed to ending violence. Even when ethno-nationalism wins, as occurred in the 1990s, ethnicity only describes the logic behind targeting of violence, but it cannot account for how, why, or when it ends.

Regardless of whether the end result is *Yugoslavism* or ethno-nationalism, the basic "recipe" for endings remains stable: consolidation of control over territory, an animating idea of the state that serves to forge local alliances, and international acceptance of the endgame. South Slav history aligns with the general insight that atrocities tend to occur during armed conflict. These wars are fought to create territorial states and end when power politics, including fighting, creates such a state or states. The atrocities occur during war and, hence, end when one side is victorious. What complicates these wars is that they involve a minimum of three local forces and at least one armed force representing a global power, be it Ottoman, Hapsburg, Axis, or, a coalition like NATO. Atrocities end as the triumphant military power consolidates its regime. Victory cannot just be a tactical battlefield success but requires a political vision or program that enjoys sufficient credibility among the political class that it can forge a coalition. Further, the vision must be aligned with regional, international, or imperial power.

Each period ends with the creation of a new state or states: the 1919 Yugoslav kingdom of Serbs, Slovenes, and Croats, 1945 Socialist Federal Republic of Yugoslavia, and the host of post-Yugoslav nation-states after 1990. Not only is a new state (or states) created, but the old one is destroyed – a fact that has implications for both the nature of the violence and, as noted earlier, the political vision animating the new state. Tone Bringa's insight on the 1990s applies to all three periods: "For the new social and political order to be implemented, Yugoslavism

3 The groups are all South Slav in terms of ethnicity; the main identity-driven difference between them is religion: Serbs are Orthodox, Croats Catholic, and Bosniaks Muslim. Muslims increasingly use the nonreligious self-identifier "Bosniak" as a parallel to Serb and Croat.

not only had to be destroyed as a state structure, buts its very founding ideas had to be purged" (Bringa 2003, p. 148).

At first glance, the last century appears as a slow, painful arrival at ethnically defined nation-states, and, while significant minority populations exist in Croatia, Serbia, and Montenegro, they cannot challenge the idea of the ethno-national state. Today, the lone post-Yugoslav state not exclusively defined by ethnic majority[4] at the federal level is Bosnia. Held together with a weak central government, it is nonetheless an ethnically partitioned state. Real power is exercised at the substate "entity" level: the Federation of Bosnia and Herzegovina (further split into areas of Bosniak and Croat political dominance) and the Serb Republic. Nonetheless, neither in Bosnia nor in the wider region was ethno-nationalism a predetermined outcome.

The South Slav political imagination plays tug of war between and within the ideas of *Yugoslavism* and nationalism. They are not inherently opposites. *Yugoslavism*, for instance, has meant many things over the past century: a single linguistic and ethnic community (Rusinov 2003, pp. 25–26); a vehicle by which dispersed ethnic communities could share a single state; a bulwark against stronger neighbors seeking to carve out new zones of influence; or a preferable compromise to the threat of domination by any single regional power. At no point were the disparities between these ideas completely overcome; the idea of a Yugoslav state triumphed when multiple visions converged.

In 1919, across the region, people were identified as peasants, as members of a clan or locality, as religious communities, by nationalities, or by linguistic community, and political ideology; but they shared a rejection of subjugation to encroaching foreign powers (Macmillan 2003, p. 120). A hastily formed coalition of Balkan leaders journeyed to the Paris Peace Conference as a single delegation to plead their case (Macmillan 2003, p. 115). The resulting state was unstable – as witnessed in post-war assassinations and the complete collapse when Germany invaded in 1941 – nonetheless, the new coalition staved off further widespread violence until 1941.

The triumph of communist Yugoslavia in 1945 was made possible by three factors: first, banned and isolated throughout much of the interwar period, the Communists were free from compromising entanglements that discredited the stronger prewar political parties (Wright 1985, p. 37). Second, their center of gravity was local. The Croatian fascist regime, led by the ultranationalist Ustasha, relied on

4 The idea of the state of Bonsia-Herzegovina is, as stated in the constitution, founded on equality of multiple ethnic groups: Bosniacs, Croats, and Serbs are defined as constituent peoples, along with "others" and "citizens" of the Federation of Bosnia and Herzegovina (Constitution of the Federation of Bosnia and Herzegovina 1994, Annex 4). The presidency is a three-member body and can be occupied only by a Bosniac, Croat, and Serb. In 2009, the European Court of Human Rights judged that this provision violates the European human rights law by discriminating against other members of the population (ECHR 2009).

German power to retain its authority. The partisans built a pan-ethnic vision that attracted all ethnic groups, granting them greater access to local resources, spread across a wider geography than other local groups (Hoare 1996). Third, and central to our question of ending atrocities, the use of widespread atrocities and tit-for-tat assaults against unarmed groups discredited all other competing local groups (Redžić 2005, p. 206). Atrocities were inherent in the political vision articulated by both Axis-aligned and Chetnik groups: total eradication of the Balkan Jews; the intensely targeted violence against non-Croats particularly in heterogeneous areas[5]; a return to the Serbian king and greater Serbian state; even "self-protection" that spurred creation of, for example, a Bosniak Nazi unit. While exceptionally lethal, the political visions behind Nazism, exclusionary Croatian nationalism, or Serb royalism were rejected by the Yugoslav population who formed an antifascist alliance. This is not to say that the partisans were innocent – they committed systematic atrocities following the end of World War II – but they won the battle of ideas and were thereby able to create the strongest coalition.

By the 1990s, there were ever fewer international and Balkan supports to bolster the idea of Yugoslavia. The economic and political structures of communism were considered moribund. The iconic World War II hero synonymous with Yugoslavia, Josip Broz "Tito," died in 1980; the party had proven unable to rise to the post–Cold War political-economic challenges; and by 1991, the army, the last unifying Yugoslav institution to collapse, put itself at service of Serbian nationalist leaders. Nonetheless, the dissolution of Yugoslavia need not have been as violent as it was. Maximalist, mutually exclusive nationalist plans ensured a return of the Yugoslav pattern of atrocities – positing that ethnic demographics, not the political borders of the republics, should define the post-Yugoslav states. The Serbian maximalist national plans advanced first and furthest, but as long as the question of creating ethnically defined states remained open, the vision fueled contestation amongst all players. After Serbian elements pursued this path in Croatia and Bosnia, Croatia did the same inside Bosnia, and Kosovar Albanians were left to wonder why they should settle for anything less when their long-standing peaceful resistance seeking political accommodation failed.

Bosnia, whose population was the most heterogeneous of the Yugoslav states, with sizeable Bosniak, Serbian, and Croat populations, suffered the highest levels of violence. Opposed to the ethno-nationalism maximalist visions that sought to destroy Bosnia entirely or fundamentally reorder its borders, the majority of Bosniaks along with some Bosnian Serbs, Croats, and others sought to face the challenges of Yugoslav dissolution by forming a government around the idea of a unified, multiethnic state. That they attempted to do this through a coalition of

[5] Biondich (2011, pp. 136–137). Ustashe forces deployed killing as the tool for demographic change at higher rates in more heterogeneous areas. Other measures, forced displacement, and conversion were the preferred tools in areas where Serbs lived in greater numbers. A similar pattern was repeated in Bosnia in 1992–1995.

nationalist political parties rather than multiethnic parties[6] meant that the state-level vision was at odds with the principles of political organization. This condition made the process of coalition building and political accommodation much slower than it might have otherwise been and, given the pace of independence and the Bosnian Serb preparations for war, time was crucially lacking in 1991.

As we will see, both the maximalist nationalist and multiethnic visions were curtailed to forge the necessary coalition to end wars and atrocities in Bosnia and Croatia. The end marked the triumph of a coalition of nationalists who agreed to recognize each other within existing political borders and to sideline those clinging to maximalist visions. This logic[7] held for Kosovo as well, where the ending followed NATO intervention to punish the Serbs into recognizing Albanian demands, and subsequent displacement of roughly half the area's Serb minority, which dropped from just under 200,000 people before the war to around 100,000 afterward, largely concentrated in the north.

Finally, international powers have played the role of kingmaker at each phase of atrocities (Woodward 2013). The South Slav region may reside at the margins of European interest, but Europe and the broader international community are often decisive for its political outcomes. Situated in what Mark Levene calls Europe's "rimlands," the wider Balkan area is situated on a geopolitical fault line[8] (Levene 2013, p. 7), and has been subject to waves of imperial, neo-imperial, and nation-state building violence invariably accompanied by mass atrocities. Given this liminal status, South Slav periods of violent instability and atrocities are intimately tied to international shifts, which have, at times, determined not only conditions for violence but also discrete actions. For example, the communist reprisal atrocities as World War II ended were catalyzed by local actors' uncertainty whether the West would allow a communist regime to establish itself in Yugoslavia. The fascist forces fought for another day and the partisans used widespread killing to ensure that those competitors were completely eliminated before the decision-making capacity shifted to international actors (Tomasevich 2001, p. 262). Exposure to outside forces further structures the region's economics: following World War II, Yugoslavia's communist regime entered what Susan Woodward has described as a "Faustian bargain" (Woodward 1995, pp. 222–259), gaining access to international financial

6 There were two non-nationalist political parties that participated in the 1991 elections. However, their connections to the then-discredited Communist Party hampered their ability to garnish votes in an era where nationalist parties, who did not pull votes from each other, cooperated to dominate the elections (see Donia 2006, pp. 254–262).

7 Macedonia was the lone exception to this logic, which faced an armed uprising by its Albanian minority in 2001 that was ended through EU-led mediation process that recognized the multiethnic character of the state. See Ilievski and Taleski (2009), who nonetheless remain wary of the limitations EU mediation given changes in enlargement policies.

8 Levene (2013) similarly describes two other "rimlands:" the areas that stretch along the Caucasus–Black Sea–eastern Anatolia, and from the Baltics, southward, including Belorussia, Ukraine, Poland, Silesia, and the Carpathian ranges.

institutions as a trade-off for providing a militarized bulwark against Soviet expansion in southern Europe. As the political winds changed in the 1980s, Yugoslavia was unable to survive the new international terms for financial support.

International forces sometimes have the perverse effect of accelerating atrocities, as noted earlier, but at other times, they have played a stabilizing role. The 1919 Paris Peace Treaty recognized many of the South Slav concerns about their borders, of which seven were disputed when the negotiations began. During World War II, the ultimate defeat of Axis powers in Russia and the West, plus the recognition of communist Yugoslav state, and later support for Tito when he broke with Stalin were crucial to stabilizing the state. So it was in the 1990s: uncertainty and lack of consensus over what Europe would accept from the new post-Yugoslav states and the internationally imposed arms embargo that crucially handicapped the Bosnian government were important factors that fueled mass atrocities. Ending political uncertainty and endorsing (where previously internationals had been suppressing) military victories in Croatia and Kosovo, and a shift in momentum in Bosnia, ultimately contributed to ending the wars during which atrocities occurred. Intensively internationalized liberal peace building has of yet proven incapable of undoing the nationalist political vision endorsed at the end of violence.

The consistently important factors in ending Balkan periods of atrocities did not change with the post–Cold War dispensation: military victories, a political vision that enabled a regional coalition of actors, and international blessing for the outcome remained the salient forces. Too often, the 1995 NATO bombing campaign is extracted from this context and fashioned into an example of the efficacy of the most potent response mechanism in an anti-atrocities toolbox. This misrecognition of the role played by coercive international force has simplified and, therefore, distorted understanding of the dynamics of atrocity endings in Bosnia. Blocked from view are both the complex tale of endings, which, as we will see later, does not allow for heroes of universal values, and confuses assessment of how Bosnian endings provide lessons for other cases (Conley-Zilkic and de Waal 2014; Conley-Zilkic 2015).

PART TWO: HOW, WHERE, AND WHEN ATROCITIES ENDED IN BOSNIA-HERZEGOVINA

Compared to other periods of South Slav atrocities and many instances of mass violence, remarkably detailed data exist for Bosnia.[9] According to the Research

[9] Yugoslavia carried out a census in 1991, providing a credible baseline from which to measure change. The conduct of the war was fairly well documented as well, particularly killing and displacement, although these figures must be treated as minimal estimates. Finally, the International Criminal Tribunal for the Yugoslavia, created through a UN resolution in 1993, has done an exceptional job gathering and reviewing evidence.

TABLE 5.2: *Fatalities of the 1992–1995 War in Bosnia-Herzegovina by ethnicity*

	Bosniak	Serb	Croat	Other	Total
Civilians	30,070	4,075	2,163	376	36,684
Soldiers	30,966	20,830	5,625	102	57,523

Source: Research and Documentation Center Sarajevo 2008

TABLE 5.3: *Fatalities of the 1992–1995 War in Bosnia-Herzegovina by year*[10]

	1992	1993	1994	1995
Civilian	21,813	4,823	1,530	9,914
Soldier	23,297	14,306	8,070	9,424

Source: Research and Documentation Center Sarajevo 2008

and Documentation Center of Sarajevo (Research and Dcoumentation Center Sarajevo 2007), a minimum total of 39,684 civilians and 57,523 soldiers were killed during the 1992–1995 war.[11] These numbers represent people killed during the war, not excess mortality, and do not capture the wider range of suffering inflicted on civilian populations: displacement, torture, wounding, sexual violence, for instance, or the widespread confiscation of property that impoverished large portions of the population.

Note that Bosniak civilians represent the overwhelming number of civilian victims and the most lethal year is 1992. Looking more closely at 1992 (Table 5.4), the weight of killing is further concentrated between April and August of 1992. The UNHCR documented over 1.8 million people displaced by the war by July 1992, out of a total of 2.2 million eventually displaced throughout the war. Beginning in fall 1992, violence largely shifted from attacks against civilians within Serb-held territory to military opposition across frontlines that at times also targeted civilians (Costalli and Moro 2012, p. 813). It was difficult to recognize this shift during the conflict, as the violence that continued until 1995 appeared the same – changes in scale and location

[10] RDC includes figures, which are numbers in the hundreds for 1991 (53 civilians and 459 soldiers) and 1996 (16 total) as well, beyond the scope of the war.

[11] The statistics developed by the Research and Documentation Center of Sarajevo (2007) are derived from data of individual documented deaths and arrived at by cross-checking multiple sources, including family and eyewitness testimony, and diverse other databases, international and national. It is the best-documented minimal number of murders from the war. Demographers from the International Criminal Tribunal for the former Yugoslavia have suggested a slight increase of the number of civilians killed, up to around 40,000.

TABLE 5.4: *Fatalities in the War in Bosnia-Herzegovina in 1992*

	Jan.	Feb.	Mar.	Apr.	May	Jun.	Jul.	Aug.	Sep.	Oct.	Nov.	Dec.	Unknown
Civilians	13	26	50	1,192	4,718	6,125	3,625	1,998	1,142	723	520	449	1,232
Soldiers	52	40	79	930	3,015	4,421	3,108	3,142	2,588	2,083	1,623	1,921	295

Source: Research and Documentation Center Sarajevo 2008

paled next to the seeming unending pain inflicted on civilians. The Human Rights Watch World Report (1994), for instance, stated: "The human rights situation in Bosnia continued to worsen throughout 1993." This is incomplete: murder and other acts of ethnic cleansing decreased, yet the stranglehold of siege and war tightened, deepening the pain of *living* conditions – and with no solution in sight.

Spring and summer 1992 were seasons of intensive atrocity as the Bosnian Serb Army (VRS: *Vojska Republika Srpska*) ethnically cleansed Bosniak and Croat populations from areas claimed for "Republika Srpska." Town after town in eastern and northern Bosnia was violently taken over by the Bosnian Serbs, including, to name only some of the deadliest locations, Kalinovik, Foca, Bratunac, Vlasenica, Rogatica, Visegrad, Zvornik, Trnovo, and Prijedor (Costalli and Moro 2012, p. 810). While there were important variations in location, victim, perpetrator, timing, and duration of atrocities – some of which are presented later – this initial wave of violence represents the dominant pattern of killing civilians during the conflict.

Mass atrocities declined starting in fall 1992 for several reasons: first, many of the Bosnian Serbs' goals were met (Melander 2007, p. 49). The Bosnian Serb nationalists shifted their goal from remaining in Yugoslavia to creating a homogenous republic within Bosnia's borders by December 1991 (Donia 2006, p. 269); by fall 1992 they had nearly achieved this. The war continued thereafter because the Bosnian Serbs refused to compromise on the maximalist national plans while they were winning the ground war. While various peace plans were tabled, none could overcome the Bosnian Serbs' reluctance to give up territory they had military conquered and the Bosnian government's insistence that the gains of mass atrocities should not be legitimized. Another factor was sustained armed resistance from the fledgling Bosnian government army (ARBiH: *Armija Republike Bosne i Hercegovine*) and the Croatian Defense Council (HVO: *Hrvatsko vijeće obrane*). While the ARBiH had difficulty advancing their lines, they and the HVO managed to halt the VRS in, for instance, Sarajevo, Tuzla, Zenica, Bihać, Konjic, Mostar, Žepa, Goražde, and Srebrenica. Third, the VRS soon ran into their internal limitations, including low morale and commitment amongst their soldiers, manifested in high desertion rates and manpower shortages (Cigar 1996). Further, relations were strained between Bosnian Serb civilian and military leaders, notably between Bosnian Serb President Radovan Karadžić and General Ratko Mladić, commanding officer of the VRS (CIA 2002, p. 32). Finally, the Bosnian Serbs relied on Yugoslavia for strategy, logistics, personnel, training, armaments, and financial support, a fact that became more important near the ending of the war (Cigar 1996, pp. 5–8). When the VRS did not take major urban areas immediately, they lacked the capacity to fight for them. They were later also affected by international scrutiny when they tried to advance their lines further, for instance, in Srebrenica in April 1993. Instead, the Bosnian Serbs opted for siege warfare, which was extremely destructive, but not accompanied by the high level of killing as when civilians were directly in their control.[12]

The speed of the initial VRS offensive was made possible because they planned for war earlier than others and received aid from Serb nationalist-dominated Yugoslav forces (*Prosecutor v. Krajišnik* 2006, paragraphs 51–61).[13] The 1990 Bosnian elections were won by three nationalist political parties: the SDS representing the Bosnian Serbs under Radovan Karadžić, the SDA for the Bosniaks under Alija Izetbegović, and the HDZ for the Bosnian Croats under Stjepan Kljuić. Throughout 1991, the SDS worked to unify and connect areas where they had won elections, created parallel state institutions, like the Assembly of the Serbian People of Bosnia-Herzegovina (Bosnian-Serb Assembly), and issued secret orders instructing SDS municipal leaders to take over the municipality and establish a crisis staff either overtly where Serbs formed a majority or covertly where they formed a minority.[14]

Self-arming campaigns began quietly amongst all three groups (Serbs, Bosniaks, and Croats) in 1991, picking up pace in 1992. However, the Bosnian Serbs were more successful in arming themselves for two reasons. First, they were more united in the goal of pursuing an armed resolution of political differences than were the Bosniaks or Croats. But more importantly, they benefitted from resources provided by the Yugoslav National Army (JNA) and Interior Ministry, under the control of Serbian nationalists, headed by Slobodan Milošević.[15] Upon negotiated stalemate to the war in Croatia on November 23, 1991, the JNA retreated to Bosnia. Milošević orchestrated the withdrawal of Serbian and Montenegrin soldiers from the force, replacing them with soldiers born in Bosnia (Silber and Little 1997, p. 218). This meant that when war began in Bosnia, the JNA personnel, command structure, and, most importantly, heavy weaponry formed a readymade force at the disposal of

12 A no-fly zone was established for Bosnia in April 1993 and patrolled by NATO airplanes (Cigar 1996, p. 8). It likely saved many lives; however, it does not help us understand the decline at the end of summer 1992.

13 For an overview of secret communications the tribunal uncovered demonstrating planning between Serbia and the Bosnians Serbs throughout 1991, see *Prosecutor v. Momčilo Krajišnik*, paragraphs 51–61.

14 On December 19 or 20, 1991, the SDS leadership circulated a memo to municipal leaders instructing them to undertake actions to “enhance the preparedness of the Serbian people and its readiness to defend its interests” (*Prosecutor v. Momčilo Krajišnik*, paragraphs 86–99).

15 Over the period, Milošević had several titles: president of Serbia from 1989 to 1997, president of the Federal Republic of Yugoslavia from 1997 to 2000, and leader of the Socialist Party of Serbia.

the Bosnian Serbs, named the Bosnian Serb Army (VRS) on May 12, 1992 (Hoare 2004, p. 34; Nation 2003, p. 157). The Bosnian referendum on independence (February 29 and March 1, 1992) – boycotted by the Bosnian Serbs – passed with a resounding support from the Bosniak and Bosnian Croat population. The war began within weeks thereafter, with a fundamental weaponry disadvantage for the Bosnian government army (ARBiH) that, with an international arms embargo placed on the region, could not be overcome.

On May 12, 1992, as violence escalated, Bosnian Serb leader Radovan Karadžić announced six strategic goals that emphasized separation of Serbs from other nationalities and outlined the geographic claims of their "Serb Republic," including the division of Sarajevo. By the end of August 1992, Bosnian Serb forces controlled over 70% of Bosnian territory, from which the non-Serb populations were displaced. The completion of this campaign marked the end of massive waves of ethnic cleansing that fundamentally altered Bosnian demographics.

By no means does this mark the end of atrocities; there remained significant variation in endings, which we briefly explore.

SNAPSHOTS OF VARIATION

Below I introduce several examples to demonstrate how, where and why violence against civilians continued thereafter 1992; this is not an exhaustive review of violence, merely illustrative. We begin with Prijedor, which follows the dominant pattern introduced above, but where endings were delayed significantly for those who were interred in camps–as was the case for camp internees across areas claimed by the Bosnian Serbs. Following is the case of Konjic, an area that experienced fighting in 1992, but where the VRS was pushed back and Bosnian Serb civilians victimized, and where violence spiked again in 1993 when a new front with Croatian forces opened. Next are three profiles of safe havens: Srebrenica, Žepa and Gorazde. These towns were rimmed by Bosnian Serb forces and vulnerable to attack throughout the war, and each experienced a distinct pattern of endings.

Prijedor

The end of atrocities in Prijedor municipality[16] follows the dominant pattern described earlier, but also exemplifies the longer period of atrocities for people detained in camps. In 1991, its population was composed of 49,351 Bosniaks, 47,581 Serbs, 6,316 Croats, and 6,459 Yugoslavs, and 2,836 people of other or unknown ethnicity (*Prosecutor v. Krajišnik* 2006, paragraph 469). By the end of August 1992, over 30,000 of the Prijedor area's total Bosniak and Croat population had fled

[16] These statistics include the town of Prijedor and the surrounding areas.

(*Prosecutor v. Krajišnik* 2006, paragraph 499). And by 1993, as noted in a Bosnian Serb Interior Ministry document, a total of 42,000 Bosniaks and 2,000 Croats had fled.[17] Demography reports generated for the International Criminal Tribunal for the former Yugoslavia by Ewa Tabeau found that an estimated 2,190 persons from Prijedor were killed or went missing, 95% of whom were Bosniaks (Tabeau 2009a, p. 167), mostly men, with specific targeting of political, social and economic leaders (pp. 173–178). By 1997, the Bosniak population of Prijedor dropped from 42% of the prewar population to 1% of the post-war population (Tabeau 2009a, p. 727).

This was achieved with overwhelming force. On April 30, 1992, the SDS crisis group officially took control of Prijedor – deploying soldiers and police to checkpoints and occupying the city's most important structures. Non-Serbs were fired from their jobs, their children were barred from schools, and their movement was severely restricted. In May, Prijedor's old town, largely inhabited by Bosniaks, was leveled, and its population forced to flee. In Prijedor and neighboring villages, men were ordered to surrender any weapons. Not all Bosniaks complied and there were skirmishes in, for example, the villages of Hambarine and Kozarac, between lightly armed Bosniak and Serb farmers. On May 22, the Bosnian Serbs demonstrated their military advantage, shelling the villages and sending in infantry. Both towns surrendered, and Bosniaks who remained suffered additional waves of violence between June and July.

Many men from these two towns, along with others deemed of special interest, were sent to the notorious Bosnian Serb-run detention camp, Omarska. Omarksa was one of five long-term detention centers of a total fifty-eight detainment camps in the area (*Prosecutor v. Krajišnik* 2006, paragraph 483). Deprivation was the norm across the camps, but some, like Omarska and Kereterm, were sites of intense brutality. Largely reserved for men, although some women were imprisoned there, detainees suffered starvation, beatings, psychological abuse, sexual assault, rape, torture, and murder (*Prosecutor v. Krajišnik* 2006, paragraph 499). The perpetrators included guards, soldiers, and local Serbs, who often pursued personal agendas in joining the brutality.

In August, international journalists – spurred by unbelievable reports of violence from displaced persons – pressured Karadžić into allowing access to the camps. In this case, media exposure had an impact in ending the brutalities of the worst camps. According to a statement by Milomor Stakić, the local SDS president, detainees were released for two reasons: "pressure from international public opinion and official policy and the steep cost of maintaining the prisons" (*Prosecutor v. Krajišnik* 2006, paragraph 496). On August 6, the process of closing Omarska began, with buses herding men to other camps, Trnopolje and Manjača. Trnopolje remained open until November 1992. Manjača was closed between

[17] *Prosecutor v. Krajišnik*, paragraph 497.

December 14 and 19, 1992 (Helsinki Watch 1993, p. 133). Most men were traded in prisoner exchanges with the ARBiH, often supervised by the International Committee of the Red Cross. Thus was ethnic cleansing aided by international humanitarian efforts to help end detention. The irony was not lost on detainees. Rezak Hukanović, held in Omarska and Manjača, described offers of asylum in Germany, Holland, the USA, New Zealand, and elsewhere: "you offer us half the world, but all we want is our Bosnia" (Hukanović 1996, p. 132). Hukanović was transferred from Omarska to Manjača, and released in a prisoner exchange on November 14, 1992. Some detainees were kept longer; Emir Beganović, for instance, was transferred from Omarksa to Manjača, and to Batković camp near Bijeljina in mid-December 1992, not released until March 4, 1993 (*Prosecutor v. Dusko Tadic* 1996, p. 1434). In Prijedor and across Bosnia, for those who suffered severe abuses during extended detention, violence continued well beyond the summer of 1992.

Konjić

The town of Konjić is situated on the strategic road that leads south out of Sarajevo, chasing the Neretva River on its way to Mostar, and then the Adriatic coast. Its path weaves through tunnels, over mountains, and across river bends. The scenic road is also of enormous strategic value: along its path in Konjić, for instance, was a former-JNA barracks, munitions factory and communications center (ICTY, Čelebići, paragraph 123, p. 49). The Neretva was designated by Bosnian Serbs as their southwestern border, and they launched an offensive to achieve this aim in 1992. However, unlike the Prijedor area, violence in 1992 took another path, and, in 1993, was followed by new fighting between ARBiH and Bosnian Croat forces (HVO)[18] and new waves of atrocities.

The prewar population of Konjić was 50% Bosniak, 26% Croat, and 15% Serb. VRS forces attacked on April 20, 1992, surrounding the town. Many in the Serbian and Croatian communities escaped, yet the population swelled as Bosniaks displaced from nearby Serb-held territories sought shelter there. Shelling began on May 4 and continued sporadically throughout the war. However, on May 25–26, ARBiH forces in coordination with the HVO mounted a successful

[18] Bosnian Croat political and military leadership was split between moderates, who saw their future within Bosnia, and hard-liners, who affiliated themselves with the maximalist nationalism emanating from Croatia, the most extreme of which envisioned completely dividing Bosnia between Croatia and Serbia; see Banac (2009, p. 466), and Silber and Little (1995, p. 306) for a 1991 meeting between Milošević and Tudjman to this effect; and regarding a May 1992 meeting between Bosnian Serb leader Radovan Karadžić and Bosnian Croat leader Mate Boban in Graz (*Prosecutor v. Prlić et al.*, paragraph 439). Boban declared an independent state of Herceg-Bosna in July 1992, even though large-scale violence did not break out until April 1993.

counteroffensive, ending the blockade and clearing the road. At this point, tensions emerged with the HVO refusing to further advance with the ARBiH.

In the course of the operation, ARBiH and HVO forces captured several Serbian villages. An estimated 700 Bosnian Serb civilians, mostly men but including women, were arrested and sent to Čelebići camp (Dzidic 2014). There, civilians suffered conditions that paralleled those in Bosnian Serb-run camps. Also like those detainees, the experience of violence extended beyond the heights of summer 1992; the last Čelebići detainees were released on December 9, 1992, when the Bosnian government closed the camp. Among those detained was Grozdana Ćećez,[19] who was arrested on May 27, 1992 ostensibly for interrogation concerning her husband's whereabouts. Hazim Delić, deputy commander of the camp, raped her the day she arrived, and over the course of her detention, she would be raped seven times by other men. She stated, "[P]sychologically and physically I was completely worn out. They kill you psychologically" (ICTY 1997, p. 551). She was released August 31,1992, and returned to Donje Selo for a brief period before leaving the area entirely.

Ćećez was wise to depart, because Donje Selo became the location of fierce fighting between ARBiH and HVO forces in mid-April 1993. By this point, the village was populated primarily by Serbs, concentrated there by fighting in 1992, and Croats, displaced by new fighting in 1993. Combat continued for two days, before the successful ARBiH forces demanded that the entire population move. During the displacement, villagers were robbed and beaten, men were separated from the women and children, and an estimated 9–12 were summarily executed (Helsinki Watch 1993, pp. 11–12). By the war's end, Konjić experienced a fundamental demographic change; by 1998, the town was 98% Bosniak.[20]

The ARBiH forces committed abuses elsewhere along this front, but not systematically in pursuit of a strategic goal of separation. This was not true of the HVO. By late 1992, the center of gravity within Bosnian Croat military and political vision shifted toward hard-liners, who pursued the idea, as expressed by Croatian President Franjo Tudjman in 1991, "it is time that we take the opportunity to gather the Croatian people inside the widest possible borders" (*Prosecutor v. Prlic et al.*, paragraph 428). Thus, HVO forces systematically and violently expelled non-Croat populations from towns taken under their control: hundreds of civilians were killed, and thousands were displaced. Mostar, for instance, was split between a Croat west and Bosniak east, the latter under complete siege from May 1993 to May 1994.

[19] Details of her story come from the full transcript of her testimony before the ICTY in the case *Prosecutor v. Mucić et al.* She was the first woman to testify publicly at the ICTY about rape, on March 17 and 18, 1997.

[20] Despite significant international investment in the town to enable minority returns, few had taken place even several years following the end of the conflict (ICG 1998).

Arguably, this wave of violence was prompted by the terms of the Vance-Owen peace plan, which envisioned the creation of ten provinces, each led by the local ethnic majority. However, the map was contested and the military adjustments required to implement its terms fueled violence. Long-standing tensions and distinct strategic goals caused the fighting, but, as Laura Silber and Alan Little wrote: "the Plan gave Bosnian Croat territorial demands a stamp of legitimacy they otherwise would have lacked" (1997, p. 297). The ARBiH won key battles, significantly diminishing HVO-controlled areas (Hoare 2004, p. 94). In February 1994, generals representing these forces signed a cease-fire under heavy pressure from U.S. diplomats. Ultimately, the hostilities, catalyzed by a peace proposal, were quieted with a new agreement. The March 1, 1994 "Washington Agreement" set the political terms for how the two groups would share power henceforward as a federation. The unity did not run deep, but the agreement was sufficient to improve the situation, calm areas where atrocities had occurred, and, discussed later, make a fundamental difference in the overall path of the war.

Srebrenica

Srebrenica, where over 8,000 Bosniaks were killed in July 1995, demands special attention in the study of atrocities in Bosnia-Herzegovina. Following ethnic cleansing of 1992, the completely surrounded town swelled to include 40,000 Bosniaks, many displaced from towns across eastern Bosnia. The isolated Bosniak fighters were able to mount enough of a defense to carve out a small zone of Bosnian government-affiliated territory deep within areas claimed as the Serb Republic. Barely eking out a living, the population faced severe deprivation and continued shelling. After nearly falling to the Bosnian Serbs in 1993, it was designated a UN safe haven. However, contrary to the agreed-upon definition of the safe haven, it was never fully disarmed, nor when the time came, was it protected from Serbian assault by either the Dutch battalion of UNPROFOR stationed there or NATO airpower.

The end began in earnest with Operational Directive 7, issued by Bosnian Serb President Radovan Karadžić on March 8, 1995, ordering:

> the physical separation of the Srebrenica and Žepa enclaves as soon as possible, preventing even communication between individuals between the two enclaves. By planned and well-thought-out combat operations, create an unbearable situation of total insecurity, with no hope of further survival or life for the inhabitants of Srebrenica or Žepa.
>
> (*Prosecutor v. Popović et al.*, paragraph 199)

Should the UN soldiers retreat from the safe haven, the order continued, the VRS would then launch Operation Jadar, tasked with "breaking up and destroying the

Bosniak forces in these enclaves and definitively liberating the Drina Valley region" (*Prosecutor v. Popović et al.*, paragraph 199). This directive was given military specificity with "Operation Krivaja 95," which began on July 6. By July 9, the initial success of the offensive soon led commanders to expand their goal to "liberation," which they achieved on July 11. That their plans altered when they met no resistance lends credence to speculation that had the international forces, either UNPROFOR or NATO, demonstrated any commitment to protecting Srebrenica, the genocide might not have occurred.

As for the Bosniak forces in Srebrenica, there was little they could do: their willpower was sapped by years of deprivation; their leader, Nasir Orić, was absent when the town fell; and, most fatally, lacking heavy weapons, they did not have the capacity to resist the concentrated VRS attack. When the UN and NATO forces manifestly failed to protect the town, the path was left open to the VRS. Fearing their fate should they fall into Bosnian Serb hands, an estimated 10,000–15,000 Bosniak men (ICTY 2001, paragraph 61) fled through the woods to try to reach government-held territory. In addition to this column of men, only some of whom were armed, 25,000 civilians sought safety at the UN compound just north of Srebrenica at Potočari (ICTY 2001, paragraph 37).

Killing started immediately, if initially sporadically, as civilians came into contact with Bosnian Serbs. The night of July 11–12 is described by Bosniaks at Potočari as filled with terror: reports of rape, murder, and torture at the hands of VRS forces coursed through crowd sheltering outside the UN compound (ICTY 2001, paragraphs 41–47). On July 12, the VRS organized evacuations of the civilians, but separated males of ages 16–60 years from the group as the Dutch UNPROFOR forces watched. The males were taken to Bratunac and killed (ICTY 2010, paragraph 340).

The column of men fleeing toward Bosnian-government-held territory came under repeated attack. The best armed men led the column and fought their way through Serb ambushes – forcing the Serbs to redeploy reinforcements away from the gathering assault on Žepa – but most of the men who followed were unarmed and the column dissolved as they scattered to avoid assaults. On July 13, several thousand men were captured or surrendered to VRS units and were taken to several holding sites: Kravica warehouse, Cerska Valley, Grbavci School in Orahovac, the "new" Petkovci School (in Petkovci), the Pilica School in Kula, and the Cultural Center in Pilica. Detained men were then moved from these holding locations to execution sites. Large-scale killing operations and mass burials were carried out in July 14–18. These were well-organized, systematic endeavors where the Bosniak men, many blindfolded with their hands tethered behind their backs, were lined up and murdered by execution squads. Buried in mass graves, their bodies were moved one or two additional times as the Bosnian Serbs sought to cover up their crime.

The end in Srebrenica was relentless. Bosnian Serb forces attempted to kill all the men they captured. In total, 8,372 people from Srebrenica[21], mostly men, but including women and children, were killed.

Žepa

In marked contrast to Srebrenica, after the Žepa safe haven fell to the VRS forces on July 25, 1995, there was no widespread killing. Three primary factors help explain the difference. First, the VRS offensive was delayed as reinforcements were needed to fight the column of men retreating from Srebrenica and to staff the killing operation, and as they met resistance from ARBiH forces in Žepa (fighting continued in July 19–24). Second, while international response to the attack on Žepa was hardly robust, the fact that UNPROFOR representatives escorted buses evacuating civilians may have saved lives (ICTY 2010, paragraphs 665–738). Despite statements of outrage in response to early tales of the massacres at Srebrenica, an international conference called in London dithered while Žepa was under attack. Even then, international diplomats clarified that NATO would only draw a line at the third eastern enclave, Goražde, seemingly offering a green light for the VRS to take Žepa (Sheridan and Daly 1995). Third, while the Bosnian Serbs killed Colonel Avdo Palić, who was negotiating the terms of surrender with Gen. Mladić, and two civilian representatives – many of the men from Žepa had time to flee through the surrounding hills before the takeover was complete. Further, they did not attempt to all flee in the same direction, but scattered in search of safe territory, including crossing into Serbia. Already overtaxed, the VRS did not have the manpower to hunt down the remaining men from Žepa.

Sarajevo

For many Sarajevans, the war ended in stunning ideological, not military, defeat when the idea of multiethnic Bosnia was abandoned. As Kemal Kurspahić, editor of the Sarajevo daily newspaper, *Oslobođenje*, wrote: "for me, the fight to preserve the multiethnic nature of Sarajevo was not just a political platform for maintaining the unity of the capital of Bosnia, but for maintaining the very essence of life there" (Kurspahić 1997, p. 239). Maintaining the multiethnic editorial board and publishing every day throughout the siege was the journalists' way of resisting the war; an act of everyday defiance, the paper's strategy echoed across Sarajevo by

[21] The precise number of people killed in Srebrenica remain contentious; the number 8,372 killed was produced by the Federal Commission for Missing Persons in Bosnia on December 21, 2008. It combined several lists of the missing and known dead, with the results of exhumations of mass graves and DNA identification of remains. See Srebrenica Genocide blog, http://srebrenica-genocide.blogspot.com/2008/12/update-8372-victims-of-srebrenica.html.

a population that refused to succumb to the nationalist vision of their state. For many, the peace that compromised this vision of Bosnia, rewarding ethnic cleansing and embracing partition, felt like a betrayal of the reasons for fighting in the first place.

Over the course of the conflict, the city's population shrank from 500,000 to 300,000, and, as Sabrina Ramet notes, half of the latter were refuges from villages that had been "cleansed" by Serb forces (Ramet 2006, p. 431). For those who remained, the siege was an exhausting experience that exposed them to hardship and terror. According to the Bosnia-Herzegovina Department of Public Health, over 10,000 people were killed in Sarajevo, over 75% of them in 1992 (Donia 2006, p. 334). Robert Donia (2006, pp. 288–289) argues that the Bosnian Serbs did not appear to want to destroy the city, but it remains unclear how much of its area they sought to control. More evident was their strategy of terrorizing the city's population as both a demonstration of power and a negotiating tactic. The VRS increased their bombardment of the city in relation to military or negotiating setbacks, as a way to punish the population before the international media who swarmed to the city (Donia 2006, pp. 289–290). Rather than military targets, the VRS pattern of targeting during the siege was intended primarily "to invoke terror," as a UN military observer noted (ICTY 2003, paragraph 569). The largest single massacre occurred on February 5, 1994, when a mortar crashed into Sarajevo's marketplace, killing 68 people and wounding 200. The UN, whose Bosnian headquarters were in Sarajevo, prioritized delivery of humanitarian supplies, which required their ability to maneuver through the VRS-controlled airport. Reliant on permission of the Bosnian Serbs, the UN was willing to make costly concessions to the VRS to maintain humanitarian access to the city.

Sarajevo is cradled in a valley, with VRS heavy weapons claiming the high ground around it. With few heavy weapons on their side, the ARBiH literally faced an uphill battle the entire war. The ARBiH launched several offensives to end the siege over the course of the war, and while they made some important gains, ultimately "the result was a protracted military stalemate" (Donia 2006, p. 317). In the case of Sarajevo, it would take superior weaponry to dislodge the VRS from their strongholds. In 1995, this took the form of the NATO bombing campaign. When a mortar hit the Sarajevo marketplace on August 28, 1995, killing 43 and wounding 75, it triggered newfound international consensus and resolve to use NATO power to punish the Serbs. Operation Deliberate Force was launched on August 30 and continued through September 14, targeting heavy weapons around Sarajevo and Bosnian Serb headquarters at Pale.

One last gasp of ethnic cleansing followed the end of the war. During the Dayton peace talks held in November 1995, which ultimately produced the agreement that ended the conflict, the Bosnian government negotiated for Sarajevo to remain unified under their control (Holbrooke 1999, p. 298), which required the Bosnian Serb military to retreat from areas they controlled. This concession was granted by

Slobodan Milošević, who represented the Bosnian Serbs at Dayton, but rejected by the Bosnian Serbs. President of the Serb Assembly, Momčilo Krajišnik, insisted on the goal of separating the Serb from the Bosniak population, and proposed to relocate all of the Serbs from the parts of Sarajevo that would be turned over to Federation administration. As the date of the handover drew nearer:

> Serb gangs roamed the suburbs of Serb-held Sarajevo, terrorizing the vast majority of Serbs into leaving . . . . The gangs removed furniture, stripped luxury apartments of plumbing fixtures, electrical wiring, doors, windows and parquet floors . . . . Gangs set fire to individual apartments and entire apartment buildings.
>
> (Donia 2006, pp. 338–339)

The few Serbs who nonetheless stayed faced intimidation and violence from Bosniak groups, further convincing them to flee. This final wave of ethnic cleansing appears to be an example of nationalist cooperation: both sides contributed coercion to incite the Serb population to leave (Boyle 2014, p. 131). While violence against individuals was not widespread or systematic, it was sufficient. This final act of demographic change cemented the city's new profile: as a city divided between the Federation and Republika Srpska, with each part far more homogenous than before the war.

Mass atrocities during the 1992–1995 war in Bosnia-Herzegovina diminished significantly following the initial wave of ethnic cleansing in 1992. Violence against civilians continued throughout the war in a range of locations and perpetrated by multiple actors, and with terrifying force in Srebrenica. These variations demonstrate how a different range of factors influenced vulnerability to violence: for those held in captivity, the duration of direct violence was longer; for those caught in the new fighting between Croat and Bosniak forces, new threats emerged in 1993; cities under siege, including the safe havens, remained vulnerable throughout, even as the intensity altered significantly over time. The endings to these other forms of violence sometimes introduced new factors: for instance, in Žepa, international monitors, the decision to flee, and the delayed VRS offensive saved lives.

The 1995 NATO bombing, often credited with creating a fundamental difference in atrocities, was not a major factor in the path of Bosnian atrocities, with the notable exception of Sarajevo, where it pounded entrenched VRS positions on the high ground. Even in the case of Sarajevo, however, the height of atrocities was in 1992, but the residents were subjected to terror, deadly sniper, and shelling throughout the war. Atrocities primarily ended through success of the Bosnian Serb plans, armed resistance by the ARBiH and HVO, and the VRS's internal limitations.

If we set aside the disaggregated picture and return to the larger dynamics of the war, we see again that the NATO bombing was but one factor that contributed to the endgame.

PART FOUR: ENDING THE WAR

The war in Bosnia-Herzegovina ended thus: sufficient consensus emerged in the political imagination of the post-Yugoslav leaders, which enabled the breaking of old and forging of new alliances. The consensus was impacted by international economic, diplomatic, and military pressure on local actors. With the new alliances in place, the momentum of the ground war shifted definitively away from the Bosnian Serbs for the first time. Only against the backdrop of the convergence of regional political and military factors can one assess the specific role of the NATO air campaign Deliberate Force.

First, by 1995 both Croatian and Serbian leadership were ready to modify their maximalist ethno-nationalist pursuits. For Serbia, of utmost importance were ending the sanctions, diminishing the financial drain of funding Serb separatists in Croatia and Bosnia, and reclaiming some international legitimacy. This meant Serbian support for maximalist ethno-nationalist plans of both Croatian and Bosnian Serbs was curtailed. Croatia, having lost the battle to assert a maximalist ethno-national plan inside of Bosnia, was willing to settle for more moderate gains within the recognized political borders. The change in position empowered a limited alliance of convenience between Croatian and ARBiH forces.

Too often discussed in isolation from each other, the conflicts in Croatia and Bosnia were intimately connected. The cease-fire of 1991 between Croatian Serb separatists and Croatia left significant portions of the country under Croatian Serb control until late 1995 when Croatia defeated the Serb separatists. Why did Croatia not push to resolve the situation sooner? There are three potential answers: international pressure, lack of capacity,[22] or the strategic decision to leave open the question of redefining borders until they could see how far they could take their own claims inside Bosnia (Žunec 2001). Whatever the reasons for the timing, it is clear that in 1995 Croatia set about to retake its own borders from separatist Serbs and did so in coordination with the ARBiH. Within days starting on August 4, 1995, Croatia convincingly defeated the Croatian Serbs. Significantly, Serbian leaders provided no help as the Croatian Serbs were pummeled and over 200,000 civilians were displaced.

Not only did Serbia tacitly allow the offensive against the Croatian Serbs, but Slobodan Milošević exerted his influence over the Bosnian Serb leadership, who never relinquished their maximalist vision. By 1995, the Bosnian Serbs overplayed their hand: holding international soldiers hostage, undermining a Russian-negotiated

[22] Much emphasis has been placed on the role of U.S. advisors from the private firm MPRI, in the final campaigns of the Croatian War; however, this question remains contentious. The former vice president of MPRI has stated (Isenberg 2010) that they had 15 generals in Croatia beginning in April 1995, insufficient time and numbers to fundamentally impact the summer-fall 1995 offensives. But given the war crimes and violations of international humanitarian law that accompanied the Croat offensives, MPRI also has reason to downplay its role.

deal concerning heavy weapons around Sarajevo, and committing genocide at Srebrenica. And, as noted later, they began to lose ground militarily. Karadžić even attempted to compete with Milošević for the mantle of leading Serb nationalist, prompting Serbian media, under Milošević's control, to attack the Bosnian Serb president (Thompson 1999, pp. 111–112). On August 27, 1995, Milošević leveraged his power over the Bosnian Serbs, forcing them to sign the "Patriarch Papers," establishing Milošević as the final arbiter for the Bosnian Serbs in peace negotiations.

The Bosnian government leadership also had to give up its vision of multiethnic, unified state to join the alliance of pragmatic nationalists. Over the course of the conflict, the Bosnian government became more isolated and nationalist; nonetheless, they remained extremely reluctant to cave to the effects of ethnic cleansing. However, given intense international and regional pressure, they did eventually sign a peace agreement that confirmed partition, granting recognition of the results of Bosnian Serb mass atrocities.

Another key factor was increased international cohesion as manifested in the U.S. diplomatic effort behind the Contact Group Plan, put forward in summer 1994, which envisioned the territorial division of Bosnia: 51% to the Bosniak-Croat federation and 49% to the Serb Republic. The international diplomatic effort had been fractured throughout the war; several changes supported cohesion behind both U.S. diplomacy and a more robust use of force. Key British and French leaders suspected of Serbian sympathies and supportive of conciliatory policies left the scene. In France, Jacques Chirac replaced Francois Mitterand in May 1995, key British negotiators Douglas Hurd and Lord David Owen resigned, Gen. Michael Rose was replaced by Gen. Rupert Smith (McCourt 2013), and the tide turned toward a new policy that was more confrontational to the Bosnian Serbs. Even the Russians, who had supported Serbian interests, were finished with the intransigence of the Bosnian Serbs. Further, careful U.S. diplomacy balanced Russian concerns over NATO expansion with their desire to play a significant role in resolving the conflict. In an exhaustive effort, U.S. diplomats led by chief negotiator Richard Holbrooke seized on the opportunities of 1995.

Critically, in fall 1995, the ground war shifted for the first time with a combined Croatian and ARBiH offensive in northwest Bosnia, and the VRS retreated en masse. The Croat-ARBiH offensive came close to Prijedor, but halted. Why remains a topic of debate: did internationals demand a halt because they did not want the ARBiH to exceed the 51/49 division of territory in the peace plan; were the Croatians, vital to the offensive, interested in a weak, divided Bosnia, and so refused to go further; or had the ARBiH moved so fast that it needed time to regroup and reinforce, during which time the VRS also prepared a stronger defense? Regardless of the balance of reasons, when the offensive ended, the VRS had lost significant ground, almost precisely matching the terms of the proposed peace plan.

No assessment of the NATO bombing campaign from August 30 to September 14, 1995 can be made without attention to the political vision for the post-Yugoslav states, re-formed local alliances, international diplomatic efforts, and the ground war. As was noted in an after-action report by Col. Robert Owen of the U.S. Air Force, "Despite its brevity and limited military scope, Deliberate Force turned out to be a complex diplomatic event influenced by military operations other than the air campaign – and by the conduct of diplomatic activities in several venues" (Owen 2000, p. 494). The NATO bombing was important to the government's war effort around Sarajevo; it sent a strong message to the Bosnian Serbs that their days were numbered; and it disrupted their communications, which did impact the ground war elsewhere. These are not insignificant factors, but neither are they proof that halting atrocities, even against "minor" actors in the global periphery, is easy to accomplish with casualty-free airpower.

Having the right conditions of possibility for a peace settlement does not mean that peace is inevitable or easy. The Herculean effort made by U.S. diplomats, led by Richard Holbrooke, to craft what would become the Dayton Peace Agreement is the final factor that fell into place. If one wants to identify a triumph of international engagement in Bosnia related to ending the war, it is diplomatic, not military.

Ultimately, the Dayton agreement created a state palatable to nationalists, with a very weak central government and strong entities. Other measures, like the right of minorities to return and vote according to their prewar homes, were intended to eventually balance the impact of rewarding ethnic cleansing, but this is not yet borne out by events. As Michael Boyle (2014, p. 101) demonstrates, nationalist parties continued to pursue policies hostile to cross-entity integration and multiethnicity; however, they carefully calibrated how much violence they could deploy without harming their core war gains. Ethnic minorities attempting to return to their prewar homes, particularly to Republika Srpska, faced intensive harassment and attack; but murder rates remained low (Boyle 2014, pp. 131–137). No doubt this record was aided by the presence of international armed forces, internationally run security sector reform efforts (particularly of the border controls and police, a European strategic concern), and the Office of the High Representative, an international position empowered to resolve disputes amongst local actors and final civilian authority in Bosnia. However, despite similarly robust international presence in Kosovo following the 1999 NATO intervention, and with half the population of Bosnia, Kosovo experienced five times the number of post-conflict murders as Bosnia did (Boyle 2014, p. 176).[23]

[23] In Kosovo, the lessons learned from Bosnia were put to perverse practice. Milošević thought he could continue to walk the tightrope of being the favored interlocutor with the West while retaining his mantle as leader of the Serbian nationalists. While Milošević is often described as a dictator, he arrived at and survived in power through elections, however manipulated. A crucial part of his electoral survival required that he control the Kosovo block of votes. He could not remain in power if the Kosovar Albanians controlled their vote within Serbia, nor, as events would reveal, could he hold on once he disappointed nationalists by losing Kosovo.

The resulting Bosnian state is structurally dysfunctional – with overwhelming advantage for nationalist parties who have established extensive patrimonial networks within the entity-level governments. It is not, however, violent.

CONCLUSION

Mass atrocities ended in Bosnia during the 1992–1995 war according to a militaro-political recipe that has not much changed in the past 100 years. Wars replete with atrocities are fought to create territorial states and end when those states are consolidated. Other key factors remain likewise consistent: the ability of local actors to articulate a vision of the state that will forge regional coalitions and win international recognition. International interest in the region shifted beginning in 1919 and ending after World War II from competing territorial aspirations to maintaining stable, Western-leaning states in a frontier region. At the end of the 1990s, the requirement for international recognition of these states was also that they perform as economic and political liberal states – which is new and we have yet to see the long-term implications of this requirement. The short-term implication was that Yugoslavia as a state could not manage the transition. The ending of atrocities and the war in Bosnia marks a continuation of these trends, rather than a sign of a new human rights–based, anti-atrocities dispensation. What was new was that international actors played a role in inhibiting military triumph in Bosnia, which may have reduced the overall level of mass atrocities, but it also produced the dysfunctional state and rewarded the initial large-scale mass atrocities in 1992 and 1995.

Why does the 1995 NATO bombing take place of pride in the evolving anti-atrocities narrative? Why are the complex mix of factors that contributed to Bosnian endings so frequently reduced to this one "tool"? There are a few factors. First, bombs are more visible and dramatic than political shifts or diplomacy. Second, embedded within genocide, a term that framed response to Bosnia particularly for those who advocated for and felt vindicated by stronger international military action, is the assumption that mass atrocities need to be terminated through international military action. Third is a humanitarian trap. Understanding of the war shifted from naturalized "Balkan" violence to a debate about the need to aid victims. International sympathy accrued based on a narrative of suffering rather than arguments about the viability or justice of the political vision of the state

Popular support, or lack thereof, determined both his rise and demise. The Kosovars discovered that nonviolent, political protest against their long-standing subordinate status would get them nowhere; new leadership arose with the goal of militarized separatism, eventually supported by NATO airpower. As Boyle (2014, p. 175) notes, many international actors assumed that Bosnia's experience of a low-violence post-conflict experience would hold for Kosovo. What they overlooked was the fact that the political vision they had midwifed, ethnic monopolies over politics, would not support the existence of a significant Serb minority in Albanian-dominated Kosovo.

articulated by the key Bosnian actors. With grievance as the sole language with which to articulate rights, the available analytical vocabulary of the war – and of the anti-atrocities agenda that would develop thereafter – only allowed for perpetrators, weak victims, and righteous international action.

This narrative, and the place it reserves for international actors above politics, relates to the final factor: the dominance of a crisis management approach to international politics, in which only the universalizable lessons, the ones that can apply to next crisis, are deemed of value. Lessons need be presented as tools ready at hand for the international community, and political dynamics are more difficult to frame as such. Following Bosnia 1995, military intervention dressed in the moral certitude of human rights ushered in an exception to the post–Cold War delegitimization of coercive international military action. While this "tool" was not used often in subsequent years, it became the cornerstone of anti-atrocity policy, limiting the imagination and exploration of what international principles contribute to atrocity prevention (Conley-Zilkic 2015).

If a lesson must be extracted, the correct one from Bosnia is that mass atrocity endings are complicated and compromised political, not humanitarian, events. Military force may indeed be a useful tool if it is subordinated to a political process with a clear endgame. The mistake in Bosnia and thereafter was confusing this endgame with a virtuous anti-atrocities agenda.

WORKS CITED

Banac, Ivo. 2009. "What Happened in the Balkans (or Rather Ex-Yugoslavia)." *East European Politics and Societies* 23:4, 461–478.

Biondich, Mark. 2011. *The Balkans: Revolution, War, and Political Violence since 1878*. Oxford: Oxford University Press.

Bosnia-Herzegovina 1994. Constitution of the Federation of Bosnia and Herzegovina 1994, Annex 4., Accessed February 22, 2015. www.ohr.int/dpa/?content_id=372.

Boyle, Michael. 2014. *Violence After Wars: Explaining Instability in Post-Conflict States*. Baltimore: Johns Hopkins University Press.

Bringa, Tone. 2003. "The Peaceful Death of Tito and the Violent End of Yugoslavia." In *Death of the Father: An Anthropology of the End in Political Authority*, edited by John Borneman, 148–200. New York: Berghahn Books.

Brunborg, Helge. 2009. "Report on the size and ethnic composition of the population of Kosovo. Expert report presented in the SLOBODAN MILOSEVIC Case (IT-02-54), August 14, 2002. ERN: K023–1607-K0230–1624." In *Conflict in Numbers: Casualties of the 1990s Wars in the Former Yugoslavia* (1991–1999), edited by Ewa Tabeau. 2009. Belgrade: Helsinki Committee for Human Rights in Serbia.

Carnegie Endowment for International Peace. 1933. *Report of the International Commission to Inquire into the Causes and Conduct of the Balkan Wars*. Washington: Carnegie Endowment for International Peace.

Central Intelligence Agency (CIA). 2002. *Balkan Battlegrounds: A Military History of the Yugoslav Conflicts 1991–1995*, Volume 1. Washington: Central Intelligence Agency.

Cigar, Norman. 1997. "Croatia's War of Independence: The Parameters of War Termination." *Journal of Slavic Military Studies* 10:2, 34–70.

1996. "How Wars End: War Termination and Serbian Decisionmaking in the Case of Bosnia." *South East European Monitor* 3:1, 3–47.

Conley-Zilkic, Bridget. 2015. "The Pistol on the Wall: How Coercive Military Intervention Limits Atrocity Prevention Policies." In *Reconstructing Atrocity Prevention* edited by Sheri P. Rosenberg, Tiberiu Galis, and Alex Zucker, pp. 31–60. Cambridge: Cambridge University Press.

Conley-Zilkic, Bridget and Alex deWaal. 2014. "Setting the Agenda for Evidence-based Research on Ending Mass Atrocities." *Journal of Genocide Research* 16:1, 55–76.

Costalli, Stefano and Francesco Niccolò Moro. 2012. "Ethnicity and Strategy in the Bosnian Civil War: Explanations for the Severity of Violence in Bosnian Municipalities." *Journal of Peace Research* 49:6, 801–815.

Donia, Robert, ed. 2012. *From The Republika Srpska Assembly 1991–1996: Excerpts from Delegates Speeches at the Republika Srpska Asssembly as Body of Evidence for the International Criminal Tribunal at The Hague*. Sarajevo: University Press.

2006. *Sarajevo: a Biography*. Ann Arbor: University of Michigan Press.

Dzidic, Denis. 2014. "Bosniaks Mark Closure of Detention Camp for Serbs." *Balkan Transitional Justice*. October 24. Accessed February 24, 2015. www.balkaninsight.com/en/article/closing-of-celebici-camp-marked.

European Court of Human Rights (ECHR). 2009. *Sejdić and Finci v. Bosnia and Herzegovina*. December 22. Accessed February 22, 2015. http://hudoc.echr.coe.int/sites/eng/pages/search.aspx?i=001-96491.

Fukuyama, Francis. 1989. "The End of History?" *The National Interest*. 16, 3–18.

Government of the Republic of Slovenia, Public Relations and Media Office. 2001. "War for Slovenia 1991." May. Accessed February 27, 2015. www.slovenija2001.gov.si/10years/path/war/.

Hagan, John and Todd J. Haugh. 2011. "Ethnic Cleansing as Euphemism, Metaphor, Criminology, and Law." In *Forging a Convention for Crimes Against Humanity*, edited by Leila Nadya Sadat, 177–201. Cambridge: Cambridge University Press.

Hall, Richard C. 2000. *The Balkan Wars 1912–1913: Prelude to the First World War*. New York: Routledge.

Helsinki Watch. 1993. *War Crimes in Bosnia-Herzegovina*, Volume II. New York: Human Rights Watch. April 1.

1992. *War Crimes in Bosnia-Herzegovina*. New York: Human Rights Watch.

Hoare, Marko Attila. 2004. *How Bosnia Armed*. London: Saqi Books.

1996. "The People's Liberation Movement in Bosnia and Hercegovina, 1941–45: What Did It Mean to Fight for A Multi-Ethnic State?" *Nationalism and Ethnic Politics* 2:3, 415–445.

Holbrooke, Richard. 1999. *To End A War*. New York: Modern Library.

Hukanovic, Rezak. 1996. *The Tenth Circle of Hell: A Memoir of Life in the Death Camps of Bosnia*, translated by Ammiel Alcalay. New York: Basicbooks.

Human Rights Watch. 1994. *Human Rights Watch World Report 1994*. New York: Human Rights Watch.

2000. "Civilian Deaths in the NATO Air Campaign." February. Accessed February 27, 2014. www.hrw.org/reports/2000/nato/.

Ilievski, Zoran and Dane Taleski. 2009. "Was the EU's Role in conflict management in Macedonia a Success?" *Ethnopolitics* 8:3, 355–367.

International Commission on Intervention and State Sovereignty (ICISS). 2001. "*Report of the International Commission of State Sovereignty and Intervention: The Responsibility to Protect.*" Ottawa: International Development Research Center.

International Commission to Inquire Into the Causes and Conduct of the Balkan Wars. 1993. *The other Balkan wars : a 1913 Carnegie Endowment Inquiry in Retrospect.* Washington: Carnegie Endowment for International Peace.

International Criminal Tribunal for the Former Yugoslavia (ICTY). 1997. *Prosecutor v. Mucić et al.* (testimony of Grozdana Čečez) IT-96–21 (March 17 and 18, 1997).

1998. *Prosecutor v. Zejnil Delalić (et al), Zdravko Mucić, Hazim Delić and Esad Landzo* (Judgment) IT-96–21-T (November 16, 1998).

2000. *Prosecutor v. Miroslav Kvočka, Dragoljub Prcać, Milojica Kos, Mlađo Radić and Zoran Žigić.* 2000. (Witness Testimony) Emir Beganović. IT-94–1-T. May 4–5.

2001. *Prosecutor v. Radislav Krstic* (Judgment) IT-98–33-T (August 2, 2001).

2003. *Prosecutor v. Stanislav Galić* (Judgment) IT-98–29-T (December 5, 2003).

2006. *Prosecutor v. Momčilo Krajišnik* (Judgment) IT-00–39 (September 27, 2006).

2010. *Prosecutor v. Vujadin Popović (et al), Ljubisa Beara, Dargo Nikolic, Ljubomir Borovcanin, Radivoje Miletic, Milan Gvero, Vinko Pandurevic* (Judgment) IT-05–88-T (June 10, 2010).

2013. *Prosecutor v. Jadranko Prlić (et al), Bruno Stojić, Slobodan Praljak, Milivoj Petković, Valentin Ćorić, Perislav Pušić* (Judgment) IT-04–74-T (May 29, 2013).

International Crisis Group (ICG). 1998. "The Konjic Conundrum Why Minorities Have Failed to Return to the Model Open City." ICG Bosnia Project. June 19. Accessed February 17, 2015. www.crisisgroup.org/en/regions/europe/balkans/bosnia-herzegovina/035-the-konjic-conundrum-why-minorities-have-failed-to-return-to-model-open-city.aspx.

Isenberg, David. 2010. "MPRI Couldn't Read Minds: Let's Sue Them." Huffington Post. August 19. Accessed February 15, 2015. www.huffingtonpost.com/david-isenberg/mpri-couldnt-read-minds-l_b_688000.html.

Kaufmann, Chaim. 1998. "When All Else Fails: Ethnic Partitions and Population Transfers in the Twentieth Century." *International Security* 23:2, 120–156.

Kaplan, Robert. 1993. *Balkan Ghosts.* New York: Vintage Books.

Kurspahić, Kemal. 1997. *As Long as Sarajevo Exists*, translated by Colleen London. Stony Creek, CT: The Pamphleteer's Press.

Levene, Mark. 2013. *The Crisis of Genocide, Volume I: Devastation: The European Rimlands, 1912–1938.* Oxford: Oxford University Press.

MacMillan, Margaret. 2003. *Paris 1919: Six Months That Changed the World.* New York: Random House.

Magaš, Branka and Ivo Žanić, eds. 2001. *The War in Croatia and Bosnia-Herzegovina 1991–1995.* New York: Frank Cass Publishers.

McCourt, David. 2013. "Embracing Humanitarian Intervention: Atlanticism and the UK Interventions in Bosnia and Kosovo." *British Journal of Politics and International Relations* 15:2, 246–262.

Melander, Eric. 2007. "Ethnic cleansing in Bosnia-Herzegovina, 1992–1995." Paper presented at the conference on "Disaggregating the Study of Civil War and Transnational Violence." University of Essex, November 24–25. Accessed February 26, 2015. http://privatewww.essex.ac.uk/~ksg/dscw2007/Melander.pdf.

Mozjes,Paul. 2011. *Balkan Genocides: Holocaust and Ethnic Cleansing in the Twentieth Century.* Lanham, MD: Rowman & Littlefield Publishers.

Nation, R. Craig. 2003. *War in the Balkans 1991–2002.* Carlisle, PA: Strategic Studies Institute, U.S. Army War College.

Norwegian Refugee Council. 2005. "Profile of Internal Displacement: Serbia and Montenegro." Geneva: Norwegian Refugee Council, September 27. Accessed February 21, 2015. www.internal-displacement.org/europe-the-caucasus-and-central-asia/serbia/2005/profile-of-internal-displacement-serbia-and-montenegro.

Owen, Col. Robert. 2000. "Summary." In *Deliberate Force: A Case Study in Effective Air Campaigning*, edited by Robert Owen, 455–522. Maxwell Air Force Base, AL: Air University Press.

Pawlowtich, Steven, K. 1999. *A History of the Balkans 1804–1945*. New York: Longman

Power, Samantha. 2001. *A Problem From Hell: America and the Age of Genocide*. New York: Basic Books.

Ramet, Sabrina. 2006. *The Three Yugoslavias: State-building and Legitimation, 1918–2005*. Bloomington, IN: Indiana University Press.

Redžić, Enver. 2005. *Bosnia and Herzegovina in the Second World War*, translated by Aida Vidan. New York: Frank Cass.

Research and Documentation Center Sarajevo (RDC). 2008. *Human Losses in Bosnia and Herzegovina 91–95*. Sarajevo: Research and Documentation Center.

Rusinov, Dennis. 2003. "The Yugoslav Idea before Yugoslavia." In *Yugoslavism 1918–1992: History of a Failed Idea*, edited by Dejan Djokić, 11–26. Madison, WI: University of Wisconsin Press.

Sadat, Leila Nadya. 2011. *Forging a convention for crimes against humanity*. Cambridge; New York: Cambridge University Press.

Schneider, Gerald. 2013. "Accounting for the dynamics of one-sided violence: introducing KOSVED." *Journal of Peace Research* 50:5, 635–644.

Sheridan, Michael and Emma Daly. 1995. "Allies Threaten Massive Air Attacks: Ultimatum to Bosnian Serbs Warns of Action If Gorazde Comes Under Fire." *The Independent*, July 22.

Siegel, Robert. 2005. "Bosnian City's Unique Statue Choice: Bruce Lee." Interview with Veselin Gatalo. National Public Radio. September 13. Accessed February 26, 2015. www.npr.org/templates/story/story.php?storyId=4845621.

Silber, Laura and Alan Little. 1997. *Yugoslavia: Death of a Nation*. New York: Penguin Books.

Tabeau, Ewa. 2009a. "Basic Demographic Characteristics and Socio-Economic Status of Missing and Killed Persons from the Municipality of Prijedor, 30.04–30.09. 1992. Expert Report from the STAKIC case (IT-97–24)." In *Conflict in Numbers: Casualties of the 1990s Wars in the Former Yugoslavia* (1991–1999), edited by Ewa Tabeau. 2009, pp. 159–184. Belgrade: Helsinki Committee for Human Rights in Serbia.

Tabeau, Ewa, Marcin Żółtkowski, Jakub Bijak, Arve Hetland. 2009. "Ethnic Composition, Internally Displaced Persons and Refugee from 47 Municipalities of Bosnia and Herzegovina, 1991 to 1997. Expert prepared for the SLOBODAN MILOSEVIC case (IT-02–54). In *Conflict in Numbers: Casualties of the 1990s Wars in the Former Yugoslavia* (1991–1999), edited by Ewa Tabeau 2009, pp. 661–876. Belgrade: Helsinki Committee for Human Rights in Serbia.

Thompson, Mark. 1999. *Forging War: The Media in Serbia, Croatia and Bosnia-Hercegovina*. Luton: University of Luton Press.

Tomasevich, Jozo. 2001. *War and Revolution in Yugoslavia, 1941–1945*. Stanford: Stanford University Press.

UN High Commissioner for Refugees (UNHCR). 1992. "A Comprehensive Response to the Humanitarian Crisis in the former Yugoslavia." UN doc. HCR/IMFY/1992/2. July 24. Accessed February 26, 2015. www.refworld.org/docid/438ec8aa2.html.

Wachtel, Andrew Baruch. 2008. *The Balkans in World History*. Oxford: Oxford University Press

Woodward, Susan. 2013. "The Long Intervention: Continuity in the Balkan Theater." *Review of International Studies* 39:5, 1169–1187.

1995. *Socialist Unemployment: The Political Economy of Yugoslavia, 1945–1990*. Princeton: Princeton University Press.

Wright, Phil. 1985. "The Political Economy of the Yugoslav Revolution." *Institute of Social Studies Occasional Papers* No. 102. Rotterdam: Erasmus University.

Žerjavić, Vladimir. 1992. *Yugoslavia: Manipulations with the Number of Second World War Victims*. Zagreb: Croatian Information Centre. Available at: www.hic.hr/books/manipulations/p06.htm Accessed 26 February 2015.

Žunec, Ozren. 2001. "Operations Flash and Storm." In *The War in Croatia and Bosnia-Herzegovina 1991–1995*, edited by Branka Magas & Ivo Zanic, 67–83. New York: Frank Cass Publishers.

Iraq

Atrocity as political capital

Fanar Haddad

INTRODUCTION

Perhaps the most consistent feature of Iraq's dense history of atrocities is the lack of closure: underlying issues fester, justice is denied, grievances mount, and the memory of much of what actually transpired is consigned to oral histories and the silent testimony of mass graves. This lack of closure rendered even the country's recent chance for an "ending" – the decline of mass atrocities after 2007 – ephemeral: violence subsided but the underlying drivers of conflict remained unaddressed; rather than an ending, the drop in violence proved to be yet another signpost along a drawn-out continuum of conflict. For this reason, the question to ask in Iraq is twofold: why did violence decline in 2007 and why did that reduction not last? Many, this author included, wrongly thought that 2007/2008 signaled an ending of sorts. Why this view proved so mistaken and why there seems to be no end in sight to the new Iraq's conveyor belt of atrocities are the central focus of this essay.

When discussing violence in Iraq, 2003 is an unavoidable turning point separating two qualitatively different sociopolitical realities. Perhaps the most striking difference between the two periods is the nature and role of the state. Partly by fault and partly by design, violence was thoroughly decentralized after 2003. The confusion that followed regime change created both the space and the demand for a variety of armed groups to emerge. The state is very much a part of this landscape; indeed, it is difficult to clearly delineate between state and non-state armed groups given that irregular forces have been a part of Iraqi security forces, and Iraqi politics, in one way or another since 2003 and never more so than after the spread of Islamic State (IS) militants over much of north and western Iraq in the summer of 2014.[1] Naturally this has complicated and perpetuated conflict since 2003. Gone is the

[1] For an overview of the role of militias in post-2003 Iraq, see Ucko (2008). For a look at Shi'a militias following the summer of 2014, see Human Rights Watch (2014) and Amnesty International (2014).

Leviathan that could end conflict through a unilateral exertion of disproportionate force and gone is the massive asymmetry between state and non-state forces.

If we look at the most relevant cases of mass atrocity in pre-2003 Iraq, the question of endings becomes intertwined with the state's capacity for coercive violence and the role of external actors. The most egregious mass atrocities of the pre-2003 period would be the Anfal campaign in 1988 and the suppression of the rebellions of 1991 in southern and northern Iraq. The Anfal campaign, which is officially recognized as genocide by several countries, was the culmination of decades of intermittent conflict between Baghdad and Kurdish guerrillas and the climax of a broader context of genocidal counterinsurgency in the late 1980s and the Iran-Iraq war of 1980–1988. It is estimated that, at the very least, 50,000 people were killed during the Anfal campaign with some estimates going as high as 180,000 (Makiya 1993; Human Rights Watch 1995; McDowall 2003). The other major case of pre-2003 mass atrocity happened in 1991. Following Iraq's crushing defeat in the Gulf War and the ignominious retreat from Kuwait, anti-regime demonstrations turned into violent rebellion with the state quickly losing control of 13 of Iraq's 18 provinces. The suppression of the rebellions was a costly affair that saw entire cities devastated and anywhere up to 300,000 people killed (Human Rights Watch 1992; Jabar 1992, pp. 2–14; Makiya 1993, chapter 2; Haddad 2011, chapter 4; Khoury 2012).

In both these cases, and other examples from pre-2003 Iraq, the beginning, tempo, and ending of mass atrocities were linked to the role of the Iraqi state and external powers. For example, Kurdish military fortunes were often hostage to the continued support of external actors, particularly Iran,[2] and the rebellions of 1991 were quelled through brute force in the south with atrocities only stopping after the state had regained control of lost territory and had collectively punished the rebellious areas. In the north the situation was calmed in 1991 largely as a result of the intervention of external powers who imposed a safe haven from which state forces were excluded. Such endings do not fit the post-2003 landscape of violence, given the state's lack of capacity and even coherence to act in the manner of its predecessor.

The legacy of authoritarianism, economic collapse, political dysfunction, social fragmentation, and international isolation that the Ba'athist state bequeathed to the new Iraq held all the preconditions for political failure and none of the preconditions for a successful transition to a more benevolent political order.[3]

[2] As most vividly illustrated by the collapse of Kurdish insurrection in 1975 as a result of the Algiers agreement between Baghdad and Tehran that led to a cessation of Iranian support to Kurdish rebels. See Farouk-Sluglett and Sluglett (2003, pp. 169–172).

[3] In many ways the Ba'ath era (1968–2003) and particularly the final 13 years during which Iraq was under crippling economic sanctions were the incubator of many of the ills that emerged in the wake of the regime's collapse in 2003. For the Ba'ath Party and the regime it led, see Sassoon (2011), Rohde (2010), and Makiya (1998). For the sanctions era, see Gordon (2012) and Cockburn and Cockburn (1999).

Making matters worse was the questionable way in which regime change was enacted: an illegal invasion that delegitimized the new Iraq, proving extremely divisive both in Iraq and internationally. The incompetence of the occupation and Iraq's new political classes ensured that the destruction of the state would not be followed by the rebuilding of a functional alternative. Furthermore, as will be shown, the political forces that were ultimately empowered by regime change were inescapably rooted in the prism of identity politics thereby ensuring that Iraq's social divisions, already strained by years of authoritarianism, economic collapse, and accumulated grievances, would become inflamed through political relevance.

As a result of these and other factors, many of the more familiar paths toward conflict resolution were closed to the new Iraq. For example, there was an absence of statesmanship or charismatic leadership, and it remains unlikely for Iraq to see the emergence of a Mandela or a de Klerk. Exhaustion seems an equally distant prospect, given the availability of resources and the role of external actors in perpetuating conflict. Lacking internal and external sovereignty, the state is incapable of initiating a meaningful reconciliation process or of successfully suppressing rivals to its authority. Moreover, the depth of political and social division today precludes the trust needed for compromise and reform in the near term. Finally, given the time needed for a generational turnover amongst political leaders and given the continuing regional instability relating to the Syrian civil war and regional geostrategic rivalries, ending mass atrocities in Iraq remains a distant prospect.

This chapter begins by examining the underlying drivers of post-2003 violence; it will be shown that at heart the conflicts in Iraq revolve around the legitimacy and identity of the state, something that is complicated by its connection to communal identities and communal relations. Second, the chapter will briefly look at patterns of violence in the years 2003–2007. Third, reviewing the existing literature and scholarly positions on the subject, the drivers behind the huge drop in violence beginning in late 2007 and that lasted until 2013 will be explained. Finally, this chapter will discuss why violence has yet again surged and why an ending to mass atrocities in Iraq remains so elusive.

POST-2003 IRAQ: A STATE OF DIVISION

To ask why mass atrocities have not ended in Iraq since 2003 is essentially to ask why attempts to build a new post-Saddam Iraq have failed so spectacularly. There were proximate causes behind Iraq's spiral into widespread violence in 2003: the power vacuum caused by the collapse of the state; the failure to secure vital infrastructure or to seal borders; the presence of an occupation and the resentment this bred in Iraq and beyond; the failure to rebuild a functioning state' and so forth (Dodge 2007). However, the root of Iraq's major political conflict lies in clashing visions, long predating 2003, over the identity and ownership of the state.

This is particularly relevant to conflict in Arab Iraq as opposed to the Kurdish region of Iraq that has long had little interest in Baghdad beyond how dynamics in the capital will impact on life in the Kurdish regions and on Kurdish national aspirations. In other words, Kurdish political actors never sought to dominate Baghdad because theirs has been an ethno-national consciousness juxtaposed against an Iraqi one. In contrast, the political struggle amongst Arab Iraqis has been about defining the contours of Iraqi national consciousness and ownership of the Iraqi state with or without the Kurdish north. For this reason, and due to the fact that Arab-Kurdish competition has not resulted in mass atrocities since 2003, the focus of this chapter will be on conflict in Arab Iraq.

For a variety of historical reasons and preexisting, overlapping societal divisions, empowering Shi'as and Kurds in Iraq was never going to be straightforward or free of controversy.[4] Yet this process was made all the worse by the political orientation and backgrounds of the political actors who were empowered by regime change in 2003. The opposition to Saddam Hussein's regime was dominated by ethnocentric and sect-centric political organizations and it was they, by virtue of their history and their weight in Iraq's exiled opposition, who ascended the political pyramid after regime change and played a leading role (amongst Iraqis at least) in shaping the new state.[5]

The Shi'a political classes, for instance, throughout their careers, were more akin to Shi'a-rights advocates than national politicians. Rather than politicians who simply happen to be Shi'a, they were *Shi'a politicians* whose political worldview was deeply rooted in Shi'a identity. For them, given that Iraq is a Shi'a-majority country, the national project was synonymous with group empowerment and the empowerment of Shi'a identities. This mindset is perhaps best described as oblivious to rather than belligerent toward the other and is best encapsulated in the highly sect-centric "Declaration of the Shi'a of Iraq" of 2002, which many post-2003 Shi'a politicians were signatories to.[6] After 2003, many if not most of the post-2003

4 This has been an issue throughout modern Iraqi and Middle Eastern history and is a result of the state's failure to manage nation building and communal plurality. For a development of these themes (see Haddad 2012a, 2014a, 2014b).

5 Most prominent amongst the exiled Shi'a opposition that attained high office after 2003 would be the Da'awa Party, the Supreme Council for the Islamic Revolution in Iraq (later renamed the Islamic Supreme Council of Iraq), and its paramilitary wing the Badr Corps (later renamed the Badr Organisation). Within Iraq there was the Sadrist movement and later a number of splinter groups all of whom were similarly sect-centric.

6 The "Declaration of the Shi'a of Iraq" was signed in 2002 by a list of prominent Shi'a figures in exile. Some of the signatories include Adil Abdul Mahdi (minister of oil at time of writing), Sami al Askari (senior advisor to former Prime Minister Nuri al Maliki), Muwaffaq al Rubaie (former national security advisor), Hussein al Shahristani (former minister of oil), Ali Allawi (former minister of defense), and Mohammad Bahr al Uloom (first president of the Iraqi Governing Council). English translation available on www.al-bab.com/Arab/docs/iraq/Shia02b.htm#Annex2. Arabic version available on www.aljazeera.net/NR/exeres/F55B05C7–517F-4692–8FA1–29440FF3E48F.htm. For an analysis of the declaration's implications, see Haddad (2011, pp. 148–150).

Shi'a political elite retained their role as sectional sectarian advocates. Their failure to make the transition from Shi'a-rights advocates to national politicians validated Sunni prejudices and fears, which were exacerbated by the fact that many of these political actors were based in or had strong links to Iran – a country Iraq had fought against for eight years and that successive regimes often portrayed as one of Iraq's archenemies.

On the other side of the sectarian coin, Sunni Arab Iraqis had long identified with – though not necessarily supported – the state. For Sunnis, the disappearance of the state in 2003 and the birth of an Iraq – midwifed by an American-led invasion – that they simply could not identify with continues to be the source of profound Sunni ambivalence toward the entire post-2003 political order. This ambivalence is rooted in the fact that the new Iraq reduced Sunnis to minority status and is ruled by Shi'a-centric forces many of whom were demonized for decades in state propaganda as Iranian aligned traitors.[7] Adding to their fears and suspicions was not just the overt sectarian entrenchment of their Shi'a competitors, but the fact that, prior to 2003, Sunnis lacked the sect-specific organizations, politicians, and even the sectarian self-awareness that were now mandated by a new Iraq that was fundamentally based on identity politics.

For many Shi'a political actors, for whom sectarian activism was part of their political DNA, identity politics were a route to empowerment and very much a welcome development. For Sunnis, identity politics were an alien political register that forced them to accept the unwelcome fact of their numerical inferiority in a system that can be described as "demography as democracy" (Jabar et al. 2014, p. 8). Yet, unfortunately for Sunnis, these were the very foundations of the new Iraq as embodied in the ethno-sectarian composition of post-war Iraq's first governing institution, the Iraqi Governing Council (IGC).[8]

In effect, regime change was a turning point in a much longer conflict: it saw the triumph and empowerment of the Shi'a-centric and Kurdish-centric opposition over the pre-2003 state. In many ways, the past 12 years have been about the effort to build a Shi'a-centric order in Arab Iraq and the violent rejection that this has produced among Iraqi Sunnis. Hence, in certain respects the violence can be

[7] The loss of an Iraq that Sunnis could identify with was perceptively described by Ahmed Hashim as a form of "identity disenfranchisement" (Hashim 2006, p. 68).

[8] The IGC was a 25-member body appointed by head of the Coalition Provisional Authority Paul Bremer in July 2003. In the name of fair representation, the composition of the IGC sought to mirror the assumed demographic weight of Iraq's major communities thereby institutionalizing majority and minority status of Shi'as and Sunnis, respectively, and turning ethno-sectarian identity into the basic organizing principle of Iraqi politics. The fact that there is little agreement on Iraqi demographics and that no reliable current figures exist has made the matter all the more controversial. The IGC, indeed post-2003 Iraq more broadly, is a classic case of how identities can be shaped by state and policy. For parallels from India and elsewhere, see Chandhoke (2005).

viewed as the continuation of a single conflict that predates regime change – which perhaps explains the zero-sum nature that Iraqi political discord has often assumed. As one recent study argues, ethno-sectarian entrenchment was not unknown in pre-2003 Iraq; however, the virulent strain of identity politics that so characterized Iraq after regime change was something different. It was the result of the:

> ... calculated objective of powerful factions that emerged after Saddam's disappearance in 2003 with explicitly sectarian agendas in mind. Shi'a supremacists, Sunni chauvinists and Kurdish maximalists all aimed to exploit the post-Saddam political vacuum to advance their narrowly defined communal interests.
>
> (Rayburn 2014, p. 73)

For "Shi'a supremacists," cementing Shi'a political ascendency in a new Iraq that reflects a particular Shi'a-Iraqi reading of recent history was paramount. This inevitably entailed an attempt to right historical wrongs as perceived by Shi'a political actors. In turn this lent post-2003 state building an at-times vengeful character that many Sunnis felt vilified and targeted them – in sum effect, nourishing Sunni rejection of both Shi'a empowerment and the entire post-2003 order. The matter was made all the more contentious by the fact that the Coalition Provisional Authority (CPA), far from being impartial observers, actively took sides in the emerging contest between Sunnis and Shi'as. As noted by the International Crisis Group, the CPA's dismantling of the old regime chimed with Shi'a and Kurdish political actors' desire to create a clean Ba'ath-free slate:

> Importantly, the old regime was perceived as based in the Sunni Arab community, a view that meshed with the predominance of opposition parties rooted in the other two principal communities, the Shiites and the Kurds. The destruction of these key institutions therefore had a sectarian aura.
>
> (International Crisis Group 2006a, p. 8)

Another example of this dynamic can be found in the early stages of the constitutional drafting process – a process that, again, was heavily backed by the CPA. According to one analyst, the first draft of the Iraqi constitution presented to the National Assembly on August 15, 2005 mirrored the sentiments expressed in the "Declaration of the Shi'a of Iraq" of 2002. To illustrate, the first draft included an article that, it was felt, implicitly vilified Iraq's Sunni Arabs in the following terms: "remembering the pains of the despotic clique's sectarian oppression of the majority" (al Kubaisi 2013, pp. 5–6). While the drafters may well protest that the intended "majority" could mean the majority of all Iraqis; critics can just as easily point out that the ethno-sectarian basis of the new Iraq left little doubt about what was implied by minorities and majorities in the heated context of 2005.

Similar examples of Shi'a sect-centric state building and Sunni rejection can be found in the policy of de-Ba'athification and the manner in which it was implemented,[9] the official line on demographics and consequently the system of ethno-sectarian apportionment and Sunnis' minority status, and so the list goes on.[10] As a result, there has existed since 2003 a latent resentment underlining Sunni views toward the new Iraq. Generally speaking, this manifests along a spectrum from begrudging acceptance to armed insurgency. The balance between these two poles is influenced by perceptions of the stability and permanence of the state and the prospects for political reform and progress. It can even be argued that one of the factors perpetuating violence today is the existence of a significant body of Sunni opinion that has been unwilling to accept the post-2003 order from the very beginning – a tendency that has hardly been assuaged by Shi'a politicians. As one commentary recently put it:

> The most significant factor behind Iraq's problems has been the inability of Iraq's Sunni Arabs and its Sunni neighbors to come to terms with a government in which the Shi'as … hold the leading role. This inability was displayed early on, when Iraq's Sunnis refused to take part in Iraq's first parliamentary elections, and resorted to insurgency almost immediately after the US invasion and fall of Saddam Hussein. All along, the goal of Iraqi Sunnis has been to prove that the Shi'as are not capable of governing Iraq.
>
> (Hunter 2014)

In effect, Shi'a political actors – through their incompetence and their own sect-centricity – validated many preexisting Sunni prejudices that distanced them from the new Iraq. This, in turn, prompted Sunni political actors – even those from within the political process – to aid efforts that aimed to destroy the post-2003 order. And, in a predictable cycle, these efforts at subversion accentuated the already-severe shortcomings of the newly empowered non-Sunni political elites (Rayburn 2014, pp. 113–115). More relevant to our purposes, this dynamic also nurtured an ambivalent relationship between Sunnis and antistate militancy that has done much to perpetuate the cycle of conflict. As illustrated by the most recent surge in violence,[11]

9 There have been persistent complaints that de-Ba'athification has been turned into a political weapon and that it is used more leniently with Shi'a former Ba'athists. One scholar described de-Ba'athification as, "closer to a pre-Islamic [*jahili*] vendetta than a legal interpellation …" (Salih 2011, p. 161). The abolishment or reform of de-Ba'athification has been a consistent demand of Sunni politicians and activists. On the evolution of de-Ba'athification, see Lafourcade (2012) and Al Marashi and Keskin (2008, pp. 243–259).

10 Demographics are a major source of contention. Many Sunnis reject the fact that they are a numerical minority. Exact population breakdowns are unknown and current estimates that give Sunnis an approximately 25% share of the Iraqi population are based on extrapolations from previous censuses. Conducting a new census has proven controversial (Haddad 2014c, pp. 155–156).

11 A renewed insurgency has been underway since spring 2013 and more so since December 2013 when former Prime Minister Nuri al Maliki ordered the shut down of the Sunni protest camps that had been demonstrating since December 2012. Since then the state has had only partial control of Iraq's Anbar province. In June 2014 insurgents led by what is today known as the "Islamic State" took over Mosul, Iraq's second city, after which the government lost

many Sunni leaders, even those who are personally involved in the political process, are nevertheless prone to voice their support for antistate (and not just antigovernment) insurgents.[12]

At heart, political violence and sociopolitical division in post-2003 Iraq have revolved around the issue of state legitimacy in a context of poor governance and failing politics. Both Shi'a and Sunni politicians have supported violent non-state actors – except that in the case of the former, these actors have been aligned with, or at least were not in opposition to, the state. In the case of the latter, these have been antistate actors. This unfortunate equation reflects the broader divide over views of the legitimacy of the post-2003 order and leads to a vicious cycle that shows no sign of abating: antistate sentiment among Sunnis feeds into antistate insurgency that then nourishes the discriminatory, heavy-handed, and sect-centric aspects of post-2003 governance, thereby exacerbating antistate sentiment among Sunnis by again validating widespread Sunni grievances (real or perceived).

VIOLENCE IN IRAQ 2003–2007

The drivers of *division* described thus far must be taken into account when considering the drivers of *violence* and Iraq's descent into civil war, which is consistently characterized by violence against civilians/mass atrocities. Division need not be synonymous with violence, nor civil war with atrocities, but given the conditions that prevailed in Iraq in the early post-war period, it is unsurprising that violence and division were amplified in mutually reinforcing ways. The invasion of Iraq was accompanied by a total breakdown of law, order, governance, and authority. There was no restraining force or guiding principle in the early days of the new Iraq. Consequently, the space emerged for all manner of groups to organize and assert their will: from new political parties to civil society organizations to militias to insurgent groups and criminal organizations (al Jaza'iri 2009). As already mentioned, the new political order was itself divisive in that it politicized ethno-sectarian identities and empowered polarizing figures

control of most of Ninewa, Salah al Din, and Anbar provinces to a patchwork of insurgent groups most prominent of whom have been the IS. The fall of Mosul is a major turning point in the renewed insurgency and may be the most critical crisis faced by the crisis-ridden post-2003 state.

12 As was common in 2003–2008, Sunni figures often distinguish between what they regard as legitimate (even if violent) resistance to the state and terrorism. As such antigovernment outlets such as *Baghdad* television (which is associated with former Speaker of Parliament Osama al Nujaifi's Mutahidun political bloc) seldom mention the likes of the IS instead describing those fighting the Iraqi security forces as "tribal revolutionaries." Even after the fall of Mosul, Nujaifi himself used the term "revolution" (a term whose positive connotations imply legitimacy) to describe the renewed insurgency while accepting that "terrorists are taking advantage of it" (Hauslohner 2014). Similarly, the Grand Mufti of Iraq, Sunni cleric Rafi'i al Rifai'i rejected the label of "terrorist" referring instead to "rebels" or "revolutionaries" ("Mufti Rafi'i al Rifai's Response to Mahdi Al Karbala'i's Statements" 2014).

and organizations. All of this was facilitated and supported by the presence of a no-less-divisive occupation force.

As a result, anti-occupation and antistate violence became intertwined. Given the perceived sense of Shi'a ownership of the new order, there was a distinctly sectarian flavor to the violence from a very early stage.[13] In many ways, with time, it became increasingly difficult to clearly delineate the logic of attacking the U.S.-led occupation, the new state or the Shi'as. In parallel, the lines separating fighting for the state, fighting terror, and attacking Sunnis also became more ambiguous over time.[14] Almost immediately after the fall of the regime, score settling and violence, political and/or criminal, became a feature of the new Iraq. It is worth noting that Shi'a militants, many of whom were affiliated with the newly empowered political elite, operated from the earliest days of the new order with their assassination squads targeting Ba'ath sympathizers and former Ba'athists.[15] A profound sense of insecurity amongst Sunnis and Shi'as at both the elite and the mass level created a classic security dilemma, whereby mutual fear led to increased group mobilization – both in the sense of armed mobilization and in the mobilization of group identity.

The details of the escalation that ultimately led to the gruesome highs of violence in 2006 and 2007 need not detain us.[16] The violence included some internal variation, but spanned most of the Arab Iraqi geography. Not all forms of violence followed the logic of the Sunni-Shi'a schism: for instance, intra-Shi'a violence (e.g., Basra 2007, Karbala 2008); the fight against Al Qaeda (e.g., Anbar and Diyala 2007); the fight against the United States (e.g., Anbar, Baghdad); and inter-militia violence (Baghdad 2006–2008; Basra 2007). Further, Sunni anti-U.S. insurgent activity declined at the time that Shi'a anti-U.S. insurgents gained momentum.

More relevant to our discussion of why mass atrocities have *not* ended is how these years, building on a legacy of authoritarianism and violence, shaped the political landscape that emerged after some measure of stability had been achieved

13 For example, in August 2003 the leader of what was then known as the Supreme Council for the Islamic Revolution in Iraq was assassinated in a car bombing that killed upwards of 80 people outside the Imam Ali mosque in Najaf – a site of particular religious significance to Shi'as. Another early example would be the multiple bombings of Shi'a religious processions in the spring of 2004 that killed upwards of 170 people.

14 For example, one study on internal displacement notes that "Sunni Arabs from conflict areas, though displaced by Coalition military operations, often view themselves as displaced by sectarian tensions, because they view US efforts to assert control over Sunni areas as part of a Shi'a plot to control Iraq . . . ." (al Khalidi and Tanner 2006, pp. 2 and 9).

15 To give an early example see "Iraq's Shi'i cleric urges killing of Saddam's Ba'athists," *BBC Monitoring*, June 13, 2003.

16 The escalation of violence in the period 2003–2007 has been the subject of much analysis. To name but a few examples: Dodge (2012), Rosen (2010), International Crisis Group (2004, 2006a, 2006b, 2006c, 2007, 2008a, 2008b, 2013, 2014), Boyle (2009, pp. 261–287), and Allawi (2007).

in late 2007. By the time Iraq's first elected government was formed in 2006, the state was composed of competing forces, many of whom were active participants in the ever-escalating violence. Most notoriously the Ministry of Interior came to play a prominent role in the civil war in Baghdad and beyond, particularly after the elections of 2005, and the granting of the Ministry to the Islamic Supreme Council of Iraq whose paramilitary wing, the Badr Corps, was now able to operate with impunity from the ministry. Sources describe the emergence of a parallel chain of command reporting to Badr-affiliated cadres and who held sway over the formal hierarchy within the ministry (Haddad, interview with Ministry of Interior 2014; Rayburn 2014, pp. 79–81). In effect, what emerged was a shadow ministry within the Ministry of Interior: above the formal ministerial structure, there existed a sect-centric militia-led force that was leading the fight against antistate militants and their support networks (Haddad, interview with Ministry of Interior 2014).

A similar pattern developed across the various organs of the state in effect halting whatever efforts existed to build the state's governing capacity. An enduring result of this dynamic is the institutionalization of violence and narrow group interests. This has resulted in a pronounced state of fragmentation across the state and within state organs. For example, intelligence officers complain that they must contend with party and militia-affiliated intelligence networks whose information and recommendations often take precedence over ostensibly national intelligence organs (Haddad, interview with Baghdad Counter Terrorism Department 2012). Furthermore, promotions, assignments, and rotations are subject to intense political interference, thereby hampering an institution's effectiveness (Haddad, interview with Baghdad police captain 2014). A member of Baghdad's Provincial Council described competing criminal, militant, and political networks within single institutions in 2006–2007:

> There were instances of real criminality [referring to extortion and strong-arm tactics for financial gain] and some unbelievable methods of killing that were happening within institutions. You may be surprised to hear that the civil war [also] happened within the institutions: people disappeared not [only] outside on the streets; many people were abducted from their offices for sectarian reasons using official orders and official channels . . . . So sectarianism was bigger than just this one is Sunni and that one is Shi'a: it affected the state's infrastructure and institutions. Gangs! It was gangs!
>
> (Haddad, interview with Baghdad Provincial Council 2013).

The councilman's recollections highlight an important point: while much of the violence was undeniably sect-coded and continues to be so, various other armed groups compete within and across sectarian lines, and within and against the state for a greater share of its power and resources (Boyle 2009, p. 268). This dynamic has continued in one form or another, highlighting the fact that the system that has emerged in Iraq is shaped by conditions of civil war: opacity, diffusion of power, dysfunction, and kleptocracy. This has been both a symptom and a cause of the failure of the post-2003 state-building project. It has allowed for the proliferation of armed groups and the perpetuation of violence. Ultimately, no other factor oils the cycle of violence more than state weakness and fragmentation.

The Iraqi state lacks the capacity to enforce a victor's peace, and Iraqi politics are too fractious and dysfunctional to enact a meaningful reconciliation process. Indeed, it can be argued that political violence, like many other ills afflicting contemporary Iraq such as identity politics or corruption, is not an anomaly but a defining characteristic of the current order. As argued by Charles Tripp:

> violence in Iraq has now become a central part of the practice of power, both by the government and by certain non-governmental agencies, some of them bitterly opposed to, but others enmeshed in webs of government practice.
>
> (2012)

Indeed, what Tripp refers to as the "grammar of violence" continues to inform political bargaining at the elite level and dictates state response to political conflict (Tripp 2007, 2013). One even suspects that political violence in the new Iraq has become so entrenched and so banal that government policy deals with it much the same way as unemployment is dealt with elsewhere in the world: as something to be managed and contained rather than something that needs eradication.[17]

Nonetheless, beginning in late 2007 and early 2008, Iraq seemed to have achieved some sort of an ending to mass violence and looked like it was set on a more positive trajectory. By any measure, a drop of monthly deaths from highs of over 3,000 killed in July 2006 to just over 600 deaths two years later in July 2008 is a remarkable achievement. Indeed the average monthly violent death toll continued to hover around 300 until 2013 (Iraq Body Count).[18] What explains the drop in violence in late 2007 and why, six years later, did it begin to soar again?

2007: THE "ENDING" THAT WASN'T

The drivers behind the reduction in violence beginning in late 2007 have been the subject of much research, particularly on the question of whether or not the U.S. "Surge" policy was the primary cause. Broadly speaking, there is consensus that no single factor, Surge or otherwise, can be solely credited with the security improvement in 2007–2008 that generally lasted until 2013. A number of interrelated and interdependent factors, difficult to recreate individually, let alone in tandem,

[17] This was certainly the impression I came away with after speaking to employees in the Office of the Commander in Chief, Baghdad, March 2014.

[18] Throughout 2006–2007 the average monthly death toll was over 2,300. In the years 2010–2012, that figure dropped to an average of just over 350 deaths per month. The highest monthly figure in the period 2006–2013 was in July 2006 with 3,297 violent deaths documented. The lowest figure for the same time period is December 2010 with just 218 deaths.

combined to create what at the time seemed like an ending. Various scholars have suggested a combination of the following: the military losses of Sunni militants to the state and Shi'a militias; the extra U.S. troops and reorientation of U.S. counterinsurgency policy afforded by the Surge; the Awakening movement; sectarian cleansing; the "freeze" or standing down of the Mahdi Army (one of the most prominent and destabilizing forces in the violence of 2006–2007); and finally the growing strength and confidence of the state and the Iraqi security forces. The multiplicity of factors, in part, reflects the multiplicity of conflicts and drivers of conflict by early 2007: sectarian violence; antistate violence; anti-occupation violence; intra-Shi'a violence; intra-Sunni violence; external subversion; criminality; and weak state institutions.

The Surge

By late 2006, Iraq seemed to be broken beyond repair. Some U.S. officials were even describing the situation as lost and a growing stream of unofficial statements implied that Iraq's more restive areas were effectively beyond control (Ricks 2006; Baker 2006). There was even debate at the highest levels of the U.S. administration as to whether a gradual drawdown of U.S. troops in Iraq should be initiated in the near future. In the event, in early 2007, then President George W. Bush decided to adopt what became known as the "Surge." The most visible feature of the new strategy was the deployment of six new brigades to Iraq, totaling some 30,000 additional troops.

However, the Surge entailed far more than a surge in firepower. It also involved a reorientation of American counterinsurgency tactics with an emphasis on the need to protect the Iraqi public. This led to a host of shifts in U.S. military practice in Iraq: strengthening relationships with local actors, some of whom were former combatants; empowering local leaders; embedding U.S. forces within local populations; encouraging localized ceasefires and reconciliation initiatives; supporting reconstruction programs; focusing attacks on key insurgency leaders and enablers; supporting job programs; assisting in governance initiatives; and so forth (Patraeus 2013). As described by the public face of the Surge, General David Petraeus, "It is important to note that the surge was ... a *comprehensive* civil-military campaign, not just a substantial number of additional forces" (Patraeus 2013). Indeed, when considered in isolation from other factors, there is no clear correlation between increasing the number of troops and increasing stability during the Surge (Thiel 2011). In fact, several positive trends commonly attributed to the Surge were already underway before Surge operations had begun.[19]

[19] This was particularly evident in Iraq's Anbar province (McCary 2009, pp. 43–59). The same report argues that extra troops had a varied utility in different areas of Iraq: "Whereas an increased tactical force presence may have helped in crowded urban areas with sparring

The infusion of additional American firepower was not irrelevant; on the contrary, it was crucial, but only as part of a wider array of factors that combined to reduce violence and end the civil war that had been raging until early 2007. The success of the Surge was dependent on local Iraqi dynamics and vice versa. U.S. military efforts would have failed to yield a satisfactory result were it not for political factors (Iraqi and American), and positive Iraqi dynamics may well have stalled were it not for the role played by the Surge (Ollivant 2011). At the very least the adoption of the Surge policy by then President Bush had a powerful psychological benefit in that it signaled a robust commitment to the Iraqi state's survival and to resolving Iraq's conflicts at a time when there were genuine fears that the United States may abandon Iraq.

THE "BATTLE FOR BAGHDAD" AND THE "AWAKENING"

Another central factor in the decline of violence was the victory of the state and its allied militias over Sunni militants in the "Battle for Baghdad." The military fortunes of the state and its allied militias, particularly when considered in conjunction with the influx of extra U.S troops and the reorientation of counterinsurgency policy, were crucial in several regards. By late 2006 Sunni militants had realized they had lost the civil war – little did anyone know at the time that this would turn out to be just one bout in a longer civil war rather than *the* civil war. This forced them to reevaluate their position and how best to secure their future in Iraq. They had to accept the reality that, by late 2006, they had little alternative to negotiating with the Iraqi state and cooperating with U.S. forces to secure themselves from both the state and Al Qaeda in Iraq (AQI).[20]

In many ways, the brutal violence of 2006–2007 finally forced Sunni militants and political actors to accept the new political landscape (albeit begrudgingly) that they had resisted and regarded as transient since 2003. As described by Nir Rosen, a journalist with unrivaled access to Sunni militant groups in the years 2003–2006:

> The balance of power really shifted in 2006. And I met resistance leaders, Sunni resistance leaders, in Baghdad and Anbar, Syria, Jordan, and they all said the same thing: "We lost. We lost." It was a huge shift in how they thought of themselves. They had once thought that they could easily overthrow the Americans and overthrow the Shi'as."
>
> (Kouddous, interview with Nir Rosen 2010)

ethnicities, such as Baghdad, a few thousand troops in the vast rural expanses of al Anbar would not have made a difference" (McCary 2009, pp. 52–53).

20 The beginnings of the turn of Sunni tribes and militants against AQI go back to mid-2005 in Anbar province. As such this is one amongst many examples of events in late 2006–2007 that encouraged positive trends already underway. It should be noted that AQI was subsumed by the Islamic State of Iraq when the latter was formed in late 2006, but the term AQI was still in use several years later.

A sense of defeat, more than anything, facilitated the Awakening movement that in turn fed into the counterinsurgency tactics of the Surge and ultimately led to the demise of the Mahdi Army, the resurgence of the state, and an end to mass violence.

The Awakening movement marked a shift within tribes and parts of the Sunni insurgency against the more unpalatable parts of the insurgency, namely, AQI. It saw former antistate and anti-occupation combatants work with the state and the coalition to defeat AQI in Sunni areas. Some of the more commonly given reasons for this change include U.S. financial incentives, revulsion at AQI's brutality, and anger at AQI's infringement on tribal authority and sources of finance – such as smuggling routes. There may be partial truth to all of these, but a crucial determining factor was the changing fortunes of the Sunni insurgency in Baghdad and elsewhere over the course of the civil war.

Parts of the Sunni insurgency found themselves losing ground to the state, Shi'a militias, and AQI. As Ollivant argues, with the tide turning, they feared that their future in Iraq would be jeopardized by a victorious Iraqi state that they had tried to overthrow. Consequently, they were more willing to turn on AQI as a means of ingratiating themselves not just with the Iraqi state but more crucially with the United States – an actor that by 2007 was regarded by many Sunnis as less of an existential threat than the Iraqi state (which many Sunnis regarded as synonymous with Iranian occupation) (Ahad 2007). Once Sunnis had turned on AQI, the Americans then set up programs that legitimized these former Sunni insurgents by turning them into quasi-governmental paramilitary units and by assuring them some measure of immunity with plans to eventually integrate them into the new Iraq (Ollivant 2011; Musings on Iraq 2012).

In sum, the success of the Awakening in 2006 and 2007 was directly linked to the success of the state in the civil war and to the Surge – all three factors were mutually reinforcing in bringing about the much-needed respite from violence in late 2007. Were it not for the defeat of Sunni militants in the violence of 2006–2007, the incentives for Sunni insurgents to de-escalate the fight against the state, turn on AQI, and win over the Americans would have been much weaker. By the same token, were it not for the Surge and the extra firepower it afforded, turning to the Americans might not have been a winning strategy – just as the extra U.S. troops without the Awakening may well have proven ineffective beyond the immediate term. The importance of this synergy is highlighted by the fact that there were attempts by Sunni tribes in Anbar to work with the Americans against AQI from as early as 2004. However, prior to 2007 such attempts were localized and lacked the urgency that became apparent once the fate of the civil war became less ambiguous. Furthermore, prior to the Surge, both the United States's insufficient troop strength and their counterproductive military doctrine hampered attempts at cooperation and ensured the failure of attempts to mobilize against AQI.[21] The Surge not only provided manpower but also fostered the trust needed for cooperation between U.S. forces and potential allies.[22]

The Ascendancy of the State

To this combination of factors can be added another ingredient: the defeat of Sunni militants in Baghdad in 2006–2007 gave the Iraqi state the confidence to regard itself as such. As our source in the Ministry of Interior put it:

> What happened in 2008 was that the state and the Shi'a militias had won the civil war. More importantly this allowed the state to adopt a more inward looking stance and began to draw limits to what these groups [militias allied to/within the state] could do as they had started to get out of control.
>
> (Haddad interview in Baghdad 2014)

This applied to several groups, but by 2007 it applied to the Mahdi Army more than any other.

The Mahdi Army's brutality was integral to the defeat of Sunni militants in Baghdad and surrounding areas.[23] Their meteoric rise in 2006–2007 was in part a reflection of the state's near-collapse as the civil war raged. The demand for the security and services that the Sadrists and their Mahdi Army were able to provide came from both the Shi'a population and the state. They penetrated key parts of the state, not least of which was the police, and went through a remarkable territorial expansion across many parts of Baghdad in the course of their ruthless fight against Sunni militant groups in 2006 and 2007. The extent of their success and the intensity of the violence are attested to by the capital's demographic shift in those years in which Baghdad turned into a less mixed and more Shi'a city.[24] The state security apparatus' complicity and cooperation in these developments is well documented and, in fact, made it difficult to differentiate between official state security forces and Mahdi Army militants throughout much of 2006–2007 (International Crisis Group 2008a).

[21] Biddle et al. outline four failed attempts in Anbar between 2004 and 2006. With insufficient troop levels, U.S. forces were unable to provide the protection or support that fighters desperately needed once they had turned on AQI (Biddle et al. 2012, pp. 7–40).

[22] For the role of counterinsurgency doctrine and the role of money and reconstruction efforts in fostering the Awakening, see McCary (2009, pp. 45 and 50).

[23] A fact commonly attested to (sometimes begrudgingly) by many Iraqis including Iraqi politician Ahmed al Chalabi, who once stated that "were it not for the Mahdi Army . . . there would not have been a single Shi'i left in Karkh [western Baghdad]." ("Ahmad al Chalabi: Were it not for the Mehdi Army not a single Shi'a would have remained in Iraq," 2011).

[24] For maps detailing the changing sectarian demographics of Baghdad, see The Gulf/2000 Project (2013).

Politically, the government of Nuri al Maliki, formed in 2006, was dependent on Sadrist support. Militarily, the state was in need of Sadrist militancy in the form of the Mahdi Army to counter antistate Sunni militants. Socially, the Sadrists provided services, and the Mahdi Army provided protection to a Shi'a population that felt encircled by Sunni militants and abandoned by the state. Describing Baghdad in 2006 and the first half of 2007, the International Crisis Group wrote:

> In a city virtually abandoned by the state, Sadrist offices in several neighbourhoods became the last and only resort for Shiite residents in need of help. Shiites living in remote areas requested military support; displaced families asked for resettlement assistance; even feuding couples turned to [Sadrist offices] for arbitration.
>
> (2008a, p. 7)

However, Sadrist fortunes turned by mid-2007, and the Mahdi Army was eventually broken by a resurgent state (Krohley 2015). Again, the factors behind this development were numerous and worked in a synergetic way. The Mahdi Army's power declined in tandem with the factors already discussed, and led to the drop in violence in late 2007. With Sunni sectarian violence waning in 2007, Iraqi forces gaining in confidence and effectiveness, and the renewed commitment of the United States to the Iraqi state, the conditions that created the demand for and growth of the Mahdi Army largely disappeared.

Just as importantly, there was increasing revulsion amongst many Shi'as at the Mahdi Army's predatory behavior and criminality that became ever more difficult to tolerate or excuse as the sense of existential threat waned. Following a serious incident of intra-Shi'a violence in August 2007 that was widely blamed on the Mahdi Army, the leader of the Sadrist current, Muqtada al Sadr, ordered a "freeze" to all Mahdi Army activity. Sadr felt that he may have lost control of what was always a decentralized movement and the freeze would offer him a chance to purge the Mahdi Army of its more troublesome elements. In any case, mercifully for Iraq, the freeze fit neatly into the constellation of factors that led to the end of mass violence in 2007.

From the Iraqi government's point of view, with the Sunni threat weakening, the rise of the Awakening movement, and the increased U.S. military presence, by mid-2007 the Sadrists and the Mahdi Army were at best a burden and at worst a threat. There was little room or need for the Mahdi Army once the political focus shifted from street warfare and winning the capital to consolidation and building state capacity. As a result, the Sadrists were eventually excluded from the ruling coalition and political cover was lifted from the Mahdi Army, leaving them vulnerable to Iraqi and U.S. operations. By 2008, violence had sufficiently decreased and Maliki (and much of the Shi'a political classes) felt secure enough to start jettisoning unruly partners who had until recently been essential allies in the civil war. This culminated in the Charge of the Knights operations of

2008 launched by Maliki, with significant U.S. military support, that were ultimately to break the Mahdi Army.[25]

Clearly, no single driver can account for the drop in violence in 2007. All of the factors discussed here worked interdependently and all were essential to the success of each other. The loss of the civil war incentivized Sunni political and insurgent forces to negotiate and work with the Americans and with the Iraqi government. This was a key driver behind the rise of the Awakening. In turn the Awakening was facilitated by the Surge, and conversely, it ensured the Surge's effectiveness, which in turn provided the opening for the state to focus on consolidating gains and building capacity. The resulting improvements in security led to the isolation of and eventual freeze on Mahdi Army activities. Ultimately this worked toward enhancing the state's legitimacy and broadened popular acceptance (begrudging or otherwise) of the post-2003 order.

These were the factors that, beginning in mid-late 2007, led to the ending of mass violence and mass atrocities.[26] They were a product of the sociopolitical moment, and are, as such, impossible to replicate – something that is particularly unfortunate given Iraq's renewed and urgent need for an end to mass atrocities. These factors do not provide a formula for ending, but rather describe a political opening that was not seized.

WHY MASS ATROCITIES HAVE NOT ENDED

The years 2007–2013 saw a lull in violence and a relative stabilization of the state that afforded Iraq a real opportunity for political progress. This was squandered as a result of several factors: the controversial elections of 2010, the withdrawal of U.S. forces, and the highly corrosive politics of Nuri al Maliki's second government (2010–2014). More fundamentally, however, the lull in violence was not accompanied by a political effort to address the underlying roots of conflict.

Clashing conceptions of the meaning, identity, and ownership of the Iraqi state were unresolved, and grievances relating to the pre- and post-2003 periods were unaddressed. Further, the state lacked the capacity – particularly after the departure of U.S. troops in late 2011[27] – to adequately suppress these issues under

25 The Charge of the Knights operations were launched in March 2008 against the Mahdi Army and then against AQI in Iraq. The operations were broadly successful and were hugely popular in that they broke the Mahdi Army and cemented recent security gains. It temporarily gave Maliki the aura of a strong cross-sectarian statesman. Indeed it was at this time that Maliki began disassociating himself and his party, the Da'awa Party, from the broad Shi'a coalition formed in 2005 and created his own State of Law coalition that still exists today. Neither Maliki's pretensions to cross-sectarian politics nor the Mahdi Army's fall proved permanent.

26 As opposed to the notion that violence dropped because sectarian cleansing had run its logical course leaving no more potential victims for sectarian militias to target – a notion easily disproved by a visit to Baghdad today (Biddle et al 2012, pp. 13–18; Rayburn 2014, pp. 90–95).

27 In the words of Iraq's former minister of defense: "Remember, there was a lot of peace and stability. Until 2010 conditions were good. Maliki's big mistake was not keeping American forces even though many Iraqi officials tried to keep them" (Ratnam 2014).

a victor's peace. In short, as one veteran of the Iraq war lamented, the drop in violence bought time, but did not solve much (Kingsbury 2014). This eventuality was predicted in the Iraq Study Group Report of December 2006. Commenting on the limits of what additional U.S. forces could achieve, the authors argued:

> Sustained increases in U.S. troop levels would not solve the fundamental cause of violence in Iraq, which is the absence of national reconciliation .... As another American general told us, if the Iraqi government does not make political progress, "all the troops in the world will not provide security."
>
> (Baker III 2006, p. 30)

There were several points between 2007 and 2013 when the cycle of Shi'a-centric state building and Sunni rejection could have been broken. But time and again a dysfunctional political system characterized by a fundamental lack of trust, political vision, and will stood in the way of political progress.[28] The most promising period was 2008–10: violence continued declining, sectarian politics were in very clear retreat,[29] militia and insurgent networks had been crippled, and many were optimistic that post-2003 Iraqi politics had come of age.[30] Sadly, whatever glimmer of hope existed began to fade in the parliamentary elections of 2010. The contest was mainly between Prime Minister Maliki's State of Law and Ayad Allawi's Iraqiya list. Buoyed by the improvement in security and by the success of several major counterinsurgency operations in 2008, Maliki had dissociated himself and his party, the Da'awa Party, from the broad Shi'a coalition formed in 2005 opting instead to form the State of Law coalition. More broadly, and reflecting the mood of the electorate, he had positioned himself as a strong, nationalist, cross-sectarian statesman. Ayad Allawi, although often portrayed as the nonsectarian alternative, can more accurately be described as the non-Shi'a-Islamist, overwhelmingly Sunni vote. His associations with former Ba'athists and with regional Arab powers made a considerable body of the Shi'a electorate regard him with suspicion as little more than a Ba'athist Trojan horse. In the event, Maliki narrowly lost the elections but, to the detriment of Iraq's political development, managed to retain the prime minister's seat through a mixture of legislative acrobatics and a return to sectarian coalition building (Visser 2009).[31] The speedy return of sectarian coalitions was

28 Some of the most contentious legislative issues have continued to linger for the better part of a decade. These include the need for hydrocarbons legislation, amnesty laws, reform of counter-terrorism laws, de Ba'athification reform, constitutional reform, an elections law, and the list goes on.

29 This was particularly noticeable in 2009 (which incidentally was an election year). For example, see Wahid (2009).

30 Writing in 2009, Reidar Visser provides an overview of the reasons for optimism and also why optimism needed to be cautious (2009). Indeed, while the January 2009 elections were largely peaceful, there were several instances of questionable electoral tactics such as the use of de-Ba'athification to exclude rivals from the elections.

31 In the end, a power-sharing government emerged in December 2010 encompassing practically every major political power in the country and leaving no room for a formal opposition

indicative of the persistence of the underlying drivers of division, and ultimately conflict. The fact remained that self-interested leaders could tap into politically salient social cleavages and their attendant fears, grievances, and senses of entitlement to rally a base who lent their support more out of fear of the other than any genuine political conviction. It was common to find Iraqis supporting a second Maliki government because they were convinced that the alternative was a return of barely reformed Ba'athists under the stewardship of Ayad Allawi. This was a continuation of a pattern going back to 2003: many Sunnis simply could not accept Shi'a-centric politicians, and many Shi'as feared the alternative, particularly given the prevalence of sectarian violence and the sense of existential threat that it bred.

Without a viable political force to tap into the desire for cross-sectarian unity, political forces capitalizing on recent traumas for political gain through aggressive identity politics easily deepened divisions and perpetuated conflict. This dynamic can be so pronounced as to constrain people's ability to choose – as Kreidi and Monroe found in their work on the Lebanese civil war:

> We were struck by the extent to which identity constrained choice for all these people … no one felt they had a choice. Each insisted they were pushed into action by "the other." No one seemed to want the conflict to continue; yet all seemed pulled towards its continuation by a feeling that they would be destroyed if they did not turn to violence.
>
> (2002, p. 19)[32]

The years 2008–2013 were the new Iraq's most promising, yet these were also the years in which the modest gains of 2007–2008 were ultimately reversed. The moment created by the Awakening movement, the tentative – albeit begrudging – Sunni acceptance of the new Iraq's political realities, the waning of sectarian entrenchment, and, ultimately, the drop in mass violence in 2007 began to vanish. By 2013 what little progress had been made on these fronts had been reversed, and the clash between Shi'a-centric state building and Sunni rejection was as relevant as ever.[33] Sunni political participation was undermined by the elections of 2010, the ineffectiveness of Sunni political leadership, the centralizing and increasingly autocratic second government of Nuri al Maliki, and particularly his targeting of top Sunni leaders in 2011–2013. Militant networks were still active and steadily gaining ground with every year of political failure that passed. In fact it was in these

let alone a thought for good governance (Visser 2010). For an analysis of Maliki's second term and Iraqi politics in 2010–2014, see Project on Middle East Political Science (2014).

32 Similarly, after expressing his heartfelt disgust of Iraqi politicians, one Iraqi claimed that "I have to vote for my [sectarian] group. That's what Iraq is now. If I don't vote for my sectarian group I would worry that the other [sectarian group] would eat me alive" (Pers. comm.).

33 The specific drivers behind these reversals are complex and include Iraqi, regional, and international drivers. For an overview see, amongst many others, Rayburn (2014, pp. 209–242); Dodge (2012), Chapter 5; Project on Middle East Political Science (2014); International Crisis Group (2013); Hill (2014); and Wicken (2013).

years that the Islamic State of Iraq was able to reconstitute itself and expand its operations *before* entering the Syrian arena and eventually launching its audacious sweep across vast swathes of Iraq in the summer of 2014 under its new banner of the Islamic State of Iraq and al Sham – soon to be rebranded into the Islamic State. With hindsight, it would seem that the return to mass violence was the unavoidable concomitant of the unsustainability of the Iraqi political order in the years 2010–2014.

In a study of elite political bargains and civil war in Sub-Saharan Africa, Stefan Lindemann hypothesized that:

> [. . .] the post-colonial trajectories of civil war versus political stability across Sub-Saharan Africa are largely determined by the varying ability of ruling political parties to overcome the specific historical legacy of high social fragmentation by forging and maintaining "inclusive elite bargains."
>
> (2008, p. 16)

Iraq's governments since 2010 have certainly been inclusive in terms of the apportionment of cabinet positions – it can even be argued that they have been inclusive to the point of dysfunction – however, they have not been inclusive in terms of sharing actual power.[34] Maliki's second government was characterized by rising authoritarianism and centralization of power. Most damagingly, this involved targeting the highest levels of Sunni political representation, illustrated by the arrest warrants issued against Vice President Tariq al Hashimi in December 2011 and against Minister of Finance Rafi'i al Issawi in December 2012.[35] These are just two examples of the failure of Iraq's political classes to forge a functioning inclusive elite bargain. The reasons behind this are far greater than just the former prime minister's incompetence. At heart, the ill-defined, yet often called-for "reconciliation" that Iraq is in need of is a reconciling of clashing visions regarding the identity, ownership, and ultimately the legitimacy of the state. The failure to adequately acknowledge, let alone address, this issue has made "reconciliation" in the Iraqi context a rather vacuous term. It has also perpetuated violence and seen a return to civil war and atrocities beginning in 2013 and more so since the summer of 2014.

A constitution, a supreme court, a piece of legislation, or an election are only effective in ordering society and moderating political contestation when they are

[34] Lindemann identifies four indicators of inclusivity in the distribution of government jobs: social composition of the cabinet; social composition of the "inner circle of political power"; social composition of parliament; social composition of the ruling party. Iraqi governments are less inclusive in the second and fourth indicators (Lindemann 2008).

[35] The move against Issawi precipitated the protest movement in Sunni majority areas that lasted throughout 2013 before the outbreak of full-scale insurgency. Whether the move against Hashimi and then against Issawi was a manifestation of sectarian policy or centralizing tendencies (irrespective of sectarian identity) is a moot point, given the impact that both episodes had on perceptions regarding sectarian identity and sectarian politics (Haddad 2012b).

viewed as having the authority that is derived from legitimacy – and when they have the backing of the coercive and regulatory power of the state. In Iraq, both legitimacy and the state's capacity to enforce its will have fluctuated over the past twelve years with a concomitant effect on insurgency and ultimately mass atrocities. The more transient the state appeared to be at a given moment, the more Sunni resentment turned into armed insurgency against what it regarded as an illegitimate state.[36] Addressing this divergence regarding perceptions of state legitimacy, as opposed to debating the division of cabinet positions amongst a political elite of questionable representativeness, should be the essence of "reconciliation."

Otherwise, and particularly in times of heightened tension, even the state's most mundane functions can be sources of resentment. State building is only welcomed by people who recognize the state: whether or not a community will see the construction of a road as a sign of progress or as a threatening intrusion will largely depend on how they view the state. As argued by Stanisland:

> Population security and state building sound good in the metropole but often look very different on the periphery; seemingly technocratic policies like governance and service provision are in fact short-hand for state coercion, homogenization, surveillance and extraction. Leviathans are far more attractive to those who will run them than to those who will be in their gun sights.
>
> (2012, p. 256)

The question of state legitimacy and its impact on political perceptions is also at the heart of why mechanisms of conflict mediation and political representation have proven ineffective. For example, the state's legitimacy deficit amongst Sunnis has limited their trust in elections to act as the arbiter of fair political representation. This is rooted in the rejection amongst many Sunnis of some of post-2003 Iraq's foundational ideas – in this case, demographics.[37] As the foundation of the ethno-sectarian apportionment that Sunnis feel has disenfranchised them, demographics are a common point of reference in Sunni martyrology. From the earliest days of the new Iraq, many Sunnis rejected the notion that they are a numerical minority,[38] being treated as one nourished their sense of victimhood. They see

[36] That is not to suggest that there is a lack of Shi'a militancy; however, precisely because of views regarding the legitimacy of the political order, Shi'a militancy is not directed against the state. Here it is worth pointing out what should be an obvious disclaimer: that nothing can, or is, being said about *all* Sunnis or *all* Shi'as. Indeed, some of the most significant battlefronts today pit Sunni tribes against IS militants. However, denying that the division regarding state legitimacy falls to a significant extent along sectarian lines would simply be counterfactual.

[37] While this negative predisposition toward the electoral process was evident since the earliest post-2003 elections, it was immeasurably worsened by the controversy surrounding the elections of 2010.

[38] The argument commonly made by Sunni Arabs is that they constitute 42% of the Iraqi population while the Shi'a account for 41%; hence alongside the mostly Sunni Kurdish north, Iraq is a Sunni-majority country. I have heard this unsubstantiated view from Sunni Arab Iraqis countless times. Public pronouncements to the same effect have been made by Sunni

themselves as people who have essentially been cheated into second-class status by nothing more than a lie. For the Shi'a, majority status is the bedrock of their sense of entitlement in Iraqi politics and a central component of the Shi'a narrative of victimhood as the long-suffering majority. Until a census is conducted – and assuming that all sides accept its results – this issue will remain contentious.

The practical implications for the electoral process and Iraqi politics are obvious. Sunni political actors who subscribe to the idea that Sunnis are not a minority will have unrealistic expectations that, when not met, only deepen their sense of marginalization, exclusion, and consequently their rejection of the post-2003 order.[39] This is partly why the electoral process has been as much a blessing as a curse to post-2003 Iraq. As long as communal identity influences voting patterns, any Sunnis with an inflated sense of their demographic weight will only be further alienated by electoral results that inevitably fall drastically short of expectations and feelings of entitlement. Indeed, for many Sunnis the elections of 2005 validated Sunni militancy and further delegitimized the state after they did not get the result they expected. As one Iraqi journalist related with reference to the elections of 2005:

> Sunni Arab leaders promised the insurgents real Sunni influence if their community participated in the elections. But they think they are 45% of the population .... After the elections, Adnan Duleimi [a leading Sunni politician at the time] publicly cried out: What should I tell the resistance now? How can I deliver on my promise?[40]

The divergence of perceptions regarding demographics and, more fundamentally, state legitimacy complicates conflict resolution in Iraq far more than is acknowledged in policy prescriptions revolving around the mantra of "inclusive government."

The Iraqi experience aligns with the results of a recent study that found greater political proportionality actually *increased* the likelihood of militancy when instituted in fractionalized societies (Foster et al. 2013, pp. 541–557). The authors argue that in fractionalized societies, proportionality will mean the inclusion of numerous smaller political groups in the legislature, which not only leads to regime instability but minimizes the legislative influence of smaller groups: "In such

figures from religious leaders such as Harith al-Dhari (general secretary of the Association of Muslim Scholars) to politicians such as Khalaf al-Ulayan, Muhsin Abd al-Hamid (former head of the Iraqi Islamic Party) and former Speaker of Parliament Osama al-Nujaifi to extremists such as Taha al-Dulaimi. In fact, as early as August 2003 Dulaimi was calling the idea that Sunnis are a minority a lie. See "*The Truth: The First Book on Sunni and Shi'a Demographics in Iraq*" 2003.

39 Needless to say, in the context of post-war Iraq, this often translated into support for militancy (Rayburn 2014, pp. 111, 121, and 129).

40 Interview with Iraqi journalist, January 2006. As quoted in International Crisis Group 2006b, p. 32. In his memoirs Dulaimi maintains that Sunnis are more than 50% of the Iraqi population (Al Dulaimi 2012, p. 153).

circumstances, proportionalism institutionalizes extreme groups' political impotence, increasing the likelihood of their use of violence against the state" (Foster et al. 2013, p. 542). For Sunni political actors in Iraq, the militarizing effects are magnified by their inflated perception of their demographic weight.

Needless to say, the longer this goes, the greater is the risk of an ever-widening disconnect between Sunnis and the state reaching an irreversible breaking point. In some areas, this disillusionment and the latent resentment discussed in this chapter have helped nourish a culture of militancy, as evidenced by the consistency of militant activity in certain parts of Diyala, Anbar, and Ninewa over the past twelve years. Such a culture of antistate militancy, although only actively taken up by a relatively small number of people, is facilitated by passive support or tolerance from broader communities. Such cases are reminiscent of Tripp's observations regarding pre-2003 Kurdish militancy: "Armed resistance in this context was thus more than a mere calculation of advantage, a weighing up of the pros and cons of taking up arms against an oppressive occupying power. It was part of a moral universe that made sense of collective existence" (Tripp 2013, p. 62).

Few examples illustrate the interaction between state legitimacy, sectarian identity, and violence in Iraq better than the parallels between 2003 and 2014. In both cases, the issue was state collapse and what the response should be. In 2003, Shi'as were, broadly speaking, more receptive to the idea of regime change than their Sunni compatriots. The reason was not that Sunnis were pro-Saddam and Shi'as were not; rather, it was that many Shi'as accorded the *state* no legitimacy whatsoever and, crucially, for many Shi'as the downfall of the regime in 2003 was as much their deliverance as a sectarian group as it was Iraq's liberation from tyranny. In 2014, the same dynamic was evident but in reverse: as IS militants surged toward Baghdad and as the post-2003 order seemed to be on the verge of collapse, Shi'as rallied to the defense of the state despite whatever resentment they may have harbored against the government. Amongst Sunnis, on the other hand, there was a considerable body of opinion that would have welcomed the collapse of the entire post-2003 order if it were at the hands of practically anyone other than IS – hence in Sunni public discourse, the role of IS was downplayed and instead repeated references were made to "tribal revolutionaries."[41]

In response to the IS threat, the highest Shi'a clerical authority, Grand Ayatollah Ali Sistani, issued a call to mass mobilization to respond to what was framed as a national threat.[42] The fact that Sistani was no supporter of then Prime Minister Nuri al Maliki's government highlights the centrality of state legitimacy in Sunni and Shi'a perceptions regarding the events of the summer of 2014. As if to underline the point, many Sunni clerics and political figures were incensed by Sistani's call to

[41] See footnote 12.

[42] The language used in Sistani's communiqué was framed in the vocabulary of nationalism and national institutions – nevertheless, it still proved divisive as expected (Kadhim and Al Khatteeb 2014).

arms believing it to be an anti-Sunni mobilization in defense of Maliki (rather than the state), who by that point had become a hate figure of mythic proportions in Sunni perceptions.[43] A question that was often heard being asked rhetorically by Sunnis was: where were Sistani's mobilizational powers in 2003 when Iraq was invaded? Herein lies the crux of the matter: neither Shi'a clerics in 2003 nor Sunni clerics in 2014 came to the defense of the state because neither considered the state legitimate and worth defending; in both cases, Sunnis and Shi'as were divided on whether it was justifiable to defend the state.

CONFLICT BEGETS VICTIMHOOD, VICTIMHOOD BEGETS CONFLICT

Many communal groups define themselves through victimhood. It nourishes group identification by providing a sense of righteousness, moral superiority, and exceptionalism borne of the conviction that the group is subject to unique suffering. This phenomenon is so widespread that it led Ian Buruma to comment that "sometimes it is as if everyone wants to compete with the Jewish tragedy, in what an Israeli friend once called the Olympics of suffering" (1999). In many ways the Iraqi state that was born in 2003 was one based on mythologized communal victimhoods whereby suffering became the measure for entitlement. Unfortunately for Iraq and Iraqis, the horrors of the last twelve years precluded any sense of closure for the traumas of preceding years, and instead drew on the legacy of violence to create a competition of communal victimhoods. This competition now revolves around the present as much as on the past.[44]

Shi'as and Sunnis each consider themselves to be the prime victim of the tragedies of the past twelve years and hence the more deserving of the political capital that is presumed to accrue from unique suffering. In such an environment, atrocities become the currency in which competing victimhoods are played out with the politics of victimhood being fueled by and fueling further mass atrocities. The legacy of the past and the realities of the present have meant that no atrocity is too awful to act as a unifier, neither through outrage nor disgust. No atrocity escapes being sect-coded and thus appropriated by one group or another in pursuit of its narrow sectional interests. Such a climate also raises people's tolerance of atrocities in the name of retributive justice – something that has been particularly evident (on all sides) since summer 2014. Such an environment precludes the trust needed for compromise and long-term solutions.

The civil war did not end in 2007; indeed, the failure of Iraq's political classes to address the drivers of conflict during the relative respite offered by the years

43 For example, see the Mufti of Iraq's on Sistani's statement ("Mufti Rafi'i al Rifai's Response to Mahdi Al Karbala'i's Statements" 2014).

44 Early on after 2003, political organizations established "human rights" departments to churn out material emphasising the victimization of the community they professed to represent (International Crisis Group 2006b, pp. 1–5).

2008–2013 has seen the reemergence of a more virulent form of mass violence since the summer of 2014. Iraq is not doomed to perpetual conflict, but mass atrocities will continue to occur as long as the militarization of political fragmentation persists and as long as the past continues to be enlisted in the service of narrow sectional communal interests. Similarly, disentangling the overlap between state legitimacy, communal identity, and violence is crucial to addressing Iraq's underlying problems and the persistence of conflict. Unfortunately, this requires a degree of trust, vision, and leadership that simply do not exist in Iraqi politics today: identity politics, Shi'a-centric state building, and Sunni rejection are so entrenched as to be definitional features of, rather than aberrations within, the current political order.

Furthermore, twelve years after regime change, the divisions that some rather dubiously considered to be the preserve of politicians and power politics have inevitably had an echo within broader society. The trust – even the desire – needed for compromise and resolution is lacking not just amongst Iraq's political leaders, but amongst many sections of Iraqi society as well. How permanent or transient this will prove to be depends on whether or not Iraq's political classes can produce alternative models of leadership dedicated to finally building a functional Iraqi state that delivers and is regarded as legitimate by a reasonable cross section of Iraqis. Without major changes in Iraqi politics and significant progress in Iraqi state building, and without resolution of the region's long-standing issues and rivalries, the dynamic of Shi'a-centric state building and Sunni rejection will continue. Left unchecked, this may eventually see Iraqi sectarian identities morphing into something more akin to race, ethnicity, or even nations. Indeed the entanglement of sectarian identity with perceptions regarding state legitimacy today is such as to suggest that this process may already be well under way.

WORKS CITED

Ahad, Ghaith Abdul. 2007. "The Jihad Now Is against the Shias not the Americans." *Guardian*, January 13.

Allawi, Ali A. 2007. *The Occupation of Iraq: Winning the War, Losing the Peace*. New Haven: Yale University Press.

Amnesty International. 2014. *Iraq: Absolute Impunity: Militia Rule in Iraq*. London: Amnesty International Ltd.

Baker, Peter. 2006. "U.S. Not Winning War in Iraq, Bush Says for 1st Time." *Washington Post*, December 20.

Baker III, James A., et al. 2006. *The Iraq Study Group Report*. Washington, D.C.: United States Institute of Peace.

Biddleet al. 2012. "Testing the Surge: Why Did Violence Decline in 2007?" *International Security* **37**:1, 7–40.

Boyle, Michael J. 2009. "Bargaining, Fear and Denial: Explaining Violence Against Civilians in Iraq 2004–2007." *Terrorism and Political Violence* **21**, 261–287.

Buruma, Ian. 1999. "The Joys and Perils of Victimhood." *The New York Review of Books*, April 8.

Chandhoke, Neera. 2005. "The Political Consequences of Ethnic Mapping." Crisis State Programme, Discussion Paper No. 14, *Developing Studies Institute at London School of Economics*, December.

Cockburn, Andrew and Patrick Cockburn. 1999. *Out of the Ashes*. New York: Harper Perennial.

Cockburn, Patrick. 2008. *Muqtada al-Sadr and the Fall of Iraq*. London: Faber and Faber.

Dodge, Toby. 2007. "State Collapse and the Rise of Identity Politics." In Iraq: *Preventing Another Generation of Conflict*, edited by Markus Bouillon, David Malone and Ben Rowsell, pp. 110–124. Boulder: Lynne Rienner Publishers.

2012. *Iraq: From War to a New Authoritarianism*. London: Routledge.

Al Dulaimi, Adnan. 2012. *Akhir al Mattaf: Seera wa Dhikrayat* (End of the Road: Life and Memories). Amman: Dar al Ma'moon.

Farouk-Sluglett, Marion and Peter Sluglett. 2003. *Iraq Since 1958: From Revolution to Dictatorship*. London: I.B. Tauris.

Foster, Dennis M. et al. 2013. "There Can Be No Compromise: Institutional Inclusiveness, Fractionalization and Domestic Terrorism." *British Journal of Political Science* 43:3, 541–557.

Gordon, Joy. 2012. *Invisible War: The United States and the Iraq Sanctions*. Cambridge, MA: Harvard University Press.

The Gulf/2000 Project. 2013. "Maps and Statistics Collection." Accessed January 26, 2015. http://gulf2000.columbia.edu/maps.shtml.

Haddad, Fanar. 2011. *Sectarianism in Iraq: Antagonistic Visions of Unity*. London: Hurst & Co.

2012a. "Sectarian Gulf." In *Critical Muslim: Fear and Loathing* 1:3, 105–119. Available at: www.mei.edu/content/map/secular-sectarians Accessed December 8, 2015.

2012b "Identity Politics in Iraq: How Much of It Is about Identity?" *Near East Quarterly* 9, December. Available at: www.neareastquarterly.com/index.php/2012/12/11/identity-politics-in-iraq-how-much-of-it-is-about-identity/ Accessed October 15, 2013.

2014a. "Secular Sectarians." *Middle East Institute*, June 17.

2014b. "'Marked' for Exclusion: The Problem of Pluralism, State-Building, and Communal Identities in Iraq and the Arab World." *Middle East Institute*, August 5. Available at: www.mei.edu/content/map/marked-exclusion-problem-pluralism-state-building-and-communal-identities-iraq-and-arab-world Accessed December 8, 2015.

2014c. "A Sectarian Awakening: Reinventing Sunni Identity in Iraq After 2003." *Current Trends in Islamist Ideology* 17, 155–156.

Hashim, Ahmed S. 2006. *Insurgency and Counter-Insurgency in Iraq*. London: Hurst & Co.

Hauslohner, Abigail. 2014. "Iraq's crisis won't be resolved by fighting, Sunni leader says." *The Washington Post*, July 12. Accessed January 22, 2015. www.washingtonpost.com/blogs/worldviews/wp/2014/07/12/iraqs-crisis-wont-be-resolved-by-fighting-sunni-leader-says/?Post±generic=%3Ftid%3Dsm_twitter_washingtonpost

Hill, Christopher R. 2014. "How the Obama Administration Ignored Iraq." *Politico Magazine*, October 2.

Human Rights Watch. 1992. *Endless Torment: The 1991 Uprising in Iraq and Its Aftermath*. New York: Human Rights Watch.

1995. *Iraq's Crime of Genocide: The Anfal campaign against the Kurds*. New York: Human Rights Watch.

2003. *The Mass Graves of Al-Mahawil: The Truth Uncovered*. New York: Human Rights Watch.

2014. *Iraq: Pro-Government Militias' Trail of Death*. New York: Human Rights Watch.

Hunter, Shireen T. 2014. "The Real Causes of Iraq's Problems." *LobeLog by Inter Press Service*, June 14.

International Crisis Group. 2004. "Iraq's Transition: On a Knife Edge." *Middle East Report* N°27, April 27. Accessed January 26, 2015. www.crisisgroup.org/en/regions/middle-east-north-africa/iraq-iran-gulf/iraq/027-iraqs-transition-on-a-knife-edge.aspx

2006a. "In Their Own Words: Reading the Iraqi Insurgency." *Middle East Report* N°50, February 15. Accessed January 26, 2015. www.crisisgroup.org/en/regions/middle-east-north-africa/iraq-iran-gulf/iraq/050-in-their-own-words-reading-the-iraqi-insurgency.aspx

2006b. "The Next Iraqi War? Sectarianism and Civil Conflict." *Middle East Report* N°52, February 27. Accessed January 26, 2015. www.crisisgroup.org/en/regions/middle-east-north-africa/iraq-iran-gulf/iraq/052-the-next-iraqi-war-sectarianism-and-civil-conflict.aspx.

2006c. "Iraq's Muqtada Al-Sadr: Spoiler or Stabiliser?" *Middle East Report* N°55, July 11. Accessed January 26, 2015. www.crisisgroup.org/en/regions/middle-east-north-africa/iraq-iran-gulf/iraq/055-iraqs-muqtada-al-sadr-spoiler-or-stabiliser.aspx.

2007. "Where is Iraq Heading? Lessons from Basra." *Middle East Report* N°67, June 25. Accessed January 26, 2015. www.crisisgroup.org/en/regions/middle-east-north-africa/iraq-iran-gulf/iraq/067-where-is-iraq-heading-lessons-from-basra.aspx.

2008a. "Iraq's Civil War, the Sadrists and the Surge." *Middle East Report* N°72, February 7. Accessed January 26, 2015. www.crisisgroup.org/en/regions/middle-east-north-africa/iraq-iran-gulf/iraq/072-iraqs-civil-war-the-sadrists-and-the-surge.aspx.

2008b. "After the Surge I: The New Sunni Landscape." *Middle East Report* N°74, April 30. Accessed January 26, 2015. www.crisisgroup.org/en/regions/middle-east-north-africa/iraq-iran-gulf/iraq/074-iraq-after-the-surge-i-the-new-sunni-landscape.aspx.

2013. "Make or Break: Iraq's Sunnis and the State." *Middle East Report* N°144, August 14. Accessed January 26, 2015. www.crisisgroup.org/en/regions/middle-east-north-africa/iraq-iran-gulf/iraq/144-make-or-break-iraq-s-sunnis-and-the-state.aspx.

2014. "Iraq: Falluja's Faustian Bargain." *Middle East Report* N°150, April 28. Accessed January 26, 2015. www.crisisgroup.org/en/regions/middle-east-north-africa/iraq-iran-gulf/iraq/150-iraq-falluja-s-faustian-bargain.aspx.

Iraq Body Count. 2013. "Iraq Body Count Database: Documented Civilian Deaths from Violence." Accessed January 26, 2015. www.iraqbodycount.org/database/.

Jabar, Faleh A. et al. 2014. "Iraq on the Brink: Unravelling Maliki's Unravelling," *Iraq Institute for Strategic Studies*, IIST Iraq Annual Crisis Report, November.

1992. "Why the Uprisings Failed." *Middle East Report* 176:22, 2–14.

AlJaza'iri, Zuhair. 2009. *Harb al 'Ajiz [The Invalid's War]*. Beirut: Al-Saqi.

Kadhim, Abbas and Luay AlKhatteeb. 2014. "What Do You Know About Sistani's Fatwa?" *Huffington Post*, July 10.

AlKhalidi, Ashraf and Victor Tanner. 2006. "Sectarian Violence: Radical Groups Drive Internal Displacement in Iraq." *The Brooking Institution – University of Bern*, Project on Internal Displacement.

Khoury, Dina Rizk. 2012. "The 1991 Intifada in Three Keys: Writing the History of Violence."In *Writing the Modern History of Iraq: Historiographical and Political Challenges*, edited by Sluglett et al., pp. 245–268. Singapore: World Scientific Publishing.

Kingsbury, Alex. 2014. "Why the 2007 Surge in Iraq Actually Failed." *Boston Globe*, November 7.
Kreidie, Lina Haddad and Kristen Renwick Monroe. 2002. "Psychological Boundaries and Ethnic Conflict: How Identity Constrained Choice and Worked to Turn Ordinary People into Perpetrators of Ethnic Violence during the Lebanese Civil War." *International Journal of Politics, Culture and Society* 16, 1:5–36.
Krohley, Nicolas. 2015. *The Death of the Mehdi Army: The Rise, Fall and Revival of Iraq's Most Powerful Militia*. London: Hurst & Co.
alKubaisi, Yehia. 2013. "Iraq: Recent Protests and the Crisis of a Political System." *Arab Centre for Research and Policy Studies*, February. Available at: http://english.dohainstitute.org/release/2b069345-dc36-445b-964a-c7cd2cdc34de Accessed December 8, 2015.
Lafourcade, Fanny. 2012. "How to 'Turn the Page.'" In *Writing the Modern History of Iraq: Historiographical and Political Challenges*, edited by Jordi Tejel, Peter Sluglett, Riccardo Bocco, and Hamit Bozarslan, 181–202. Hackensack, NJ: World Scientific Publishing Co.
Lindemann, Stefan. 2008. "Do Inclusive Elite Bargains Matter? A Research Framework for Understanding the Causes of Civil War in Sub-Saharan Africa." *Crisis States Discussion Papers*, February.
Makiya, Kanan. 1993. *Cruelty and Silence: War, Tyranny, Uprising and the Arab World*. London: W. W. Norton & Co.
1998. *Republic of Fear: The Politics of Modern Iraq*. London: University of California Press.
AlMarashi, Ibrahim and Aysegul Keskin. 2008. "Reconciliation Dilemmas in Post-Ba'athist Iraq: Truth Commissions, Media and Ethno-Sectarian Conflicts." *Mediterranean Politics* **13**:2, 243–259.
McCary, John A. 2009. "The Anbar Awakening: An Alliance of Incentives." *The Washington Quarterly*, **32**:1, 43–59.
McDowall, David. 2003. *A Modern History of the Kurds*. London: I.B. Tauris.
Musings on Iraq. 2012. "Reassessing the U.S. Surge, and Recognizing Iraqi Agency in Ending the 2005–2008 Civil War in Iraq, an Interview with New America Foundation's Douglas Ollivant." *Musings on Iraq* blog, February 27. http://musingsoniraq.blogspot.com/2012/02/reassessing-us-surge-and-recognizing.html.
O'Ballance, Edgar. 1973. *The Kurdish Revolt, 1961–1970*. London: Faber & Faber.
Ollivant, Douglas A. 2011. "Countering the New Orthodoxy: Reinterpreting Counterinsurgency in Iraq." *New America Foundation*, National Security Studies Program Policy Paper.
Patraeus, David H. 2013. "How We Won in Iraq." *Foreign Policy*, October 29.
Project on Middle East Political Science. 2014. "Iraq Between Maliki and the Islamic State." *POMEPS* Briefing 24, July 9.
Ratnam, Gopal. 2014. "Spring Offensive Against ISIS in Iraq 'Unrealistic'." *Foreign Policy*, Novemeber 13.
Rayburn, Joel. 2014. *Iraq After America: Strongmen, Sectarians, Resistance*. Stanford: Hoover Institution Press.
Ricks, Thomas. 2006. "Situation Called Dire in West Iraq." *Washington Post*, September 11.
Rohde, Achim. 2010. *State-Society Relations in Ba'thist Iraq: Facing Dictatorship*. London: Routledge.
Rosen, Nir. 2010. *Aftermath: Following the Bloodshed of America's Wars in the Muslim World*. New York: Nation Books.

Salih, Qasim Hussain. 2011. *Al Shakhsiya al Iraqiyya: Al Madhhar wa al Jawhar [The Iraqi Persona: Appearance and Essence]*. Baghdad: Dhefaf.

Sassoon, Joseph. 2011. *Saddam Hussein's Ba'th Party: Inside an Authoritarian Regime*. Cambridge: Cambridge University Press.

Scott, James C. 2009. *The Art of Not Being Governed: An Anarchist History of Upland Southeast Asia*. New Haven: Yale University Press.

Stanisland, Paul. 2012. "States, Insurgents and Wartime Political Orders." *Perspectives on Politics* 10:2, 243–264.

Thiel, Joshua. 2011. "The Statistical Irrelevance of American SIGACT Data: Iraq Surge Analysis Reveals Reality." *Small Wars Journal*, April 12.

Tripp, Charles. 2007. "Militias, Vigilantes, Death Squads: Charles Tripp on the Grammar of Violence in Iraq." *London Review of Books* 29:2, 30–34.

2012. "The Seductions of Violence in Iraq." *Open Democracy*, March 23.

2013. *The Power and the People: Paths of Resistance in the Middle East*. London: Cambridge University Press.

Ucko, David. 2008. "Militias, Tribes and Insurgents: The Challenge of Political Reintegration in Iraq." *Conflict, Security and Development* 8:3, 341–372.

United States Department of State. 2003. *Mass Graves in Iraq: Uncovering Atrocities*. Washington, D.C.: U.S. Department of State, Human Rights Review.

USAID. 2004. *Iraq's Legacy of Terror: Mass Graves*. Washington, D.C.: USAID Bureau of Public Affairs.

Visser, Reidar. 2009. "Post-Sectarian Strategies for Iraq." *Historiae.org*, Last modified March 18. http://historiae.org/post-sectarian.asp.

2010. "Iraq Moves Backward." *Middle East Report* 255, 2–7.

Wahid, Ahed. 2009. "Suwar rijal al din al siyasiyeen tufariq al manazil wal sayarat" (Pictures of political religious figures leave houses and cars). *Al Hayat*, September 22.

Wicken, Stephen. 2013. "Iraq's Sunnis in Crisis." *Institute for the Study of War*, Middle East Security Report, May 11.

MULTIMEDIA SOURCES

"Ahmad al Chalabi: Were It Not for the Mehdi Army Not a Single Shi'a Would Have Remained in Iraq." YouTube video, 0:49. Posted by "Mowaly4ali," July 26, 2011. www.youtube.com/watch?v=IIvNhwfIfOQ.

"Iraq's Shi'i Cleric Urges Killing of Saddam's Ba'athists,"*BBC Monitoring*, June 13, 2003.

Kouddous, Sharif Abdel. 2010. "Nir Rosen on 'Aftermath: Following the Bloodshed of America's Wars in the Muslim World." DemocracyNow! video, 41:26, November 10, 2010. www.democracynow.org/2010/11/10/nir_rosen_on_aftermath_following_the.

"Mufti Rafi'i al Rifai's Response to Mahdi al Karbala'i's Statements." YouTube video, 14:30. Posted by "Pressnews10," June 14, 2014. www.youtube.com/watch?v=kl9XO63TGAM

"The Truth: The First Book on Sunni and Shi'a Demographics in Iraq," October 2, 2003. http://islammemo.cc/2003/10/02/2626.html

AUTHOR INTERVIEWS

Interview with senior career officer in criminal intelligence unit in the Ministry of Interior. Baghdad, March 2014. Interviewee requested anonymity.

Interview, senior officer in Baghdad Counter Terrorism Department. Baghdad, February 2012. Interviewee requested anonymity.

Interview, police captain, Baghdad, March 2014. Interviewee requested anonymity.

Interview, member of Baghdad Provincial Council. Baghdad, March 2013. Interviewee requested anonymity.

Index

For EU product safety concerns, contact us at Calle de José Abascal, 56–1°,
28003 Madrid, Spain or eugpsr@cambridge.org.

www.ingramcontent.com/pod-product-compliance
Lightning Source LLC
LaVergne TN
LVHW011522200926
848484LV00001B/112
* 9 7 8 1 1 0 7 1 2 4 3 7 0 *